WORLD RELIGIONS VOLUME 3

WORLD RELIGIONS VOLUME 3
FAITHS OF THE FAR EAST
YOUNG OON KIM

Golden Gate PUBLISHING CO.
4 West 43rd Street, New York, New York 10036

© Copyright 1976 by Young Oon Kim

All rights reserved. Except for the inclusion of brief quotations in a review, no part of this book may be reproduced or utilized in any form or by any means, electronic or mechanical, including photocopying, recording or by any information storage and retrieval system, without permission in writing from the publisher.

First Edition 1976

Artwork and design by Gil Roschuni

Printed in the United States of America

Library of Congress Catalog Number 76-23739

If the subject matter in this book interests you,
correspondence is welcomed by the author,
and may be addressed through:

Golden Gate Publishing Co.
4 West 43rd Street
New York, New York 10036

contents

Preface	ix
BUDDHISM	1
I. DISTINCTIVE MAHAYANA PRINCIPLES	2
Absolute Mind	2
The Three Buddha Bodies	5
Ethics and Enlightenment	7
Bodhisattvas and the Spirit World	9
II. BUDDHISM IN CHINESE HISTORY	15
From the Han to Manchu Dynasty	15
Attacks on Buddhism	23
Three Buddhists Sects	28
Milo Fo, The Chinese Messiah	34
III. THE MODERN PERIOD: FROM THE MANCHUS TO MAO	38
Neo-Buddhist Leaders	38
Buddhism in the Chinese Republic	41
Persecution by Mao	43
New Buddhism for a New China	49
IV. KOREAN BUDDHISM	51
Early Buddhism	51
Ech'adon The Martyr	52
The Hwarang Do	53
Wonhyo	55
Koryo Buddhism	58
The Yi Dynasty and Afterwards	60
V. JAPANESE BUDDHISM	62
Gift From Korea	62
Eminent Monks and Buddhist Teachers	63
Brief History of Nipponese Buddhism	64

The Nichiren Revival   70
Buddhist Teachings Today   78

Bibliography   84

TAOISM   87

I. LAO-TZU, THE TAOIST SAGE   88
The Most Exalted Old Master   88
Teachings of Lao-Tzu   89

II. CHUANG-TZU   99

III. VARIETIES OF EARLY TAOISM   103
The Hygiene School   104
Yin-Yang Philosophy and the Five Elements School   104
Later Taoist Philosophers   107

IV. TAOISM IN THE MODERN AGE   116

Bibliography   120

CONFUCIANISM   121

I. THE LIFE OF CONFUCIUS   122

II. THE CHINESE CLASSICS   124

III. THE CONFUCIAN ETHIC   127

IV. CHINESE PIETY   135

V. APOSTLES OF CONFUCIANISM   139
Mencius   139
Hsun Tzu, The Confucian Pessimist   142
Chu Hsi   144
Wang Yang-Ming   148

VI. CONFUCIANISM IN THE MODERN WORLD   150

VII. SOME CONFUCIAN GIFTS   156

Bibliography   159

SHAMANISM AND SHINTOISM	161
I. SHAMANISM	162
Shamanism Defined	162
Shamanist Cosmology	164
Nostalgia for Paradise	166
The Social Role of the Shaman	169
Shamanism in the Far East	170
Korean Shamanism	173
Messages from Spirit World	182
II. SHINTOISM	191
History of Shintoism	191
Shinto Myths and Scriptures	192
Respect for the Dead	194
Three Modern Japanese Thinkers	196
Bibliography	202
Postscript	203
Acknowledgements	205
Index	207

preface

WHATEVER THE title men use for God, whatever aspect of His nature is emphasized by different groups of people, God is the Father of all mankind and all are His children. However varied the doctrine and forms of worship, I see two universal features in all faiths: God is seeking His children everywhere and they are anxious to return to Him. Neither God nor man has ever stopped such longing; the efforts of each have continued and even intensified through the centuries. In olden times people may have expressed their faith in a simple way; whereas in modern times they have developed more logically and rationally to suit sophisticated minds and also the deepened spiritual experiences of individuals within each community of faith.

Rather than merely repeating a history of other men's religions or trying to refute their faith in order to promote Christianity, it is my aim in this book to show how profoundly people in each great religion have experienced the holy, encountering God, and testifying to His work throughout history—in other words, how clearly God has been revealing His will and heart to them. We might find something common, universal, consistent among all religions. If there is something different, unique in their ideology, this could be an emphasis on different aspects of the one God and His work.

Religious differences and prejudices based upon misunderstanding have caused too much hostility and bloodshed in the past. Hence it is important for us to look at each great religion with an open mind. It was so hard to explain in a few pages the theology and history of religions which have developed over a long period. Humbly admitting the inevitable superficiality I only wish that the reader may be stimulated to begin friendly dialogue with people of other faiths. Thus men of all creeds should unite in their efforts to bring about His Kingdom on earth for His sake and our own.

I want to express my gratitude for the diligent research work of Reverend Royal Davis and associate editing of Mr. John Dolen.

Washington, D.C. Young Oon Kim
September 1, 1976

WORLD RELIGIONS VOLUME 3

Mahayana Buddhism

The religion of the Buddha goes not, comes not, loves not, hates, not. Like a shadow it follows in silence. Its influence lies in the mind only. How great its power! Such was the master Sodang: a man who cast the world aside that he might give his whole soul to the onward march of the Buddha.

> Memorial inscription
> to Korean great priest Sodang[1]
> (784 A.D.)

---

1. Quoted in J. S. Gale, History of the Korean People, 1972 reprint, p. 166.

I. DISTINCTIVE MAHAYANA PRINCIPLES

Absolute Mind

IN HIS experience of enlightenment, Prince Siddhartha of Nepal became the Buddha. Henceforth, his path of liberation from the wheel of karma would be followed by millions. In India, however, his success as an Indian guru produced two distinct groups of followers. In the south a Buddhist group called the Theravada spread the message of the "noble fourfold truth" to Sri Lanka, Thailand, Burma and Cambodia. In the north a group called the Mahayana—"Big Vehicle"—took Buddhism to Tibet, China, Korea and Japan. In our study of Far Eastern religion Mahayana is the form of Buddhism which we must consider. For although the Chinese studied Theravada scriptures, it was the distinctive features of the Mahayana philosophy which commanded their loyalty.[1]

In a world of ceaseless change, decay, and suffering, Mahayana Buddhism seeks the unchanging Absolute. In one of the famous Mahayana scriptures[2], the permanent factor in and behind our universe is the absolute Mind. In that scripture the story is told of a maharajah, who, listening to the Buddha teach, asked for more information about the "imperishable principle"—the mind—since in his own experience he could find nothing that was not subject to decay and destruction.

Buddha asked the maharajah, "How old were you when your first saw the Ganges River?"

The king said, "When I was but three, my mother led me by the hand to pay my devotions by the river."

"Was the river different when you were thirteen?"

"No, just the same as when I was three; and now that I am sixty-two there is still no change in its appearance."

Buddha said, "Now that you are aged, white-haired and

---

[1] The Theravada school and the basic teachings of Buddha are discussed in volume II.
[2] *Surangama Sutra,* for selections see E.A. Burtt, *Teachings of the Compassionate Buddha,* Mentor Book, N.Y., 1955, pp. 181-194.

wrinkled, has the sight which enabled you to see the Ganges in former years become also wrinkled?"

"No."

"Maharajah, although your face has aged, your power of sight has not altered its essential nature. That which becomes old and decrepit is by nature changeable and that which does not is unchangeable. Hence, that which changes is subject to destruction, but that which changes not must be from its origin incapable of either birth or death."

On the basis of simple illustrations such as this, which point to evidence that both outside man and within him there are signs of permanence, Buddha taught that each one's mind is coextensive with the universe, and that all things in the universe are merely the primeval mind of Bodhi ("Enlightenment").[3] This Mind is universally diffused and comprehends all things. Mind is present in every minute hair, while including infinite worlds in its embrace.[4]

Mahayana Buddhists speak of this transcendent unchangeable reality as "absolute *Suchness.*" Free from all modes of limitation and conditionality, it is beyond our ordinary logical comprehension. Everything we say about it therefore would be an attempt to limit it, and so all our descriptions must be in negative terms. The Absolute is not "this" or "that," because *Suchness* is by nature all-inclusive and transcendent. It is beyond tangible categories or rational classification. As the Indian Mahayana philosopher Nagarjuna wrote,

> Between thisness and thatness,
> Between being and non-being,
> Who discriminates,
> The truth of Buddhism he perceives not.[5]

Reality, as we know it through sensory experience, is quite unlike the Absolute, "the Void," "the Emptiness of Emptiness,"

---

[3] Bodhi is sometimes translated "awakening", meaning the act of total awareness.
[4] Burtt, *Ibid,* pp. 191-192, 194 (abridged).
[5] On this important metaphysician, see K. Venkata Ramanan, *Nagarjuna's Philosophy,* C.E. Tuttle, Rutland, Vt., 1966.

to use Buddhist terminology. When the "Unconditioned" which is beyond our five senses appears to us as a panorama of diversity and individuality, *Suchness* becomes *Thisness*. When the work and existence of *Suchness* are manifested in mathematical, chemical and biological forms, the unconditioned Absolute is seen as *conditioned Suchness*. Thus, Buddhism delivers us from the world of ceaseless change and awakens us to the inexhaustible, indescribable reality of *Suchness* itself.[6]

Is *Suchness* another name for God? According to Mahayanists, there is present in our world a reality which transcends the limitations of phenomena, immanent everywhere and manifesting its full glory all about us. In that reality we live and move and have our being. Buddhists use various words—*Dharmakaya, Amitabha-Buddha,* etc.—for this reality. *Dharmakaya* denotes a living, willing, knowing being—a vital spirit manifesting itself in nature and our thought. As absolute perfect intelligence, this reality is a fountainhead of love and compassion.[7] It is forever serene and eternal, comes from nowhere and goes nowhere, illuminates all creation, is free of all opposites yet works in all things to lead them to Nirvana.

However, besides being an all-powerful will and intelligence, the *Dharmakaya* is described as all-embracing love. Possibly in reply to Christian missionaries, contemporary Buddhists stress the loving heart of *Dharmakaya*. They insist that the Absolute is an incarnation of mercy: its hands direct our lives toward the actualization of supreme goodness.[8] They quote a Mahayana text:

> With one great loving heart
> The thirsty desires of all beings he quencheth
> with coolness...
> With a great heart compassionate and loving,

---

[6] D.T. Suzuki, *Outlines of Mahayana Buddhism,* Luzac and Co., London, 1907 (1963 reprint), chapters V and IX. Noting the similarity to Vedanta, this scholar sharply contradicts western scholars who interpret Buddhism as a nihilistic philosophy. But Mahayana doctrine so greatly resembles Hindu monism that many fail to see why Gautama was condemned by Indians as a skeptic and nihilist.

[7] *Avatamsaka Sutra,* quoted in Suzuki, *Ibid,* pp. 223-224.

[8] Suzuki, *Ibid,* pp. 232-233.

All sentient beings by him are embraced;
With means which are pure, free from stain,
and all excellent,
He doth save and deliver all creatures innumerable.[9]

Are there then no differences between the Mahayana *Dharmakaya* and the Christian concept of God? Professor D.T. Suzuki believes that there are. He states that the *Dharmakaya* is not a creator who produced the world out of nothing, caused the fall of man, and touched by remorse, sent down his only son to save the depraved.[10]

The Three Buddha Bodies

Buddhists derive their concept of the Ultimate from their reflection on the life of Buddha. As Christian theology grows out of Christology, so the *Dharmakaya* is derived from Buddhology.[11] The Nepalese prince who left his palace and family to bring men the bliss of enlightenment provides the clue to the mystery of the cosmic order. Buddhists hence developed a theory of the three bodies of Buddha.

First is the *Nirmanakaya* (Body of Transformation) or the historical and human Gautama. Then there is the *Sambhogakaya* (Body of Bliss) or transfigured, celestial Buddha, the glorified Blessed One. Above these and far superior to them is the *Dharmakaya* (Law Body), the formless cosmic Buddha, the Absolute. According to a Japanese Buddhist scholar, Christians can understand the doctrine of the three bodies if they compare the *Dharmakaya* to the supreme Godhead, the *Sambhogakaya* to the transfigured, resurrected Christ and the *Nirmanakaya* to Jesus of Nazareth.[12]

---

[9] *Avatamsaka Sutra.*

[10] Suzuki, *Ibid,* p. 219. Many Christian theologians, however, would claim that this description of the Christian God is vastly oversimplified and to some degree misleading.

[11] For the gradual development of Indian Buddhology over five centuries, see S. Dutt, *The Buddha and Five After Centuries,* Luzac and Co., London, 1957.

[12] D.T. Suzuki, *Outlines in Mahayana Buddhism,* p. 256. For a modern interpretation of the Three Body doctrine and how it arose, see Suzuki, "The Doctrine of Trikaya", *Ibid,* chap X.

Of the three bodies, the Body of Bliss *(Sambhogakaya)* is the most difficult to explain. According to the first century Mahayana philosopher Asvaghosha, Buddha's Bliss Body possesses infinite forms, has infinite attributes, exhibits infinite kinds of excellence and is bestowed with infinite merits. It comes directly from *Dharmakaya,* can manifest itself anywhere and is boundless in its perfection. The Bliss Body also serves as a bridge which spans the wide gap between the human Sakyamuni and the Absolute.[13]

Buddhists have long held a variety of views about the nature of Buddha. Some would affirm the importance of two Buddhas—the cosmic Buddha *(Dharmakaya* or *Amitabha)* and the historic Gautama. Others say that Gautama was only the most recent of four or eight or one of innumerable Buddhas. A third group, especially in Tibet and China, believe that every age has a "living Buddha" (the Dalai Lama, for example) or more than one. Among contemporary Mahayana Buddhists there are also those who say that Sakyamuni was the revelation of the *Dharmakaya* to Indians and Jesus Christ was the same *Dharmakaya* for Semites.

According to Dr. Suzuki, the *Dharmakaya* is the archetype of all the Buddhas and all beings—that which is immortal in everything which lives. Because this reality seems too abstract to command the loyalty of ordinary men, the human Sakyamuni was idealized as a personification of the Absolute. This idealized Buddha and personified *Dharmakaya* was called the Body of Bliss. As for the earthly Gautama, he represents the Body of Transformation.[14]

Buddha provides the model for each man; thus each individual possesses these same three bodies, though in our ignorance we are often only aware of the first.[15] In fact all existence is divided into three worlds—the sensual, the world of form, and the Formless—though we usually live only at the lowest level, limiting our existence to the enjoyment of physical pleasures. If,

---

[13] Theravada Buddhists would generally agree with the Mahayana concept of the *Dharmakaya* and *Nirmanakaya.* For them, however, the *Sambhogakaya* refers to Gautama's supernatural ability to appear in two places at once.

[14] *Ibid,* p. 273.

[15] John Blofeld, *The Jewel in the Lotus,* Buddhist Society, London, 1948, p. 42.

however, we discover the spiritual pleasures of contemplation, we become aware of the second dimension of existence. But to enter the highest realm, we must, in the Dalai Lama's words, have *"only a bare mind, void of distraction,"* dwelling entirely *"in a state of equanimity."* [16]

Thus Buddha, knowing that these three worlds exist and that man was unaware of the way to reach the third world of pure spirit, felt pity, as stated in a Mahayana poem:

> Because he saw mankind drowning in the great sea of birth, death and sorrow...
> Because he saw that men wallowed in the mire of lust...
> Because he saw them fettered to their wealth, their wives and their children...
> Because he saw them consumed by fires of pain and sorrow, yet not knowing where to seek the still waters of contemplation...
> Because he saw them living in a time of war, killing and wounding one another, and knew that because of riotous hatred flourishing in their hearts they would be doomed to pay an endless retribution...
> Because he saw worldly men plowing their fields, sowing seed, trafficking, buying and selling yet in the end winning nothing but bitterness,
> For this Buddha was moved to pity.[17]

Ethics and Enlightenment

Gautama Buddha's life becomes for the Mahayana school an authoritative norm for the life of goodness: because he achieved Nirvana, by following in his footsteps so can any man. When one

---

[16] Dalai Lama, *My Land and My People,* McGraw Hill, N.Y., 1962, p. 242.
[17] Abridged and adapted from C. Humphreys, *The Wisdom of Buddhism,* Harper and Row, N.Y., 1960, pp. 36-37; also E.A. Burtt, *Teachings of the Compassionate Buddha,* pp. 240-241.

applies the moral commandments of the eightfold path, he can be liberated from the wheel of rebirth and fully realize his own Buddha-nature. As Shen-hsiu wrote in the seventh century,

> The body is the tree of enlightenment,
> And the mind is like a bright mirror stand,
> Always cleanse them diligently,
> And not let dust fall on them.[18]

What did Chinese Buddhists mean by not letting dust fall on the mirror of the mind? Buddhism was designed for monks who completely renounced the ways of the world. Nothing is to disturb their peace. In China this involved cutting oneself off from secular pursuits, abandoning one's home and family, not paying taxes or serving as a soldier, no longer participating in Confucian ancestor worship, and taking a new name. Nothing less would enable one to achieve Nirvana in this lifetime.

Yet, besides the strict Buddhism of the monks, Mahayana sects recognized an easier Buddhism for the layman. While no one could possibly attain Nirvana apart from the strict regimen of a monastery, the pious layman could make this life preparation for the next—in which he would be able to endure the austerities of a monk. Hsi Ch'ao (336-377 A.D.) composed a manual for such lay persons who had become Buddhists: *Feng-Fa Yao* (Essentials of Religion).[19]

In this manual, Hsi Ch'ao defines the Buddhist faith. First, faith implies surrender and full devotion to these three jewels: taking refuge in the Buddhas of the past, present and future; accepting the authority of the Buddhist scriptures; and participating in the life of the Buddhist community. And in all this, the devotee must cherish thoughts of tenderness towards all living creatures and wish that they might attain emancipation.

---

[18] Quoted in K. Ch'en, *Buddhism in China,* Princeton Univ. Press, Princeton, 1964, p. 355.

[19] Full text in E. Zurcher, *The Buddhist Conquest of China,* E.J. Brill, Leiden, 1959, pp. 164-176.

Second, Hsi Ch'ao lists five basic rules for the Buddhist layman: not to kill, not to rob, not to commit acts of unchastity, not to lie, and not to drink wine. For him, the virtue of equanimity is the greatest. Nothing is quite equal to patience or the ability to endure humiliation. If a Buddhist is scolded or abused, he will remain silent. If he is punched or beaten he will not complain. If he meets with anger and hatred, he will face his opponent with tenderness. In this way an evil man—if his heart be not made of wood or stone—will be moved by actions of goodness and truth.

Having practiced such virtues, the Buddhist can look forward to attaining Nirvana. Since this goal is often defined in negative terms like "the Void" or the "Emptiness," Hsi Ch'ao attempts to be more explicit about what it means "to practice Emptiness within Emptiness." Belonging to an enormously wealthy family famed for its patronage of Taoism, and being himself an eminent scholar in the Confucian classics as well as a prominent statesman, he was aware of the criticisms made against Buddhism. The Chinese protested its anti-social behavior, its ascetic philosophy of world negation, and its mystical nihilism. In such an atmosphere, Hsi Ch'ao's intepretation of Nirvana reconciles Buddhism and the traditional Chinese ethic. He said that those who practice the Way must keep their foothold in this world; that Buddhism does not deny the value of secular concerns—all it does is warn against attachment to them. If a man rids himself of anxiety about worldly success, he can safely participate in secular activities. Then, when no longer blinded by the allure of this world, a man can be said to practice Emptiness within the realm of Emptiness. For Hsi Ch'ao, Nirvana seems to refer to the achievement of spiritual tranquillity in this life or elsewhere: the true Buddhist is in the world but not of it.

However, for laymen no less than monks the path to Nirvana represents a long, arduous climb upward. But for Mahayana Buddhists at least, we can be helped by the Bodhisattvas.

The Bodhisattvas and the Spirit World

In Far Eastern Buddhism, the faithful are promised a variety of celestial helpers. Within a Chinese temple, one sees many statues; while none of these figures represents a god in the ordinary sense, all are superterrestrial beings to whom the pious should pay respect and from whom they can expect aid in reaching Nirvana.[20] These are the Bodhisattvas.

This Mahayana belief is in direct opposition to the doctrine of Theravada monks. The latter believe that each Buddhist must work out his own salvation, however many lives may be used up in the process. Upon abandoning the world, the monks vow: "One single self we shall tame, one single self we shall pacify, one single self we shall lead to final Nirvana."[21]—their own. Though Buddha pointed the way and proved that enlightenment is possible, each Buddhist must rely on his own power to reach that goal.

Mahayana Buddhism in China must however be understood in the light of its birth and centuries of development in north India, where popular Hinduism was polytheistic and sectarian Hinduism believed that the saving gods Vishnu and Siva became incarnate whenever necessary. Buddhism of course differs from Hinduism in its denial of creating and saving gods. Gautama was a man and so are the Bodhisattvas—at least in theory. A Bodhisattva is not a god who descends to earth, but a human who has prepared himself for Nirvana, yet prefers to help others reach this blissful state. While his wisdom entitles him to Nirvana, his compassion impels him to forego final enlightenment on behalf of the salvation of all creatures. Unable to enjoy perfect peace while a single living being struggles and suffers, the Bodhisattva vows:

> However innumerable beings are, I vow to save them.
> However inexhaustible the defilements are, I vow to extinguish them.
> However immeasurable the dharmas (requirements)

---

[20] J. Blofeld, *The Jewel in the Lotus,* pp. 170-175. For a description of the statues in a Japanese Buddhist temple, see D.T. Suzuki, *Manual of Zen Buddhism,* Grove Press, N.Y., 1960, pp. 153-186 (with illustrations). For Korean Buddhist iconography, see C.A. Clark, *Religions of Old Korea,* Christian Literature Society, Seoul, 1961 reprint, pp. 46-64.

[21] From a Buddhist text, C. Humphreys, *Ibid,* p. 146.

are, I vow to master them.
However incomparable enlightenment is, I vow
to attain it.[22]

For Mahayanists, the Theravada ideal—in which very few souls could ever reach Buddhahood, and those could only liberate themselves—was cold, and hard-hearted. How could the solitary monk so calmly ignore the suffering masses? Hence Mahayana sages pleaded," Let's abandon the thought of entering Nirvana by ourselves. Such a concept of Nirvana extinguishes the fire of the heart, leaving only the cold ashes of the intellect. Rather, as Bodhisattvas, let's be filled with compassion for all creatures and turn over all our merits, great or small, to their benefit."

This Mahayana doctrine led to a redefinition of man's original nature. The essence of man is *Bodhicitta,* "Intelligence-heart." The human heart is a reflection of the Absolute heart, just as the moon is reflected in the water of a lake on a clear night. If one understands his Buddha-nature, he sees everything with a loving heart, for love is the essence of this nature. *Bodhicitta* is the highest value, the deepest revelation of the Absolute. All Bodhisattvas find their purpose for existence in this cosmic loving heart.[23]

Not only humans but all sentient beings possess this "Intelligence-heart" to some degree. In the Buddhas it is fully awakened; in ordinary mortals it is dormant, blinded by the world of sensuality. The silver light of the moon is reflected—as surely in muddy pools as in every dew drop. Regardless of how lost in illusion men are, there flows a constant stream of compassion from the "lake of the Intelligence-heart" through the Bodhisattvas.

Ti-tsang, a Bodhisattva for the underworld of the dead, was a Korean prince named Chiao Kioh who became a monk during the Tang dynasty (circa 754 A.D.), and as the story goes, he wandered

---
[22] Quoted in C. Humphreys, *Wisdom of Buddhism,* p. 143. For two rather different evaluations of the Bodhisattva ideal, contrast H. Zimmer, *Philosophies of India,* Meridian Book, N.Y., 1951, pp. 534-551 and D.T. Suzuki, *Outlines of Mahayana Buddhism,* pp. 277-330. These two equally eminent scholars may differ because one looks at Buddhism from an Indian perspective while the other views it in its Japanese form.

[23] Suzuki, *Ibid,* p. 298.

about with his faithful white dog until he came to China. Impressed by the beauty of the "nine flowery mountains" overlooking the Yangtze valley, the monk made them his home. For seventy years he sat in the same spot, meditating, teaching disciples, blessing pilgrims and seeking enlightenment. At last, when he was ninety-nine, Chiao Kioh attained the great illumination. Nevertheless, as a devout exemplar of Mahayanism he refused the opportunity to enjoy Nirvana's bliss, preferring to continue assisting suffering men as a Bodhisattva.

When it came time for Prince Chiao to depart from this earth he slowly sank into one of the clefts in the mountain where for so long he had meditated. A shrine has since been erected there and the mountain was covered with monasteries, temples and pagodas. In hell, *Ti-tsang* continues his preaching, protecting the dead from the merciless demonic torturers and comforting their victims with hope for their final release. With the aid of pious Buddhist laymen on earth (who remember the fate of the damned), and priests (who perform rites for the dead), *Ti-tsang* implants a root of goodness in the heart of the sinner so he can be released from hell. In temples dedicated to this Korean savior, a great bronze bell is rung regularly, carrying a message of sympathy to the land of the shadows.[24]

Fear of hell is a prominent aspect of Chinese Buddhism. However, belief in the spirit world long antedated the appearance of Buddhism in China. Some scholars, taking Confucian humanism as the norm for interpreting the Chinese mind, believe that the Han civilization was largely agnostic in regard to the spirit world and almost exclusively this-worldly. This is not true. Buddhism came to a nation already committed to the veneration of ancestral spirits, practicing divination and astrology, and believing in the existence of numerous demons who needed to be exorcised—as well as plentiful beneficent supernatural beings, residing on mountaintops, in rivers and at secluded woodland holy places. From the oracle bones of the primitive Shang period to the poetic mysticism

---

[24] K. Reichelt, *Religion in Chinese Garment,* Philosophical Library, N.Y., 1951, pp. 139-141. Also see Francis C.M. Wei, *The Spirit of Chinese Culture,* Charles Scribner's Sons, N.Y., 1947, p. 117.

of the Taoists, pre-Buddhist China provides abundant evidence of the people's faith in a spiritual realm.[25]

But Buddhism did add considerably to the Chinese conception of man's nature and destiny, mainly through its promulgation of Indian metaphysics. The monks introduced concepts like karma, reincarnation and Nirvana, as well as the Hindu doctrines of heaven and hell. Chinese Buddhism eventually became a creative cultural synthesis of these borrowed Indian beliefs, Taoist philosophy, Confucian ancestor worship and ancient folk piety.

Though the concept of a region of punishment for evil men is found in Indian Buddhism, the Chinese seemed to have placed more emphasis upon it because of their preoccupation with correct social behavior. According to Buddhist cosmology there are eighteen great hells and two supernatural judges who supervise the tortures of the sinful. However there are also a multitude of smaller hells and devils to torment the sinners. Nevertheless, hell is only a place of temporary punishment to purify the depraved; once this cleansing process is completed, the individual is released to continue his journey from life to life until he attains Nirvana.

Chinese Buddhists believe that spirits have been assigned to record every good or evil deed. The world is divided into separate parcels of land, each of which is watched over by an earth god. Above these local guardian spirits are the city gods and the rural locality gods. Thus a spiritual hierarchy exists to report to heaven, just as imperial China had an elaborate bureaucracy which reported regularly to the emperor.[26] Traditionally, the Chinese believed that from the spirit world one could get specific advice about daily life and that one's prayers or rites would have an effect on the spirits. Buddhism offered new ways by which ancestral spirits could be released from hell or be given additional blessings in heaven.

Just as the Buddhist believes in many regions in hell, so he believes in twenty-eight different heavens, providing a hierarchy

---

[25] Reichelt, *Ibid*, pp. 9-33. The *I Ching*, considered so valuable that even the agnostic Confucius made it part of his canon, rests on the belief in the existence and power of the spiritual world.

[26] Reichelt, *Ibid*, pp. 108-109.

of states of bliss, increasing in value as one approaches the ultimate goal of Nirvana. Yet no one—not even the gods—lives in heaven forever. After an appropriate length of time when the virtues of a particular soul have been rewarded, it returns to the earth in a new body, befitting its status. When an individual has been born and reborn sufficiently, he becomes mature enough spiritually to attain Nirvana or take the vows of a Bodhisattva.

The most beloved of the Chinese Bodhisattvas is *Kuan-yin,* the Buddhist Madonna. No one has a sharper eye, a more open ear, or a warmer heart for people in trouble. She is the personification of womanly charity and tenderness. Because she is always able to help, she is said to possess a thousand arms and a thousand legs. Concerning the origin of this goddess of mercy there are many stories; the following account is but one. At a time when Buddha was establishing cloisters for nuns, an Indian princess named Miao-suan longed to join the Buddhist sisterhood. Knowing that her father opposed her desire, she secretly entered a convent. Her father traced her whereabouts and sent out soldiers to bring her home. They caught her, then burned down the convent, killing all of the nuns. But as punishment for such a terrible deed, Miao-suan's father was suddenly struck blind. Miao-suan, however, realized that her father acted out of misguided love and prayed that his sight might be restored. She was then told that he could recover the use of his eyes only if she was willing to become blind for his sake. This she agreed to do, and spent the rest of her life sightless. Because she dared to disobey her father in order to become a nun and because she voluntarily sacrificed her own eyes on behalf of the very one who had caused her so much suffering, she became the Bodhisattva *Kuan-yin.* In light of such a story it is no wonder that numerous temples have been dedicated to her and her birthday is celebrated by million of Buddhists.[27]

---

[27] Reichelt, *Ibid,* pp. 146-148.

II. BUDDHISM IN CHINESE HISTORY

From the Han to Manchu Dynasty

One night in a dream Emperor Ming (reigned 58-75 A.D.) of the Han dynasty saw a golden god flying around in front of his palace. Rather curious about the meaning of this night visitor, the ruler consulted his experts in such matters. One of the seers explained that he had heard rumors of an Indian who had become a god named Buddha, that this man possessed the supernatural ability to fly and that his body was of a golden hue. Naturally, the emperor sent envoys to India to learn more about Buddha. When the delegation returned, they brought to Ming the famous Buddhist text *The Sutra in Forty-two Sections*. Greatly impressed, the emperor took the images of Buddha the envoys had obtained, images identical to the figure in his dream, and built a temple for them outside the walls of the capital city.[1]

However, our earliest description of a Chinese Buddhist temple comes a century later. In the last decade of the second century, an imperial official, Chai Jung, built a large temple in which he placed a huge bronze statue of Buddha, coated with gold leaf. Soon, from five to ten thousand Buddhists were gathering regularly to hear the chanting of *sutras* and lectures on the *dharma*. This is the oldest extant account of the religion's attraction for the masses.[2]

Buddhism probably first arrived in China when Indian (or other) traders entered the country along the overland route in the northwest or by ships docking at southeastern ports. At least initially it was a foreign faith practiced only by visiting or resident aliens. According to the imperial annals, there were no Chinese monks until the fourth century. By then, for about two hundred years Mahayana texts had been translated and were widely circulated among the literati.

---

[1] See K. Ch'en, *Buddhism in China,* pp. 29-31 for a critical analysis of Ming's dream.

[2] *Ibid,* pp. 40-42. Other early references to Buddhism are found in a poem by Chang Heng (78-139 A.D.) and Buddhist observances by Ying, Prince of Ch'u, in 65 A.D. On the basis of such evidence modern historians conjecture that Buddhism entered China very early in the first century A.D.

Why did Buddhism take root in China? After three hundred years of relative peace and prosperity, the Chinese empire created by the Han dynasty had been shaken to its foundations. The once powerful emperor became a puppet of rival factions. Violent hatreds and vendettas divided the upper classes. Oppressed and abused without restraint, the peasant masses waited for the moment to rise in rebellion.

The empire simply exploded. In 184 and 189 A.D. the Yellow Turban Taoist revolts broke out, resulting in millions of deaths. Then came a bloody attack on the palace eunuchs and their friends by a temporary alliance of nobles and literati. Finally appeared the war lords, ruthless military adventurers leading armed mobs of vagabonds, ex-convicts, landless peasants and amoral mercenaries.[3] Into such a world came the message of the all-compassionate Buddha who could show men the peace of Nirvana.

In 311 A.D., the invading Huns captured the Chinese capital at Loyang—a disaster as shocking as the fall of Rome to the Goths in 410 A.D.—and the emperor who boasted of being the Son of Heaven had to flee for his life. Within a few years the whole of North China, the heartland of Han civilization, was in alien hands. For the next three centuries, the Chinese tried to preserve some slight remnant of their former brilliance at the new capital of Nanking while barbarians ruled much of the old empire.

Refugee courtiers and intellectuals dominated the culture replanted in the Yangtze river valley. No longer committed to Confucianism because it seemed outmoded in an age of troubles and fully aware of the way Taoist nihilism and permissiveness had weakened the moral fibre of Han civilization, many literati and gentry converted to Buddhism. One such notable was Hui-yuan (334-416), a Confucian teacher who had become attracted to Taoism. He attended a lecture given by a Buddhist monk, recognized the metaphysical superiority of Mahayanism, entered a monastery and spent his talents reconciling the teachings of Lao-tzu and Buddha. Like others of his class, he used Taoist concepts to

---

[3] A.F. Wright, *Buddhism in Chinese History,* Stanford Univ. Press, Stanford, Calif., 1959, pp. 23, 25, 27.

explain Buddhism and used Buddhist ideas to solve some of the intellectual problems raised by Taoists. Locating his monastery in a mountain area of great scenic beauty, Hui-yuan extolled the saving grace of Amitabha Buddha and prepared the foundations for the Pure Land sect.

Emperor Wu (ruled 502-549) illustrates the appeal Buddhism made to the ruling class. At a Buddha Birthday celebration Wu ordered his whole court to forsake Taoism for the Middle Path. To demonstrate his personal faith, the emperor more than once literally gave himself to a Buddhist temple and made his officials donate vast sums to the monks to buy him back. In 517 A.D. he even more vigorously aided the Buddhist cause by destroying all Taoist temples and requiring their clergy to become laymen. To symbolize his role as a religious monarch Wu accepted the new title "Emperor Bodhisattva."

During this period Chinese monks in the south designed a new concept of holy vocation. As calligraphers, book collectors, philosophers, painters and poets, they interpreted Buddhism to mean a life of withdrawal and speculation. Henceforth, they pursued their scholarship and serene devotion at some temple set in the midst of lovely scenery—far removed from the troubles of the palace or nation. That ideal, one of tranquil detachment, proved to be very attractive right down to the collapse of the Chinese empire in the 20th century.

In the north, conditions were far less pleasant. A succession of barbarian rulers became infamous for their tyranny. However, the Hun warrior Lo who captured the Chinese capital of Loyang was so impressed with the magical powers of a Buddhist missionary that he became a patron of the religion. Fo-t'u-teng, who arrived while the capital city was still being burned, appeared before the Hun, filled his begging bowl with water, burned incense and chanted a holy spell; after which—to everyone's amazement—a blue lotus appeared in the bowl, its bright flowers dazzling the conqueror's eyes. In such a manner Buddhists won over the invaders. Instead of reyling on the intellectual subtleties of Mahayana philosophy or the moral excellence of the Middle Path,

Buddhists claimed to possess occult powers. At will they could bring rain, win wars, relieve sickness and astound the credulous.

Several more important factors led to Buddhist success in north China. Unlike the Confucian scholars, Buddhists were not completely identified with the fallen Han empire. They could be trusted as advisors and public servants by the Huns. Because Buddhist monks had no families and had severed their connections to their relatives, they were completely dependent on the ruler's favor and therefore served him faithfully. Also, since Buddhism was a foreign religion and the new rulers were also aliens, there was common opposition to traditional Chinese racism and isolationism. Finally, Buddhism proclaimed a universalistic ethic which would help to heal the divisions between Han and Hun, Chinese and alien, ruled and ruler, for centuries to come.

With the support of the autocratic rulers, Buddhism permeated society. The emperors and rich aristocrats gave lavish presents of cash and land to the monks, erected costly pagodas, and encouraged such artistic masterpieces as the cave temples of Yun-kang and Lung-men. Under such conditions the peasants embraced Buddhism en masse. For emperor and serf the preferred form of Buddhism was faith in Amitabha, the Bodhisattva of compassionate grace, who promises his devotees rebirth in the Pure Land paradise. Only a small minority of intellectuals and deeply spiritual men were practitioners of Ch'an mysticism.

Shrewd north Chinese emperors quickly recognized the need to keep Buddhism from getting out of control. Once the monastic community became large and wealthy, the secular rulers put it under the direct control of the government. Repeated attempts were also made to restrict the number of monks, confiscate excessive temple wealth and limit future building activities. While anti-Buddhist emperors learned that they could not simply outlaw the faith by imperial edict—a method tried more than once—they could at least exercise a large measure of government control over religious activities.[4]

---

[4] For greater detail see A.F. Wright, *Buddhism in Chinese History,* pp. 42-64.

In 589 the Sui dynasty reunited China after more than three centuries of political division. The Sui emperors and their successors, the T'ang, made it imperial policy to patronize the Buddhist faith on a lavish scale while recognizing Taoism and making the Confucian classics official textbooks for government examinations. This tolerance for all three religions henceforth became more or less normative. From 590-906 A.D. Sui and T'ang emperors ruled China, greatly expanding the size of the empire, stimulating an intellectual and artistic renaissance and creating a civilization comparable to that of Europe's High Middle Ages.

Yang Chien (541-604) founded the Sui dynasty and exemplifies its aggressive spirit. As an ambitious official in the weak Chou court of north China, he successfully deposed the boy emperor, slew fifty-nine princes, dethroned the emperor of south China at Nanking, and then proceeded to subjugate neighboring territories.[5] The interesting thing is that whereas emperor Asoka of India gave up his military activities when he converted to Buddhism, Yang Chien used Buddhism to defend his martial exploits: "With a hundred victories in a hundred battles, we promote the practice of the ten Buddhist virtues. Therefore we regard the weapons of war as having become like the offerings of incense and flowers presented to Buddha, and the fields of this world as becoming forever identical with the Buddha-land."[6]

Although the Sui and T'ang dynasties revived the Confucian concept that the emperor was the Son of Heaven, they often employed Buddhist ideology and institutions to make him the pivot of a reunited empire. Great festivals and impressive rites were developed for the accession of a new ruler, the birth of an imperial prince and commemorative services for the emperor's ancestors. Naturally, the reigning monarchs rewarded such examples of Buddhist enthusiasm. For example, Emperor Wen of the Sui dynasty once donated to a single temple fourteen thousand pieces of satin, two hundred pieces of the finest silk, as well as cash,

---

[5] L. Carrington Goodrich, *Short History of the Chinese People*, Harper and Brothers, N.Y., 1959, p. 115.

[6] Quoted by A.F. Wright, *Ibid,* p. 67.

cereal and one thousand balls of silk floss.[7]

Warfare often resulted in the wounding and mutilation of the participants. Chinese had a horror of a disfiguring death in battle or a burial far from home. By emphasizing the negligible importance of the physical body, Buddhism removed one of the drawbacks to a soldier's life. Then too, the pro-Buddhist Sui and T'ang emperors built commemorative temples on the battlefields at which perpetual prayers were conducted for the spirits of the war dead. If a soldier sacrificed his life for the sake of the Middle Kingdom and the Son of Heaven, he would demonstrate his devotion to something nobler than mere personal safety, like the Bodhisattva who gave up the bliss of Nirvana to help men. If he died a hero he would be assured of an imperial shrine and a nation's prayers forever. What could be more comforting or more inspiring in an age of conflict?

Summing up this period of Chinese history, a scholar writes: "...Buddhism flourished as never before. Supported by the lavish donations of the devout, guided by leaders of true piety and brilliance, graced by the most gifted artists and architects of the age, Buddhism was woven into the very texture of Chinese life and thought. These centuries were the golden age of an independent and creative Chinese Buddhism."[8]

Fa-tsang (643-712) illustrates the philosophical subtleties of Sui and T'ang dynasty Buddhism. Puzzled (understandably so) by Buddhist metaphysics, Empress Wu asked Fa-tsang to clear up her doubts. He did so, we are told, by pointing to the golden lion guarding the palace hall as a concrete example of the way the universal and particulars are related: the animal figure (a tangible object) is only a specific manifestation of the more substantial gold which symbolizes the Absolute.[9]

Fa-tsang's pupils were still baffled. The Buddhist sage explained his position with an ingenious device. To illustrate how the

---

[7] K. Ch'en, *Buddhism in China,* p. 276.

[8] A.F.Wright, *Ibid*, p. 70.

[9] Fung Yu-Lan, *History of Chinese Philosophy,* Princeton University Press, Princeton, N.J., 1953, volume II, pp. 340-359.

Buddha-nature or Absolute is related to existing phenomena, he took ten mirrors and arranged them with one at each of the eight compass points, one above and one below. Each was placed ten feet apart, yet all faced one another. He then placed a statue of Buddha in the center so that its image was reflected from one mirror to another. Each mirror reflected the image of the other mirrors plus all of the images reflected in each of the mirrors. In this way, the doubling and redoubling of reflections continues without end. Similarly, the Absolute is reflected in each existing particular and the eternal Buddha in each living thing.

Armed with such sophisticated logic and technique, Buddhism was fully and triumphantly established in China by the eighth century. Then disaster after disaster struck the faith. From the late ninth century onward, decline set in. When the T'ang empire was weakened by civil war and foreign assaults, the ruling classes became fearful of any potential sources of social discontent. Since the Buddhist self-governing monasteries appeared to be an empire within the empire, the imperial bureaucracy decided to suppress them. Declaring that the clergy had become corrupt, that the temples had amassed an excessive amount of wealth and that the monks were idlers, the emperor in 845 A.D. confiscated all Buddhist property throughout China. A later edict ordered the destruction of 4600 temples, the secularization of 260,500 monks and nuns, the demolishing of 40,000 shrines, the confiscation of millions of acres of Buddhist-owned land and the liberation of 150,000 slaves held by the temples. Never again would Buddhism be the preferred religion of China.[10]

When the T'ang dynasty collapsed, political chaos followed. Chinese historians speak of the next period as "the five dynasties and the ten independent states." Buddhism again suffered. In 955 A.D., 30,336 monasteries were destroyed by imperial edict, leaving only 2,694.[11] Then came the Sung dynasty (960-1279), an age which saw the Muslim conquest of India—with its widespread suppression of Buddhism—and the rise of neo-Confucianism as

---

[10] L.C. Goodrich, *Ibid*, pp. 129-131.
[11] *Ibid*, p. 146.

the official Chinese ideology. Chinese civilization of the eleventh and twelfth centuries probably outdistanced that of the rest of the world. But Buddhism had lost its hold on the governing class, its appeal for the scholars and its charm for the artists. The golden age had vanished.

Nevertheless, the next seven centuries were not totally hostile to the Buddhist cause. While the Sung emperors ruled part of China, three non-Han dynasties exercised considerable power elsewhere from 907-1368. The Liao emperors of Mongol background made Buddha's birthday a national holiday—though not that of Confucius. They also printed a fine edition of the Chinese *Tripitaka,* the basic Buddhist scriptures, a set of which was presented to the Koreans. The Chin dynasty gave imperial support to Buddhism: the first emperor provided an annual feast for over ten thousand monks and nuns; and during the reign of the second emperor over a million monks were ordained. In the Yuan dynasty, Genghis Khan was favorably impressed by Buddhist monks and Kublai Khan had a Buddhist ex-monk as his closest advisor. The latter emperor even made Lamaist Buddhism the national religion of the Mongol people.

When the Mongol dynasty was overthrown, the new Ming emperor had been a Buddhist monk and after assuming imperial office he often convened assemblies of monks to which he would personally give lectures on the *sutras*. After about three hundred years of Ming rule, the Manchu dynasty called Ch'ing seized control of the empire. Naturally, the Manchus who came from the north favored Lamaist Buddhism. In fact, since "living Buddhas" were a normal part of Tibetan faith, the founder of the Ch'ing dynasty claimed to be an incarnation of the Bodhisattva Manjusri, the lord of wisdom. While the Manchu capital at Peking was famous for its distinctive Tibetan architecture and the Ch'ing emperors used their nominal patronage of Tantric Buddhism as a convenient means for displaying their legitimate rule over Mongolia, Manchuria and Tibet, on the whole Buddhism continued to stagnate. The one favorable omen was the appearance of prominent laymen who were dedicated to the reform and revival of

Buddhism.[12]

It would be a gross exaggeration to say that the last thousand years have witnessed the steady decline of Chinese Buddhism. In spite of numerous reverses, Buddhism remained one of China's three historic faiths. Yuan-hsien (1578-1657) proposed that Confucius and Buddha were sages whose teachings complemented each other, the former with his this-worldly practicality, the latter with his other-worldly spirituality.[13] Yet even such a useful synthesis gradually lost its original meaning when most Chinese became preoccupied with practical affairs. For the upper classes brief visits to a Buddhist monastery provided a relaxing pause in their busy schedules while for the peasants Buddhist priests were convenient to have around if one was sick, deeply troubled or desirous of an abundant harvest and a male heir. Neither of these utilitarian purposes, however, expresses the deepest intent of Buddhist devotion.

Attacks on Buddhism

As long as Buddhism was primarily the faith of a few resident foreigners, the Confucian intellectuals and the Chinese government could (and did) tolerate or ignore it. However, once it had become a rather widespread religion, making an appeal to the masses and at times winning imperial favor, the situation changed. Confucian criticism in particular became fierce and dangerous, as the Confucian scholars and statesmen were the defenders of the traditional Chinese ideology.

From one standpoint, the attack that was launched against the Buddhist monks could be viewed as a conflict between the spiritual ideals of a religious community and the cynical materialism of Confucian bureaucrats, politicians and warlords. However, from another standpoint, the conflict could be seen as the collision of two differing religious cosmologies, as the traditional Chinese worldview, which the Confucianists represented, contained a considerable religious element. Society was seen as a divinely-

---

[12] See pp. 44-46.
[13] K. Ch'en, *Ibid*, p. 439.

constituted part of the total universe. The state, which was personified in the emperor, possessed to a great extent a religious aura. As a Chinese general and spokesman for the imperial court explained, "To sustain one's father and to serve the ruler—these are indeed the most perfect of the natural relationships."[14] The emperor, in the eyes of the Confucian, makes life possible for all his subjects. He personifies the creative powers of nature. His rule then, reflects the mandate of Heaven; his success or failure could even have repercussions in the processes of nature. To question his authority is to violate the preordained harmony of heaven and earth. However, the Buddhist monk denied the importance of the family and considered himself free from the duties of a subject: in effect he rebelled against the emperor. Thus the Buddhist was guilty of anti-social, illegal and blasphemous behavior.

The economic aspects of popular Buddhism also caused a critical reaction on the part of Confucian statesmen and courtiers. Since the monasteries were autonomous, self-governing units free from government supervision, officials suspected they were hiding places for all sorts of undesirable people—lazy vagrants, bandits who evaded arrest by seeking monastic refuge, and potential or actual political dissidents. Worse, the privileges which monks expect—freedom from taxes, exemption from military service, not being required to labor on government projects—naturally encouraged men to abandon their civic responsibilities for the leisurely life of the monastery. This complaint was not altogether unjustified: the central government was struggling against an ever-increasing mass evasion of taxes and forced labor. According to one high official of the fourth century, tax-evaders filled the monasteries, and those escaping labor service would gather from a hundred miles around in the Buddhist temples. For him, the "extravagance of the monks" was exhausting the imperial treasury.[15]

Naturally, from a Confucian perspective, Buddhist other-

---

[14] Huan Ch'en (402 A.D.), quoted in E. Zurcher, *The Buddhist Conquest of China,* vol. I, p. 232.

[15] Huan Hsuan (circa 400 A.D.), quoted in Zurcher, *Ibid,* p. 260.

worldliness was a waste of time, talent and money. What concrete, visible benefits did it give to the nation? As one Chinese official asked, Have the monks added a single year to the life of the emperor? Have they made crops more abundant or the people richer? Can they prevent natural disorders like floods or eliminate epidemics? For the Chinese, a philosophy was expected to improve conditions in this world. Although the Buddhists had collected vast sums of money, built highly ornamented pagodas and established numerous monasteries, there was no evidence whatsoever that they had harmonized yin and yang in the natural world or in society.

Nirvana specifically posed a problem for the Confucianist. For him, the Buddhists should teach men to conform to righteousness instead of making people "hanker after Paradise." Or, rather than trying to "frighten them with Hell," monks should urge men to rectify their lives with reason. By extolling the bliss of Nirvana, Buddhism makes men lax in their practical duties. How can one be truly good if he acts merely in order to achieve a hundredfold reward in heaven? No temporal social benefits could be expected from a religion which concerns itself with the afterlife.

The followers of Buddha also had to contend with the charge that theirs was a primitive philosophy taught by an Indian, and while it might be suitable for barbarians, it was completely unfit for the far superior Chinese. Popular thought had it that China was located at the exact center of the earth in order to manifest its cultural superiority and to enlighten the ignorant barbarians dwelling beyond its boundaries. Hence Buddhism was at best an inferior faith. Confucian scholars insisted that if Buddha's path had merit, it would have been mentioned in the Chinese classics and historical annals. As a fourth century writer declared, "things from abroad should not be studied by Chinese."[16]

According to some Confucians, Chinese and non-Chinese were completely different in natural constitution. The barbarian foreigner is created with a hard, obstinate nature; from birth he is

---

[16] Ho Ch'eng-t'ien (370-447 A.D.), quoted in Zurcher, *Ibid,* p. 265.

filled with evil desires and an inclination towards hatred and violence. By contrast, the Chinese inborn nature is pure, altruistic, harmonious. Every Chinese is gifted with a love for righteousness. The fact that barbarians were obstinate and arrogant by nature thus explained why Buddha taught such a mess of supernatural and otherworldly theories: he had to awe them into submission in order to make them obey the rules of ordinary decency.

Taoists had their version of the racist doctrine too. According to their anti-Buddhist writings, true Chinese mysticism (i.e. Lao-tzu's) corresponds to the element of wood and the principle *yang*, whereas Buddhism is an inferior religion corresponding to the element of metal and the feminine principle *yin*. Thus Buddhism is effeminate compared to the healthy masculinity of Taoism. In addition, the alien Indian faith is preoccupied with death rather than life. Monks fast because they really want to die. In fact, some Taoists asserted that Buddha taught the Indians to be ascetics and celibates in order to wipe out the uncivilized barbarian races.[17]

Taoists and Confucianists both were simply astounded by the Buddhist disregard for the family—the base of ancient Chinese society and the cornerstone of collective morality. For the Chinese, filial piety was paramount; each individual without exception was expected to subordinate his personal happiness to the well-being of the family. Marriage, of course, was indispensable to ensure the continuation of the paternal lineage. Thus the Buddhist—who severs family ties, vows celibacy, and withdraws from the household estate to become a monk—unashamedly violates all of the moral axioms.

Buddhism not only denies the central importance of the family, it advertises its defiance with outward signs. The monk shaves his head, wears strange clothing, and abandons his family name for a religious one. Confucian ethics taught that one must honor his hair as a gift from his parents; it is not surprising then that the monk's tonsure was highly offensive to the Chinese public. Worse, it was a standard practice for the Chinese to punish criminals by

---

[17] Zurcher, *Ibid*, p. 306.

shaving their heads, yet the Buddhists treated the shaved head as a mark of piety.

Though Indians accepted physical mortification as a normal method of attaining spirituality, the Chinese were shocked by any mistreatment of the body. Following Indian precedents some Buddhists practiced mutilation and a few even resorted to the final "sacrifice of the body" in religious suicides. Several cases are recorded of pious monks who wrapped themselves in oil-soaked bandages and burned themselves in the presence of a crowd of spectators.[18] Despite the fact that Buddha himself opposed the extreme ascetic practices of Hinduism and espoused a middle path between self-indulgence and self-negation, it is easy to understand how the Buddhist escape to Nirvana could be interpreted by over-zealous monks as an excuse for self-immolation.

Even without such rare cases of voluntary martyrdom, Buddhism appeared disgustingly immoral to the traditional Chinese moralist. As Confucian critics charged, the Buddhist monk forsakes those who gave him birth. He rejects his kinfolk and prefers the company of strangers. He disfigures his natural appearance by cutting off his beard and shaving his head. When his parents are still alive, the monk does not support them. When they are dead he does not perform the traditional rites of ancestor worship. In sum, in a tight-knit, family-oriented society, the Buddhist treats his relatives no better than strangers. "There is no greater disregard of right principles and violation of human feelings than this!"[19]

Nevertheless, Buddhism continued to attract converts. Despite angry protests and occasional outbursts of government persecution, the once-foreign religion became so thoroughly a part of Chinese civilization that it was repeatedly described as one of the three legs of imperial culture, the others being Confucianism and Taoism. In fact, Buddhism survived the empire and was experiencing a remarkable revival when the Communists seized the Chinese mainland.

---

[18] *Ibid*, p. 282.
[19] Quoted in *Ibid*, p. 283.

Three Buddhist Sects

In India Buddhists rather quickly broke up into rival schools; the same sort of division occurred in China. Three of these Buddhist denominations were particularly important: the T'ien-t'ai, the Pure Land and the Ch'an.[20]

Chih-i (538-597 A.D.) established the T'ien-t'ai school. He became a monk after witnessing the ransacking and burning of a library by pillaging soldiers; on that occasion he realized that man's uncontrollable passions are the cause of all sorrow. After studying for a time under a famous Buddhist teacher from north China, he went to Mt. T'ien-t'ai and made his home there. In a short time he began to attract large numbers of pupils. When he was thirty-nine his fame had already become so great that the emperor ordered all revenue from the district around the mountain to be reserved for his monastery.

As a devout Buddhist, Chih-i opposed the killing of any creature. He soon was even able to persuade his neighbors to give up fishing. Emperors continued to be impressed by Chih-i. One invited him to preach in the capital city regularly, and another bestowed upon him the admiring title "Man of Wisdom."

Chih-i attempted to harmonize Theravada and Mahayana scriptures. In doing so, he systematized and classified Buddhist sacred writings. He taught his followers that Buddha's original doctrine was the mystical monism of the Mahayana *Lotus Sutra,* but, because few could understand its profundity, Buddha was forced to resort to a simpler message. This was the Theravada doctrine of the four truths and the eightfold path. After winning large numbers of converts to this basic message, Buddha spent the next eight years trying to educate his followers to go beyond the elementary Theravada gospel. For twenty years after that he taught about the nature of the Absolute, and in his last eight years he explained that it was his mission to save all creatures. With such a chronology, Chih-i succeeded in recognizing just about every form of Buddhism. But more than that, his scheme gave each kind a proper place, with the *Lotus Sutra* taught by Buddha at both the

---

[20] John Blofeld, *The Jewel in the Lotus,* pp. 121-125.

beginning and the end of his mission. Most Chinese consequently came to see that the *Lotus Sutra* contained the essence of Buddhism, and interpreted all other scriptures from its perspective.

Chih-i and his T'ien-t'ai school emphasized the idea of an ultimate mystical totality in which all contrasts become unified: if one can only break through the barrier of subjective illusions, the all-embracing absolute Mind can be recognized. As the T'ien-t'ai Buddhists put it, the whole and its parts are really identical: the entire universe and all of the Buddhas may be present in one grain of sand or the tip of a single hair. Imagine a single hair pore and then imagine a large city—the small and the great are equally manifestations of the mind that is all-inclusive.

How then can one explain the fact of individual differences? If the absolute Mind embraces everything, and all things in our world depend on this mind for their existence, what divides the absolute into the particulars we see and touch? The T'ien-t'ai Buddhists say that the absolute Mind contains two natures, the pure and impure. The pure nature allows us to see the eternal Buddhahood, and the impure, the myriad objects in the phenomenal world. In essence the absolute Mind is one, undivided; however, in its functions and activities it is diverse, producing endless variety.

Our blindness to the reality of absolute Mind can only be removed by concentration *(chih)* and insight *(kuan)*. Through concentration, the Buddhist carefully analyzes a particular object until he realizes that it is made up of a series of illusions. A flow of invisible, intangible, completely non-sensory energy-events have taken a visible, tangible form in the object. However, though it is necessary to realize by concentration the reality behind any object, it is also necessary to realize that there is a purpose for the illusions created by the mind, and therefore man must act *as though* he exists in a world of physical objects.[21]

Inevitably, one sect of monks in this school identified the absolute Mind doctrine with pantheism and acted accordingly.

---

[21] K. Ch'en, *Ibid,* pp. 303-313.

Since all life is a manifestation of the absolute Mind, then what is the special value of monasteries? Monks who thought that way soon began sleeping in courtyards and spending their days mingling with the crowds in the marketplace. They further asked if all is a revelation of absolute Mind, why worry about reading sacred scriptures or bowing in front of statues? This sect as a consequence began to speak contemptuously of book learning and temple worship. Because the Buddha-nature pervades everything, they thought that all people—whatever their station in life—should be treated like potential Buddhas. Monks would suddenly prostrate themselves before passing strangers in public and hail them as Buddhas—in complete disregard of conventional Chinese etiquette. They even went so far as to shock crowds by bowing down in front of dogs—for each dog is a future Buddha. Strangely enough, such bizarre behavior attracted attention to the basic beliefs of the sect. In fact, because the devotion of the monks was so apparent, people were often moved to give alms. Hence, their temple at the capital city became known as the Inexhaustible Treasury, so great were its financial resources.[22]

Though the T'ien-t'ai school flourished, a sect which was far more popular, making up 60-70% of the Buddhists before World War II, was the Pure Land School. Based on the teachings of the *Pure Land Sutra,* this sect offered China a religion of free grace. According to the sutra, long before the birth of Gautama, a monk was granted his wish to become Buddha Amitabha—the Lord of infinite light and immortal life who presides over the ideal Buddha-land known as the Western Paradise. There is a lake whose bottom is covered with pure gold sand, and whose waters hold miraculous power. Lotus bloom there with flowers as big as cartwheels. Surrounding the lake are towering palaces. Cranes, peacocks and swan sing there day and night, proclaiming Buddhist teachings. It is populated by countless persons who have been brought to the realm through the merit and grace of Amitabha Buddha. He has vowed, so believers hold, that anyone who calls

---

[22] *Ibid,* pp. 297-300.

upon him sincerely will be reborn in the Pure Land. Working beside Amitabha is the ever-present Avaloketsvara *(Kuan-yin)*, the always compassionate Bodhisattva who will go anywhere and do anything to lead the faithful to the land of perpetual bliss.

While the original faith of the Pure Land school came from India, and their sacred sutras were composed in Sanskrit, Chinese Buddhists accommodated the teachings to the new cultural environment, sometimes quite drastically.[23] The worship of Kuan-yin illustrates the radical nature of this adaptation. Avaloketsvara was a male Bodhisattva, whose portraits often showed him with a mustache. But sometime in the eighth century, as we noted earlier, during the T'ang dynasty, Tantric Buddhists in China introduced a female version of Kuan-yin—using the same name—who was clad in white and could give children to any woman who prayed to her. The mustached male gradually fades into the background, giving way to the female Kuan-yin, who becomes in popular Chinese religion a Madonna-like figure, the "goddess of infinite compassion."

Besides offering the masses an easy path to celestial happiness through the simple recitation of the name of Amitabha, Pure Land Buddhism won converts by its vivid portrayal of the hell that awaited unbelievers. Some became scared enough to give support to the Buddhist cause. At its best, Pure Land Buddhism encouraged men and women to experience a deep religious life based on faith, devotion and practical holiness. At its worst, it degenerated into meaningless repetition of the holy name.

The Ch'an school of Buddhism is popularly known by its Japanese name, *Zen*. Ch'an refers to a practical religious discipline aimed at tranquilizing the mind. Through such an effort, the monk is able to preserve a serenity of spirit and cheerfulness of disposition even in a turbulent world. Ch'an techniques were imported from India, but soon became thoroughly Chinese. Bodhidharma, an Indian missionary, brought Ch'an methods to China about 526 A.D. At one point in his career, he was said to have faced a blank

---

[23] *Ibid*, pp. 338-350. On Tantric Buddhism see J. Blofeld, *Ibid*, pp. 149-158.

wall for nine years. So engrossed did he become in his meditation that he refused to take notice of those who came to learn from him. That is, until one would-be disciple cut off his arm to prove his sincerity.

Ch'an Buddhism exhorts one to rid the mind of all conscious thoughts in order to attain enlightenment. Since the Void *(Sunyata)* is the goal of meditation, there is no value in reciting sacred scriptures, meditating before statues of Buddha or performing the traditional ceremonies in the pagoda. Neither is there any value in following the teachings of the eightfold path. All of these practices keep the ego at work, begetting karma and reinforcing attachment to external objects.

The true monk should allow his mind to operate freely, spontaneously, naturally. Bodhidharma himself described Ch'an as: "A special transmission outside the scriptures; no dependence upon words and letters; direct pointing to the soul of man; seeing into one's own nature."[24] Bodhidharma's purpose was "to make short work of the prevailing speculative thought and its companion, salvation by faith."[25]

Ch'an Buddhism was at the same time an affirmation of the original spirit of Buddha and a vigorous protest against popular Buddhism. As Buddha criticized the authority of the *Vedas,* Ch'an devotees opposed reliance on the Buddhist sutras. As Buddha had discouraged his disciples from debating the ontological theories of Vedanta, followers of Ch'an disregarded Mahayana metaphysics. Ch'an also pushed aside devotion to Buddhas and Bodhisattvas, much as Gautama Buddha had condemned reliance on the gods and goddesses of Hinduism. In protest against both the Pure Land's promise of a Western Paradise and popular Buddhism's veneration of sacred relics—such as Buddha's tooth, hair or collarbone—Ch'an emphasized the personal quest for enlightenment, the "direct pointing to the soul of man."

The difference between folk Buddhism and Ch'an is superbly illustrated by the Chinese emperor's interview with the Zen patri-

---

[24] C. Humphreys, *Buddhism,* Pelican Book, Harmondsworth, England, 1969, p. 67.
[25] *Ibid,* p. 67.

arch. The ruler asked the patriarch what merit he could expect to receive from his building of temples and monasteries, from his promotion of Buddhist scriptures and his support of a multitude of monks and nuns. The patriarch replied, "None whatever, your Majesty!" Shocked by the Ch'an master's disregard for his pious work, the emperor then asked the monk, "Well, what *is* the first principle of Buddhism?" The patriarch responded, "Absolutely nothing." Exasperated, the monarch said, "And who are you?" "I have no idea," said the master. While the Ch'an patriarch was quite serious, the Chinese emperor was not converted to such a strange form of Buddhism.[26]

Among the masters of Ch'an Buddhism was the eighth century monk Hui Hai, commonly known as "The Great Pearl." Like all the Ch'an, he minimized the importance of scripture. Once one awakens to reality by achieving enlightenment, the Buddhist can forget about formal doctrine; for when a fisherman catches his fish, he has no more need for a net.[27] "Walking, standing, sitting, lying—all are the functioning of your nature," said Hui Hai. "In what (way) are you out of accord with it? Just go now and take a rest (i.e., set your mind at rest) for a while. As long as you are not carried away by external winds, your nature will remain like water for ever still and clear. Let nothing matter. Take good care of yourselves!"[28]

If one is not bothered by external matters, he does not get upset over religious differences. In Hui Hai's time, many were debating the respective virtues of Confucianism, Taoism and Buddhism. The Ch'an master refused to get involved in such sectarian disputes. This monk said that when employed by men of great capacity, Buddhism, Taoism and Confucianism are the same. All of them spring from the functioning of a single self-nature. They differ when they are understood by men of limited intellect. Whether an individual remains deluded or not is solely dependent upon his own will—not upon differences in doctrine.[29]

---

[26] *Ibid*, p. 181.
[27] J. Blofeld, trans., *The Zen Teaching of Hui Hai*, Rider & Co., London, 1962, p. 123.
[28] *Ibid*, p. 128.
[29] *Ibid*, p. 103.

Ch'an Buddhism had three advantages over other Buddhist sects when persecution broke out in China. Because it did not depend on scriptures, statues or pagodas, it could function even when the Taoists and Confucianists had the emperors suppress Buddhism. Unlike other Buddhist sects, Ch'an could not be accused of being a social parasite, as all Ch'an monks were required to perform some useful labor instead of begging. In addition, the similarities between Ch'an and Taoism were so apparent that interreligious hostility was kept at a minimum. However, by its very nature, Ch'an had a limited appeal and could never become as popular as Pure Land Buddhism.

Milo Fo, the Chinese Messiah

Maitreya, the "coming Buddha" of Indian religion, was called Milo Fo[30] when Buddhism was brought to China. According to the Buddhist sutras, he waits in the highest heaven for the time when he will be most needed. At that point he will descend to earth—to save mankind. As with Christian messianism, ardent longing for the advent of Milo Fo coincided with periods of political disaster and social upheaval. During the Northern Wei period, a time of widespread turmoil, the statues of Sakyamuni and Milo Fo were most popular. However, in the more peaceful T'ang period primary attention was focused on Amitabha, the loving Buddha of the Pure Land Sect.[31]

Tao-an (312-385), the leading monk of his time, was an ardent believer in the imminent coming of Buddha. A noted translator of Sanskrit texts and an imperial advisor, he organized a cult centered on Milo Fo, conceiving of his own mission as preparation for the messiah's advent.[32] His teaching and views became widespread, explaining in part the large numbers of Milo Fo images that appeared in the next few centuries. Privileged classes and the masses alike awaited the appearance of Milo Fo, who would bring blessings to the earth, and by making use of the emperor, unify all of mankind.

---

[30] Sometimes spelled "Mi-le-fo".
[31] K. Ch'en, *Ibid*, p. 172.
[32] *Ibid*, pp. 100, 178.

In the tenth century a curious transformation of the Buddha-to-come concept occurred.[33] It began with a certain fat, jovial and eccentric monk, whose name is unknown, who began to attract public notice. At first his fame spread because of his uncanny ability to predict the weather. When men saw him wearing wet sandals they could expect a storm; when they saw him squatting on a bridge sleeping contentedly, they could look forward to good weather. The monk was also known for always carrying a hemp bag. Whenever curious children would ask what the bag contained, he would empty the contents one by one, then methodically place them back in the bag. To inquisitive adults who asked him to explain the significance of the bag, like a Ch'an mystic, he would simply reply that it was as old as space. Another story is told of someone who had seen him bathing at the river; the observer noticed that the strange pot-bellied man had a third eye—a sign of occult wisdom—on his back. Henceforth, the villagers suspected that he might be the future Buddha in the flesh.

Long after the monk's death, stories and poems still circulated about how Milo Fo had appeared on the earth disguised as a fool, his fat belly uncovered and a big smile on his face.[34] Artists in particular became enchanted with the idea that a pot-bellied monk with a hemp bag symbolized the Maitreya ideal. Porcelain images of the Laughing Buddha soon appeared and were exported throughout the Far East.

Although Milo Fo resembles the European Santa Claus, behind his joviality is expressed a deep-seated longing for the kingdom of God to be established on the earth. Chinese foresaw and spoke of a new world to come, ruled under "the Mandate of Heaven." Therefore, like the Christian and Jewish messianic hope, the Maitreya cult was often used as justification for political or social revolt. As a result emperors and bureaucrats looked upon devotees of Milo Fo with suspicion.

Though most of the time Buddhists were inoffensive monks

---

[33] K. Ch'en, *Ibid,* pp. 405-408.

[34] Cf. the Russian Orthodox concept of "Christ the fool", by Dostoievski in his novel *The Idiot.*

cultivating detachment and quiet meditation, they could—and did—turn into social critics and political rebels: sometimes by acclaiming a charismatic figure as the long-awaited Maitreya, sometimes by identifying a specific social protest as preparation for the advent of the Buddhist Messiah. In 613 A.D. two different monks claimed to be the expected Milo Fo; one of them even set himself up as the legitimate emperor for the new age of prosperity and peace. Both of them, however, were promptly arrested and beheaded. A more successful messianic pretender followed about a century later; she was the Empress Wu who rebelled against the T'ang emperor on the grounds that she was an incarnation of Maitreya, and as such was better qualified for the throne. Though she won a throne she brought no stability to China.

In the subsequent Sung Dynasty, Maitreya societies again caused trouble. The societies of the Hopei province (where Peking is located) united under the leaderhip of an army officer named Wang Tse in rebellion against the imperial government. When Wang Tse had left his home to join the army, his mother tattooed the word "fu" on his back, which meant "blessedness," undoubtedly as a good luck charm. But for the Maitreya cult members in rebellion the tattoo was considered a supernatural omen. Therefore, for them, Wang Tse was either the Messiah himself or the divinely appointed earthly ruler who would set the stage for Milo Fo's appearance. Unfortunately for the rebels, imperial troops quickly marched on their stronghold in Hopei and suppressed the revolt (circa 1047). All Maitreya societies were immediately outlawed.

Next to make trouble was the White Lotus Society. Formed about 1128 to promote Buddhist devotions, it soon ran afoul of the authorities. Because men and women met together, the group was accused of debauchery. Because it was a secret society, members were suspected to be demon-worshippers. And because they adopted white as their color they were also suspect, as white was associated with the outlawed Maitreya cult. For two centuries the organization was banned. Yet imperial disapproval forced the White Lotus Society to go underground. It provided a meeting place for all sorts of people from bandits to freedom-fighters. Rebellions were often plotted there to drive the usurpers out of the country.

In 1337 another revolt took place, this time led by one Pang Hu, who claimed that he was preparing the way for the imminent advent of Maitreya. A generation later the "Red Kerchief Bandits" appeared. Their leader, Han Shan-t'ung, gathered an army, preaching that "the country is in great confusion, and Maitreya is coming down to be reborn." Enthusiasts traced their leader's ancestry back to a former emperor, and the revolt was expected to herald the restoration of the Sung dynasty. As an emblem of their cause they wore red kerchiefs and as a mark of their devotion they burned incense to Milo Fo.

Though Han Shan-t'ung and his insurrectionists fell to the Mongols in 1362 after gaining control of a sizable part of north China, their cause persisted. A red kerchief rebel monk named Chu Yang-Chang (1328-1398) finally drove the Mongols out of China and founded the Ming Dynasty which ruled from 1368-1644. As soon as he became emperor, he quickly suppressed all secret societies like the one which had made his own rule possible. Every political dissident was executed. As a result, many Chinese Buddhists prefer to forget the White Lotus Society.[35]

Though several messianic revolts occurred during the last imperial dynasty, Buddhists were not among the revolutionary forces. The Taiping rebellion against the Manchus (1850-1865) was led by a Christian psychic who claimed to be the younger brother of Jesus. His commission was to bring the kingdom of heaven to earth. Four other revolts were carried out by Muslims who resented the second class status forced on the minorities in the empire.[36] The Boxer rebellion (1900) was a futile effort of political reactionaries, ultra-traditionalist Confucians and anti-Christian mobs to rid China of the European imperialists. As for Sun Yat-sen's republicanism, Chiang Kai-shek's nationalism and Mao's communism, these revolutionary movements were all western-

---

[35] K. Ch'en, *Ibid,* pp. 429-431.
[36] Goodrich, *Ibid,* p. 225.

oriented, anti-Confucian and anti-Buddhist as well, to varying extents. At any rate, Milo Fo had lost his appeal for the Chinese in modern times.

III. THE MODERN PERIOD: FROM THE MANCHUS TO MAO

During the Ch'ing dynasty which survived almost to World War I, China confronted the West. Opening the door of China against her will became the avowed policy of Christian missionaries, European diplomats, and western generals. China's response to the West, both positive and negative, provides the clue to an understanding of her turbulent history for the past two centuries. As one of the three major religions of the empire, Buddhism faced a challenge of unparalleled magnitude. That it survived at all is one of the wonders of modern history.

Neo-Buddhist Leaders

Yang Wen-Hui (1837-1911) was the first great apostle of modern Chinese Buddhism. Born two years before the Opium War in which Great Britain attacked China and dying two days before the establishment of the republic, Yang lived through the first chapter of his nation's tragic encounter with the West. Although the political disasters of the time surely proved Gautama's fourfold truth that man's suffering results from his worldly craving, Yang's Buddhism resulted from more personal trials. When he was three years old, he was engaged to a girl of nine who later caught smallpox and became badly disfigured. Yang gallantly refused to break off the engagement and married her. Later, he found a girl whom he wished to take as a second wife. However, his first wife had just given birth to a son and refused to share her husband. Yang became depressed and it was in such a state that he found a book of Buddhist scriptures. Henceforth nothing else seemed important.

Because of his duty to support his family, Yang remained a layman. Yet his devotion to Buddhism persisted. With the help of friends he set up a printing press for the publication of Buddhist scriptures, many copies of which had been destroyed during the Taiping rebellion.[1] He also obtained Buddhist books from Japan which he reprinted and distributed. While this literary revival in no way compared to the mass of Christian books published by missionaries, at least it was a start in counteracting the ignorance and bigotry with which Protestants and Catholics treated China's religious heritage.[2]

When Dharmapala, the Ceylonese Buddhist renovator, came back from the Parliament of Religions at Chicago in 1893, he met Yang in Shanghai, kindling in him hope for a world-wide Buddhist mission. By 1908 Yang had prepared a textbook for monks and begun a missionary training school in his mansion. When that failed he started a Buddhist research institute which sponsored weekly lectures on the sutras for laymen. In three ways Yang was the father of the Buddhist revival: 1) by encouraging the publication and distribution of religious literature, 2) by promoting the creation of modern Buddhist seminaries, and 3) by stimulating an international outlook among Chinese Buddhists.[3]

T'ai-hsu (1890-1947) was Yang's well-known and active disciple. Ordained a monk at the age of fourteen, when he was seventeen he underwent an experience of spiritual enlightenment comparable to a Christian conversion experience. By reading books on political and social reform by Chinese intellectuals, he became an enthusiastic radical. Associating with anarchists and socialists. T'ai-hsu even attended secret meetings of revolutionaries and studied the writing of Marx, Kropotkin and other anti-capitalist agitators.

After Sun Yat-sen became provisional president of the new Chinese republic, T'ai-hsu organized the Association for the Ad-

---

[1] Cf. Amaury de Riencourt, *The Soul of China*, Coward-McCann, N.Y., 1958, pp. 150-152.

[2] Cf. Holmes Welch, "Christian Stereotypes and Buddhist Realities", *The Buddhist Revival in China*, Harvard University Press, Cambridge, 1968, pp. 222-253. Unwittingly the missionary attacks on Confucianism and Buddhism provided ammunition for the later Maoist assault on all religions.

[3] For details, see Welch, *Ibid*, pp. 2-10.

vancement of Buddhism with government approval. With the help of socialist laymen he next tried unsuccessfully to take over China's most famous monastery—Chin Shan located on the Yangtze river. His intention was to turn it into a modern school for monks committed to "a new Buddhism in a new China." Outraged, the conservatives organized the Chinese General Buddhist Association to protect the monasteries from radical reformers or government leaders who wished to seize Buddhist buildings for secular use. Repeatedly T'ai-hsu tried to gain control of this organization. Not until 1945 could he accomplish this ambition; but three months before the first national conference opened at Nanking in 1947, T'ai-hsu died of a stroke. At the time of the Communist usurpation of power on the mainland, the Chinese Buddhist Association claimed 4,620,000 members.

T'ai-hsu's activities on behalf of organizational unity were a small part of his contribution to Chinese Buddhism. He published a Buddhist magazine, opened a seminary and from 1923 on started ecumenical conferences for Buddhists. After conventions held in China and Japan, the monk persuaded Chiang Kai-shek to pay for him to make a tour of Europe and America on behalf of the Buddhist cause. In 1939 the Nationalist government sponsored another world lecture tour for him. While in Ceylon, T'ai-hsu encouraged Dr. Malalasekera to found the World Fellowship of Buddhists, which he did in 1950.[4] Despite almost insuperable obstacles and numerous setbacks the Chinese monk had sown seeds which could have produced a rebirth of Buddhism on the mainland.

There were several other leaders of the neo-Buddhist movement but these two at least reveal the direction it would have taken, if political conditions had been more favorable. While missionaries, foreign visitors and a variety of Chinese reformers reported that Buddhism rapidly declined during the Ch'ing dynasty and was in a state of decay when China became a republic, such analyses are highly suspect. It was not true that the Buddhist

---

[4] See Welch, *Ibid,* pp. 15-18, 28-33, 41-71.

monastic community had dwindled. In 1667 China had 110,000 monks, in 1930 there were 500,000.[5] Rather than declining, Buddhism was in the midst of a renaissance when China became a republic.

Buddhism in the Chinese Republic

Most monks took no part in the stormy events which toppled the Ch'ing dynasty and created a republic. But the majority of Confucian scholars, Taoist priests and Christian clergymen were not directly involved either. However, there were some ardent champions for national reconstruction. Tsung-yang, a well-known monk, painter and poet, met Sun Yat-sen in Japan and raised funds for his revolutionary activities.[6] T'an Ssu-t'ung, executed by the Dowager Empress for his part in an abortive Chinese reform movement, was a student of the neo-Buddhist group. Monks at the Jade Buddha monastery in Shanghai actually organized a brigade to fight in the 1911 rebellion. In another area the abbot used monastery supplies to aid the republican troops.

When the republic was born, the Buddhists represented by far the largest organized religious group in China. While many of the successful revolutionists were indifferent to religion and a sizeable number were hostile, Buddhists still played a significant role in the leadership of post-Ch'ing China. Two Buddhist laymen served as heads of state, four as prime ministers, one as minister of agriculture, two ministers of communications, one minister of finance, one president of the supreme court and eighteen provincial governors.[7]

The political misfortunes of the republic had repercussions in the area of religion. Sun Yat-sen personally admired the American form of government but by necessity during his early years had to accept support from anyone who offered it: anarchists, ambitious politicians out of power, Marxists, impractical idealists, even a variety of foreign agents. Without the resourcefulness and deter-

---

[5] *Ibid*, pp. 227-237.
[6] *Ibid*, p. 17.
[7] Names given in Welch, *Ibid,* pp. 330-331.

mination of Generalissimo Chiang Kai-shek, the government would have collapsed long before 1949. From 1911 on, the republic faced assaults from regional warlords, Communists and Japanese invaders.

Under the Ch'ing emperors rigid laws had been passed to restrict the expansion of Buddhist monasticism yet protect its existing institutions and properties. In many cases the Sun Yat-sen government tried to curb Buddhism and in more cases could not protect its property. For a century, the monks had faced enemies like the Confucian literati, the Christian missionaries, the Chinese modernizers, predatory officials and bandits. The situation worsened after 1911. The republic tolerated the widespread destruction of monasteries and the ruthless expulsion of monks in many provinces. On one pretext or another, monasteries were expropriated for public schools, administrative offices, hospitals, barracks, orphanages and homes for the aged.[8]

Except for hastily-organized committees of monks, few raised their voices against what took place. Followers of John Dewey and Bertrand Russell, the two most popular western philosophers in republican China, encouraged campaigns against religion and/or superstition. Missionaries were delighted to see the eradication of rivals, especially as the Christians could rely on powerful foreign governments for their own protection. Modernizers, like the eminent Hu Shih[9], believed a new China could only be built after the old China was reduced to rubble. As for the Communists, they looked upon the destruction of Buddhism as preparation for a later elimination of all religion.

In 1911 a Cantonese mob seized Buddhist statues from the temples and dumped them into the river. In 1929 Kwangsi province prohibited the burning of incense and candles. In 1931-32 General Feng's troops in Honan province systematically pillaged Buddhist temples, breaking off the stone heads of the statues and using the wooden ones for firewood—a policy recommended by his Chris-

---

[8] Welch, *Ibid*, pp. 25-26, 132-159.

[9] Cf. Jerome B. Grieder, *Hu Shih and the Chinese Renaissance*, Harvard University Press, Cambridge, 1970, pp. 163-164.

tian advisers.[10] In 1935 Yunnan province made it illegal to make obeisance to an image of the Buddha. Yet no prohibition of religious practice was ever incorporated into national law.

In defense of President Chiang, it should be said that he rather quickly recognized the danger of Marxist subversion, allied himself with responsible businessmen and political moderates, and purged his government of Communist agitators. At the same time he tried to stabilize the parts of China under his control, imposing restraints on mob violence and providing greater protection for Buddhist institutions. There was never general or official persecution of Buddhism during his regime. Although there was considerable encroachment on monastic property, and their farmlands were subject to taxation, monastic premises remained tax-exempt. Monks were not required to serve as soldiers if they preferred to enlist on first-aid teams. Most important, the government at no time tried to turn the monastic community into propaganda agents for the ruling Kuomintang party. After examining all the available evidence, a scholar concludes, "monks appear to have fared as well as the rest of the population, if not better."[11]

Then came Mao and the Peoples Republic, by every standard—political, moral, philosophic, artistic, and religious—the worst scourge a long-suffering China has experienced in four thousand years.

Persecution by Mao

Because of the West's preoccupation with the tragic suppression of the Christian churches by the Maoist dictatorship, little publicity has been given to the Red Chinese persecution of Buddhists. More recently, since efforts have been made to normalize

---

[10] Welch, *Ibid,* p. 148. Missionaries frequently praised Feng as "the Christian general".

[11] Welch, *Ibid,* pp. 155-156. For a detailed report on what it was like to be a monk in 20th century China, see the biography of Abbot Miao-Chi (1895-1930) written by his friend, the Norwegian Lutheran missionary K.L. Reichelt: *The Transformed Abbot,* Lutterworth Press, London, 1954. Miao-Chi, a disciple of T'ai-Hsu, was one of the leaders of neo-Buddhism on Japanese-occupied Formosa, turning Christian two years before his death. Missionary bias is minimal until the final chapters of the book.

relations between the United States and the People's Republic, the brutal aspects of Mao's regime have been carefully hidden. For example, a popular handbook on China states that as for religion, there have been no conflicts of major consequence. Confucianism, Buddhism and Taoism are not organized religions, we are told, so they have no politically conscious theology that would clash with government ideology. Nor do they possess any entrenched power by which to resist the implementation of state socialism. Therefore the handbook reports that the Communists experienced little difficulty in confiscating Buddhist monastic lands or expropriating temples for use as offices and schools. Buddhist monks "accepted" government orders to abandon their profession and took up productive jobs like any lay citizens. The People's Republic allows certain harmless ceremonies to continue among the older folk but it knows that religion lacks appeal to youngsters and will die out.[12] Although this picture of contemporary China has become the fashionable one in colleges and among "progressive" historians, it ignores half the facts, completely distorting the situation as we shall show.

Once Maoist armies had successfully subjugated the Chinese mainland, the Communists launched a savage attack upon Buddhism. According to a Japanese Buddhist magazine, using information obtained at the third World Buddhist Conference at Rangoon, prior to 1949 there had been 130,000 temples in China; by 1955 less than a hundred had survived. In Peking, long famed for its magnificent temples, only three still remained even physically intact, two of these having been converted into factories while the third served as a concentration camp for monks. Shanghai, Nanking and Hangchow, formerly filled with hundreds of temples, were reduced to one each. Large numbers of priests, monks and nuns had been murdered when the Communists came to power; many committed suicide in despair, died in jail or were executed as enemies of the regime. By 1955, not more than 2500 Buddhist monks and nuns remained alive in Red China. Fortunately,

---

[12] Ping-Chai Kuo, *China*, Oxford University Press, London, 1963, p. 109.

a considerable number had escaped to Taiwan where they could be protected by the Chiang Kai-shek Nationalists.

The destruction of Buddhist property by the Marxists was appalling. Many Buddha images of artistic value or historical significance were transferred to the Soviet Union in exchange for military supplies. Others were simply smashed by Maoist soldiers or revolutionary mobs. Buddhist scriptures in the temples, many of which were priceless antiques, were burned. Laymen were ordered to surrender their religious books to local Red authorities who promptly destroyed them. Again, however, some rare books and precious religious art were carried to safety by the Nationalists.

Such acts of brutal suppression and pillage were in accord with the dialectical materialist ideology of the usurpers. While some looting and vandalism were to be expected in a period of national turmoil, when Maoist authority was imposed on the populace, Red officials legalized the closing or destruction of most Buddhist temples and monasteries. A German theologian who made a careful examination of the available data concluded that the Buddhist priesthood and the monastic communities were decimated.[13]

By brutally liquidating the Buddhist leadership and virtually eliminating Buddhism as a religious, educational or cultural force in China, Mao was simply following the Stalinist party line. According to the *Great Soviet Encyclopedia* (1938 edition), Buddhists are guilty of suppressing workers' protests against feudal exploitation because of their exhortations to be peaceful, compassionate and humble, making no resistance to evil. In Marxist opinion, monasteries provide strongholds of the counterrevolution and seedbeds for imperialistic espionage. Yet there were a half dozen factors in the Chinese situation which made the classic hostility of Russian Marxism to the Orthodox Church

---

[13] Ernst Benz, *Buddhism or Communism,* Doubleday and Co., N.Y., 1965, p. 178. Legal measures enacted against Chinese Buddhism took several forms: government seizure of all lands owned by monasteries and temples, condemnation of the religious leaders as reactionary landlords, classification of monks as social parasites and execution of some priests and abbots as enemies of the people (K. Ch'en, *Buddhism in China,* pp. 462-463).

inapplicable to Buddhism: 1) Chinese Buddhism was neither the state religion nor the representative of pre-Communist national ideology; 2) Buddhism had already suffered greatly as the result of the West's impact on 19th and 20th century China; 3) Christian missionary schools and publications had long condemned Buddhism as an old-fashioned and backward faith unsuitable to the new China; 4) Communists could treat Buddhism as the basis for an ancient Asian culture which was non-Western yet international so potentially useful; 5) Buddhism was far less a political or ideological threat than Christianity; and finally, 6) from Sun Yat-sen's time on, some form of state socialism was advocated by most of the architects of China's republican ideology, including the Buddhist intelligentsia.[14]

Hence, in the light of this situation, once the Maoists had stripped Buddhism of its wealth, lands and leadership, they could transform it into "a kind of religious museum under state supervision."[15] Although there could be no real place for a living Buddhism in Maoist China, the dead Buddhism of the past nineteen centuries could be praised as a precious cultural heritage. Historic temples and pagodas were restored as national monuments. Government archaeologists began excavating ancient ruins. Buddhist art masterpieces received government protection. Scholars were encouraged to write articles for the great encyclopedia of Buddhism being produced in Sri Lanka and did so. In 1956 the Chinese Buddhist Academy was opened to study the Buddhist heritage in Chinese literature and to correspond regularly with Buddhist scholars in other countries. Classic scriptural texts and commentaries have since been translated into Chinese and published in attractive editions.

When non-Marxist Japanese delegations were at last allowed to visit Red China, they saw Buddhist temples being restored, young monks studying at the Buddhist University in Peking and many active Buddhist societies in China's large cities. Chinese representatives at the Rangoon ecumenical conference claimed

---

[14] Benz, *Ibid*, pp. 179-182.
[15] *Ibid*, p. 183.

that the Communist-authorized Buddhist Association of China had 263,125 charter members, represented 4,500,000 Buddhists, administered eleven colleges and eleven other schools, supervised six libraries, ran three publishing houses and published eight magazines. Representatives from the Buddhist Association took part in conferences held in Rangoon, Colombo (Sri Lanka), Tokyo, Kyoto, and Cambodia.[16]

In the opinion of Maoist theoreticians, Chinese Buddhism could serve two useful purposes: be a reminder of China's cultural superiority by contrast with the "decadent West"; and also, provide a convenient propaganda agency in promoting friendly relations with neighboring Buddhist nations of Asia. Both as a means for reinforcing China's pride and as a convenient tool of Maoist foreign policy, Buddhism could and has been helpful.[17]

From the Chinese Communist standpoint, the People's Republic was virtually encircled by enemies: a reconstructed Japan, democratic India, American-supported Korea, the Nationalist stronghold of Taiwan protected by the U.S. fleet, and a Soviet Union which too often meddled in the internal affairs of the Chinese nation. By creating the image of being a friend of Asian self-determination and a patron of international Buddhism, Red China resolved to gradually influence her neighbors, producing a ring of nations sympathetic to her cause. Promoting Buddhism was one technique employed by the Maoist foreign ministry in pursuit of its long-range goal to dominate the Far East.

When the Chinese invaded and conquered Tibet, mercilessly massacring large numbers of lamas, ruthlessly destroying most of the Buddhist institutions and causing the Dalai Lama to seek asylum in India, what had happened to Buddhism in China was repeated on a smaller scale, though with far greater savagery. While the International Commission of Jurists condemned the Maoist subjugation of Tibet as "genocide," Chinese Buddhist

---

[16] According to their magazine *Modern Buddhism,* the Chinese Buddhist Association in 1960 represented 500,000 monks and 100,000,000 Buddhist laymen. K. Ch'en believes these figures are just guesses. (*Buddhism in China,* pp. 464-465).

[17] Benz, *Ibid,* pp. 188-189.

spokesmen defended their government's foreign policy. To the sixth Buddhist ecumenical conference meeting in Cambodia in 1961, the Chinese delegation explained that the Dalai Lama and his fellow refugees were reactionaries from the Tibetan upper classes who had imposed feudalistic slavery on the masses. Maoist intervention had cleansed Buddhist monasteries so they could recover their original usefulness. Destruction in Tibet was caused not by the Chinese liberators but by reactionary Tibetans who had fomented an unsuccessful rebellion against the masses. China has rebuilt the monasteries and was helping the lamas restore the pure doctrine of Buddha, it was said.[18]

However, according to the Dalai Lama, the former chief executive of the Tibetan government and the highest authority in Tantric Buddhism, the Maoist occupation army indulged in a mad orgy of destruction and massacre.[19] Tens of thousands of Tibetans were summarily executed without trial on suspicion of being anti-communist, hoarding money or belonging to the upper classes, but mainly because they would not renounce their religion. Lamas were especially persecuted on charges that they were unproductive parasites living off the earnings of the masses. "The Chinese tried to humiliate them, especially the elderly and most respected, before they tortured them, by harnessing them to ploughs, riding them like horses, whipping and beating them, and other methods too evil to mention. And while they were slowly putting them to death, they taunted them with their religion, calling on them to perform miracles to save themselves from pain and death."[20]

When the West did nothing and the United Nations passed useless resolutions, the Dalai Lama declared:

"We should not seek revenge on those who have committed crimes against us, or reply to their crimes with other crimes. We

---

[18] *Ibid*, pp. 196-200.

[19] Cf. "The Question of Tibet and the Rule of Law" and "Tibet and the Chinese People's Republic" (International Commission of Jurists, Geneva, 1959, 1960) for confirmation of the Maoist atrocities. The International Commission is an independent association of lawyers from fifty nations.

[20] The Dalai Lama, *My Land and My People*, p. 222.

should reflect that by the law of Karma, they are in danger of lowly and miserable lives to come, and that our duty to them, as to every being, is to help them to rise toward Nirvana, rather than let them sink to lower levels of rebirth.... My hope rests in the courage of Tibetans, and the love of truth and justice which is still in the heart of the human race; and my faith is in the compassion of Lord Buddha."[21]

New Buddhism for a New China

In the opening decade of the present century, Chinese intellectuals busied themselves with plans for a national reawakening. While some tried to turn their back on the present, notably the Dowager Empress Tz'u Hsi, and some were ardent Westernizers, a few maintained that Confucius was the true guardian spirit of the Han civilization and his teachings should become the official state religion for the new China. Liang Ch'i-ch'ao (1873-1929), a brilliant political philosopher whose knowledge of western thought matched his reformist enthusiasm, looked instead to Mahayana Buddhism for guidance in reconstructing his nation.[22]

For Liang, religion was to be judged by its ability to motivate men for moral and political action. A vital religion should give men hope, inspiring them to better themselves and society. Because believers are sure of the existence of the soul and an afterlife, they never despair. Secondly, religious faith should encourage people to transcend worldly satisfactions and entanglements, keeping them resolute in their devotion to righteousness. Thirdly, the devout should overcome the natural fear of death and become a fountainhead of courageous spirit.[23] On the basis of this psychological and sociological definition of religion, Liang felt justified in commending Buddhism as the best faith for the new China.

Rejecting Confucianism because it was not really a religion,

---

[21] *Ibid*, p. 234.

[22] Hao Chang, *Liang Ch'i-ch'ao and Intellectual Transition in China, 1890-1907*, Rainbow-Bridge Book Co., Taipei, 1971.

[23] Chang, *Ibid*, p. 231. Liang used as historical examples Oliver Cromwell, Prime Minister Gladstone, Lincoln and Japanese Zen Buddhists.

he also pointed out the superiority of Buddhism to its Chinese rivals, Taoism and Christianity. Instead of playing upon men's addiction to superstition, Buddhism generates faith in philosophical enlightenment which has transforming power. As the Mahayana sacred writings teach, men attain Buddhahood when they cultivate compassion and wisdom. There can be no incompatibility between reason and religion, as Hu Shih and other secularists alleged, when both extol the quest for enlightenment.

Liang commended Buddhism over other religions because it, more than the rest, sought universal rather than merely individual perfection. As the Bodhisattva vows to labor for the sake of others, Buddhists in the new China would selflessly devote themselves to the nation and its welfare. In Liang's mind the Bodhisattva could provide a model for the patriot, citizen and public servant. The basic Mahayana spirit of sacrificial service could save China and restore the whole world. According to the sutras, Buddha should descend into hell and stay to make hell perfect.[24]

For Liang, another mark of Buddhism's superiority is its teaching that all men are equal because all can become Buddhas. Other faiths ask men to bow—Confucianists to the Son of Heaven, Christians to God the Father. For Buddhists, the same Buddha-nature exists in every human mind. Buddhism recognizes no unbridgeable gap between Buddha and the ordinary man.

Also, Buddhism teaches that one can be saved only through his own efforts. The law of karma means a man is rewarded or punished on the basis of his deeds alone. In the Buddhist philosophy, the new citizen of China can find inspiration for both voluntarism and activism. Of course, in describing Mahayana in such terms—as a call to energetic self-reliance and strenuous public-spiritedness—Liang ignores both the monastic side of Buddhism and the popular Pure Land cult of the saving Amitabha.

History, however, never gave Liang's neo-Buddhism an opportunity to be tested, except to a limited degree at Hong Kong and on Taiwan. In neither case has Buddhism been a government-sup-

---

[24] Chang, *Ibid*, p. 235.

ported faith but only one of many contesting ideologies. Still unknown then are the effects of a "new Buddhism in a new China".

IV. KOREAN BUDDHISM

Early Buddhism

Buddhism was brought to Korea in the middle of the nine-hundred-year Three Kingdom Period—when Korea was composed of three kingdoms: Koguryo, Paekche and Silla. It was the first of the world religions to be imported to that country. A king from north China sent the monk Sundo with copies of the scriptures and a statue of Buddha to the Koguryo court of King Sosoorim in 372 A.D. Two years later the monk Ado arrived and the next year two temples were erected, showing how quickly Buddhism took root.[1] Chinese Buddhism emphasized the value of *one* vehicle by which all men attain Nirvana and therefore was a faith which embraced both Theravada's "little" vehicle and Mahayana's "big" one. It was this teaching which was introduced into Korea. Koguryo Buddhism was derived from Nagajuna's interpretation of the Middle Path and represented a pioneering effort of the *Sun* (Ch'an) school.

The kingdom of Paekche received Buddhism in 384. A monk named Marananda came from India by way of China as its first missionary. In Paekche Buddhism prospered and from there were sent the earliest missionaries to Japan (545 A.D.).[2] Unlike the *Sun* Buddhism of Koguryo, that in Paekche emphasized dharma—the law, doctrine, scriptural study—so was called *Kyo* ("dogmatic") Buddhism.[3]

A little later Buddhism from Koguryo was brought to the Silla kingdom by the monk Ado during the reign of King Nulji (417-

---

[1] Ilyon, *Samguk Yusa,* Tae-Hung Ha and G.K. Mintz translation, Yonsei University Press, Seoul, 1972, Book III, chapter lix, p. 177.
[2] *Ibid,* p. 178.
[3] Tong Sik Yu, *Korean Religions and Christianity,* Seoul, 1973, pp. 40-67 (in Korean).

458). However, it encountered much resistance—Silla had a strong sense of cultural self-identity and naturally objected to the spread of an alien faith. But once the foreign religion won acceptance it experienced healthy growth. Because of Silla's vitality and confidence, it was here that Buddhism reached new heights.

According to modern historians[4], Korean Buddhism was like a child during the Three Kingdom period and experienced its youth during the subsequent five centuries of the unified Silla period. The five-hundred-year rule of the succeeding Koryo dynasty should be thought of as the adult period (935-1392), and its successor the Yi dynasty, 1392-1910, represents an age of rapid decline, when most of the time Confucianism was the favored state ideology and Buddhist monks retreated to secluded mountain monasteries to live as hermits.

As mentioned above, unlike Koguryo and Paekche which eagerly welcomed the new religion from T'ang China, Silla had to experience labor pains in order for Buddhism to appear. Because Silla had a strong indigenous faith and philosophy, numerous obstacles were placed in the path of the Buddhist missionaries for about a century. Until the courtier Ech'adon showed that Buddhism was worth dying for, the faith was strongly opposed and its adherents treated with scorn.

Ech'adon the Martyr

In 527 A.D., during the reign of King Pophung, a minor court official named Ech'adon, only twenty-five years old, realized that the monarch longed to build a temple and spread Buddhism in his nation so that all the people might receive eternal blessings. However, the royal desire had been thwarted because of opposition from courtiers who felt that temple-building was a wasteful extravagance for a small and poor country. Convinced that the king's wish represented the divine will, Ech'adon went ahead and ordered that trees be cut down to erect the sanctuary. In fact, he told the workmen that his orders had come from the king. He deliberately

---

[4] Hong Il Sik, *Yukdang Studies,* Il Sin Sa, Seoul, 1959; also Tongsik Ryu, *Christian Faith Encounters the Religions of Korea,* Christian Literature Society, Seoul, 1965.

lied, knowing that he would be killed for issuing orders without proper authorization, because he believed his nation would accept Buddhism only if he offered his own life as a sacrifice. When the shocked and angry courtiers accused Ech'adon of acting illegally, the king had no alternative but to execute the young man, even though he recognized his noble intentions.

Summoned before the court and threatened with death, Ech'adon replied, "One man's earthly life is precious, but the eternal lives of many people are far more valuable. If I vanish with the morning dew today, the life-giving Buddhist faith will arise with the blazing sun tomorrow."[5]

According to the *Samguk Yusa,* when the executioner's sword came down on the young official's neck, the spouting blood turned as white as milk and the head flew up into the air and dropped far away on Diamond Mountain at the outskirts of the capital. Suddenly dark clouds covered the sky, followed by thunder, lightning and wild rain. It seemed as if heaven and earth had turned upside down, reported the chronicler.[6]

King and courtiers were astounded. They immediately recognized that the execution should never have taken place and were terrified by the anger of heaven. In the presence of the now-repentant nobles, the monarch solemnly announced that they should all resolve to devote their lives to Buddha and commanded that the whole nation would henceforth follow Buddhist teachings. Although the details of this story may be questioned, there is no reason to reject its substance. Through Ech'adon's martyrdom, Silla Buddhism underwent rapid development and expansion.

The Hwarang Do

When Chinhung ascended the Silla throne in 540 A.D. he devoted himself to the spread of Buddhism. According to the *Samguk Yusa,* he founded the military order of *Hwarang Do* ("Flower Youth"), a chivalrous band roughly comparable to King Arthur's knights of the Round Table. Believing he could enhance

---

[5] *Samguk Yusa,* bk. III, lxii.
[6] *Ibid,* pp. 186-189.

his rule by training an élite corps, the monarch gathered together youths from good families who were physically attractive and morally pure. These men were taught the five cardinal principles of human relationships—kindness, courtesy, justice, wisdom and trustworthiness—as well as being instructed in the arts of archery, horsemanship, calligraphy, mathematics and court etiquette.[7]

Religious dedication also played an important part in the *Hwarang Do*. To be initiated into the Order of the Flower, the youthful candidates would make a trip deep into the Korean mountains where they would engage in special exercises of self-discipline and pray for the gift of mystical power. At the conclusion of their devotions they communed with the mountain god, asking him to consecrate them and bless their swords. Later, whenever a national emergency arose, the *Hwarang* would return to the mountain for solemn prayers, before going to war.

The *hwarang* spirit soon became the foundation of the Silla national morality. Basing their lives as warriors and courtiers on a five point moral code, the flower knights 1) served their king with unquestioning loyalty, 2) honored their parents with filial piety, 3) treated friends with sincerity, 4) fought bravely and 5) killed living things mercifully.[8] Thus, the *Hwarang Do* produced loyal officials, dutiful sons, brave generals and dedicated soldiers willing to live and die for the nation.

Silla Buddhism was characterized by an affirmation of the oneness of the sacred and the secular. Primitive Buddhism required that one leave his family and abandon the householder's life so that through meditation and monastic discipline he could achieve enlightenment and enter Nirvana. By contrast, Mahayana Buddhism is less concerned about the mode of achieving tranquillity of spirit—whether by leaving one's home or remaining a householder—but rather stresses the ultimate goal of attaining enlightenment for oneself and others through inspiration derived from the Bodhisattva ideal. Whereas Theravadins aim for personal perfec-

---

[7] Han Woo-keun, *History of Korea,* Eul-You Pub., Seoul, 1970, pp. 61, 80, 107.

[8] "Five Commandments of Hwarang", a moral code worked out by the 6th century Buddhist monk Won-gwang Daesa.

tion by becoming Buddhas, Mahayanists work for the perfection of the nation and all society through compassionate devotion to the welfare of the multitudes. According to the Silla Buddhists, both individual and social perfection are needed. Hence, *Tongbulgyo*—the unique creation of Korean Buddhists—went beyond both Indian Theravada and Mahayana teaching. It surpassed also the Chinese combination of the two classical schools. Silla monks sought the one, all-embracing truth which reconciles and sublates the sacred and the secular. This higher synthesis was called Tong Buddhism.

Wonhyo

At the heart of Silla Buddhism was the thought of Wonhyo (617-686). His teaching represents not just the core of Silla Buddhism but also the apex of Buddhist philosophy in Korean history. According to some modern scholars, Indian Buddhism was introductory and Chinese Buddhism was sectarian but Korea established "conclusive Buddhism." Or to express it in another way, "the Bodhi tree had its roots in India, branched and blossomed in China and bore fruit in Korea."[9] If this claim be true, it was due to Wonhyo's contribution to Buddhist philosophy.

In fact, of all the Buddhist intellectuals from Korea he is unquestionably the most important. Even though he did not enter the monastic order until he was twenty-nine, he rather quickly attained fame as a speaker and author, abbot and royal advisor. An amazingly productive writer, Wonhyo prepared more than 240 volumes. Often the king and nobles asked him to preach, so that he had enormous influence as a public leader and became the chief spokesman for Korean unity. As a Confucian scholar and Buddhist philosopher, Wonhyo won praise from Chinese monks and was also highly esteemed in Japan.

Living at the time when the Silla kingdom subjugated its traditional rivals, Paekche and Koguryo, Wonhyo sought an ideology which could unify Korea. But first of all, he had to unify the

---

[9] Chong Ik Gi, *Life and Thought of Wonhyo* (in Korean).

Buddhists. A unified Buddhism was necessary for a united nation.[10]

At age thirty-four Wonhyo achieved enlightenment. While on his way to T'ang China for further study, he accidentally fell asleep between two graves. Awaking late at night, he felt thirsty and began searching for something to drink. In the darkness he found some water in a container and drank it. Next morning, much to his horror he found he had drunk from a human skull. Yet at that moment, Wonhyo attained enlightenment. Suddenly he realized that one's attitude determines the worth and even the existence of things. As he put it, when the heart is dead, there is nothing left but an empty skull. What we call the three worlds are merely mind; all objects are nothing but data of consciousness.

Once he had achieved enlightenment, there was no longer any reason for studying abroad. While his fellow-monk continued his trip to China, Wonhyo returned home and turned his house into a training center for monks.

Henceforth Wonhyo taught that everything originates in the human heart. This idea was the basic concept of the Flower Garland sect which originated in China and was based on the *Avatamsaka* Sutra.[11] However, for Wonhyo its truth was a matter of personal experience and direct insight. "Oneness of heart" was the meaning of his enlightenment. He realized that there is nothing but consciousness: feelings of impermanence and suffering are only subjective. They appear and disappear within the mind and have no external reality. Individual objects likewise only appear to stand over against each other. In the state of enlightenment, an individual recognizes how everything interpenetrates everything else; the real world is "Boundless," in which all are one and one is all. Differences vanish: substance and phenomena are alike; contrast is sameness; being is the Void.

For Wonhyo, because reality is boundless, life and death are one. Suffering and emancipation cannot be separated. Buddha and

---

[10] Hong Jung-Shik, "Thought and Life of Wonhyo" in Chun Shin-Yong, ed., *Buddhist Culture in Korea,* International Cultural Foundation, Seoul, 1974, pp. 15-30.

[11] Called the *Hwaom* sect (Korean) or *Kegon* and *Hosso* sects (Japanese).

the ordinary masses of people have a common origin, common nature and common destiny. Upon this fundamental *Hwajiang* concept, Wonhyo based his entire philosophy.[12] His thought and his life exemplified the sole reality of the Boundless.

Applying the *Hwajiang* idea to the religious situation, Wonhyo created *Tongbulgyo,* all-encompassing Buddhism. In China Buddhism had split into thirteen rival sects; in Korea in the 7th century there were five sects and nine schools, each with a shrine on nine different holy mountains. Wonhyo's Tong Buddhism was designed to harmonize conflicting interpretations and unify the competing sects.

According to Wonhyo, all the sutras were parts of scripture, just as a single great river might have ten thousand tributaries. By becoming attached to one text or one school, Buddhists ignore the Boundless. Therefore, by ridding themselves of attachments and becoming disinterested or detached, as Gautama taught, Buddhists would once again recognize the harmony and vitality of their faith. Truth can be found in each of a hundred theories, because when an individual looks at them without prejudice, all are one and one is all.

Wonhyo also applied the *Hwajiang* ideal to the alleged contrast between the sacred and the secular. In the light of the Boundless, how can there be a difference between this world and Nirvana? What substantially differentiates the layman from the monk? According to Wonhyo, since there are no real barriers which separate ordinary people from the Buddha, all men therefore possess the Buddha-nature. Throughout his life, Wonhyo desired to evangelize the whole world by awakening every individual to his true status as a Buddha. In the spirit of a Bodhisattva, he roamed the streets, dressed in secular garb and lived outside the monastery. Like a wandering minstrel, he sang, danced and beat on a gourd, spreading Buddhism among the masses. Sometimes he

---

[12] Cf. the similar teachings of contemporary Won Buddhism called "Everytime Zen, Everywhere Zen": "Creation is the incarnation of Buddha-nature, therefore even a blade of grass, a tree, a bird or beast is none other than Buddha." *Manual of Won Buddhism,* Iri City, Korea, 1974, p. 7.

dressed like a beggar and at other times he wore the robes of an abbot to preach in a temple. Refusing to be restricted by laws, tradition or formality, he was the Bodhisattva of emancipation. Wonhyo was never tied down, and even went so far as to break the vow of celibacy, producing a son.[13] Because he believed in the Boundless, he was both the great abbot and an unfrocked monk. In his eyes, since all is the Void, nothing separates the robed priest chanting holy sutras at a shrine from the common laborer drinking and singing in a pub. The secular was sacred and religion was daily life. For the chief philosopher of Silla Buddhism, the ideals of universalism, harmony and practicality were essential for a perfect faith.

Koryo Buddhism

Although the Silla period is customarily described as an age of youthful vitality, the Koryo period which followed did not produce a fully mature Buddhism. Only the first hundred years (935-1035) were something Buddhists could be proud of, but even that time represented external expansion and the opportunity to exercise temporal power rather than an enrichment of the content of the religion. At best Koryo Buddhism merely utilized the faith inherited from the Silla age. Furthermore, after a brief period of visible prosperity, Buddhism declined in spiritual power during the Koryo dynasty and ultimately caused the kingdom to decline as well.[14]

Buddhism's alliance with the throne was a major factor in its outward growth, but also its most serious weakness. Wang-kun, who founded the Koryo dynasty, believed that his ascent to the throne was due to Buddha's help and therefore he made Dosun, his favorite monk, the royal priest and proceeded to erect 3800 temples. In addition he gave vast farmlands to the monasteries and proclaimed that two Buddhist festivals were henceforth to be celebrated as national holidays.

During the Koryo period, monks became directly aligned

---

[13] *Samguk Yusa,* CIII.
[14] Cf. Allen D. Clark, *Religions of Old Korea,* Seoul, 1961, pp. 11-90.

with the secular power structure.[15] But expanding power and wealth for the monks inevitably led to abuses and corruption. Gradually the average man became disenchanted by what he saw going on in the temples. In addition, Confucian scholars at court voiced strong opposition to Buddhism. There was widespread hostility to the excesses of monks; especially toward those like Sin Ton, who virtually ruled the palace in the final years of the Koryo dynasty.[16]

Buddhism has always found it easy to absorb the beliefs and practices of the indigenous folk religions. This syncretism also greatly damaged Koryo Buddhism. Numerous shamanistic elements became attached to the faith. Divination based on the yin-yang theory was almost universally practiced; and in some cases the fortune teller guided every action of the king. Buddhism soon lost its original identity: believers treated it as a magical way to avert disaster, bring worldly blessings and assure physical happiness.

Finally, at a time when the government had depleted its wealth in expensive shrines and elaborate Buddhist festivals, opposition at every level—from the court, the scholars and the masses—greatly increased. Efforts were made to reduce the number of monasteries, expropriate temple lands, discourage candidates for the priesthood and suppress the immorality of monks and nuns. Confucianism was extolled as a superior philosophy. Weddings and funerals were conducted according to Confucian rather than Buddhist rites in order to cut down the usefulness of the priestly class. Thus, even in the Koryo period, preparation was taking place for the official repudiation of Buddhism by the dynasty to follow.

In spite of the merely external splendor of Koryo Buddhism and the superstitions of the masses, the age did produce a few great abbots. The most famous was Uichun, a king's son who became a

---

[15] Tae Hung Ha, *Korea—Forty Three Centuries,* Yonsei University Press, Seoul, 1962, pp. 50, 65-69.
[16] Cf. R. Rutt, *History of the Korean People,* Royal Asiatic Society, Seoul, 1972, pp. 213-216.

monk. He studied both Buddhism and Confucianism, completing his education with a trip to Sung China. Recognizing the greatness of Wonhyo, he attempted to carry out the One Mind and *Hwajiang* concepts by unifying the two rival Buddhist sects of Sun and Kyo. Also worthy of mention is Ilyon (1206-1289), author of the *Samguk Yusa* (Memoirs of the Three Kingdoms).

The Yi Dynasty and Afterward

For a thousand years Buddhism in Korea enjoyed unhindered growth and for most of the time it benefitted from unlimited state patronage. Yet repeatedly the monks abused this freedom and their privileged position. As historians point out, Korean Buddhism gradually became so decadent that it almost invited supervision from the government, and at the end of the Koryo dynasty nearly everybody was calling for reform. As a result, the new Yi dynasty initiated what was to become a long period of persecution. From 1392-1910 Yi kings conducted their campaign of oppression, although the intensity of the persecution varied greatly and occasionally a ruler favored the Buddhist cause.

Under the first Yi monarch, opposition to Buddhism became government policy. Temple lands were seized by the state. Monks and nuns were encouraged and sometimes forced to become laymen. Buddhist holidays were abolished, temple treasures were taken by the government. No longer were Buddhist prayers recited in the palace; and for a time, no monk was allowed to set foot in the capital city.

After the most extreme measures were carried out, a reaction took place, giving Buddhism a temporary revival. Great abbots like Sosan Daesa and Samyungdang emerged. When the Japanese invaded Korea in the sixteenth century, these men organized and led armies of monks against the enemy. Consequently, for a brief period Buddhism rewon popular support and official favor.

On the whole, however, the many centuries of Yi rule were disastrous for Buddhism. From the 16th century on, it looked as though the religion would be reduced to the point of extinction. Later, the situation did not improve when in addition to the enmity of Confucian scholars, the Buddhists faced both Christian missionaries from the West and a popular new indigenous religion, *Chondogyo*.

After the Japanese annexation of Korea, Buddhist conditions improved somewhat. Besides having its own historic interest in the Buddhist cause, Japan began to promote the religion as a tool of its imperialistic ambitions in the Far East. With its social position made more favorable, Korean Buddhism began to see light again. The monks and nuns were never pro-Japanese but they welcomed the removal of the Yi dynasty oppression.[17]

Independence came to Korea at the end of World War II; Buddhism then experienced an even greater revival. Whereas in 1920 the census takers found 150,000 Buddhists, by 1974 the number had risen to more than eight million.[18]

Looking back over fifteen hundred years of Korean Buddhism, one can see that it has been predominated by Wonhyo's emphasis on oneness. In addition to Wonhyo's *Tongbulgyo* of his own time, Uicheon of the Koryo period borrowed Wonhyo's ideas when he tried to unify the two sects and nine schools which divided Buddhism in his day. Then, in the Yi dynasty, Great Abbot Sosan Daesa was also a disciple of Wonhyo, urging monks to study both Sun and Kyo. According to his plan, Sun monks should be trained in Kyo doctrine and practices as a preliminary to their use of Sun meditation. He insisted that chanting and Zen are both necessary if Buddhists wish to be successful in mass evangelism. As the founder of the Chogye-jong sect, his whole life was dedicated to the ideal of religious harmony. In every period of Korean history, the noblest monks were spokesmen for the unifying spirit.

---

[17] Among the most famous Buddhist monks was Han Yong-woon (1879-1944): signer of the 1919 Declaration of Independence, novelist, poet and religious reformer. Cf. Yom Mu-Woong, "Life and Thought of Han Yong-woon" in Chun, ed., *Buddhist Culture in Korea*, pp. 97ff.

[18] According to the Korean Overseas Information Service, in 1975 there were an estimated 7,986,000 Buddhists.

V. JAPANESE BUDDHISM

Gift from Korea

Buddhism was introduced to Japan from Korea with gifts of books, statues and sacred banners from the king of Kudara (Paekche) to the emperor in the year 545 A.D. Later the Korean monarch sent to the Japanese court a Buddhist priest, a nun, an ascetic, an image-maker and a professional chanter of the sutras. Although the new faith was opposed by traditionalists who warned that the Shinto gods would get angry if an alien faith were allowed, in time Buddhism won the allegiance of powerful courtiers and the favor of the emperor.

Particularly valuable was the support of Crown Prince Shotoku (574-621). During the thirty-five year reign of his imperial aunt, he controlled the administration of the government and served as a patron for the Buddhist religion. Korean priests became his spiritual tutors and through them Chinese culture was spread widely throughout the empire. Besides commissioning the erection of Buddhist statues and encouraging the public celebration of Buddhist festivals, Prince Shotoku welcomed the introduction of the Chinese lunar calendar, the yin-yang philosophy, paper making, the use of India ink and the science of astrological astronomy. As a result of his religious zeal, the crown prince has been called the Constantine of Japanese Buddhism.[1]

Shotoku was attracted to the imported faith because of his own belief in the teachings of the Mahayana *Lotus Sutra* and also because of the usefulness of Buddhism as a symbol of the advanced Chinese civilization. While recognizing Buddhism as the religion of the throne and empire, Shotoku continued to respect the Shinto shrines and promoted the social ethic of Confucianism. According to him, Shinto explains Japan's divine beginnings, Confucian morality guides man's present life, while Buddhism reveals the nature of the afterlife.[2]

---

[1] Hajime Nakamura, *History of the Development of Japanese Thought,* Japan Cultural Society, Tokyo, 1969, vol. I, pp. 1-38.

[2] Robert C. Armstrong, *An Introduction to Japanese Buddhist Sects,* Hunter Rose Co., Canada (privately printed), 1950, p. 7.

Eminent Monks and Buddhist Teachers

Japanese Buddhism was shaped by a succession of remarkable monks who combined the talents of the scholar, administrator and sectarian leader.

1. Kobo Daishi (774-835 A.D.) showed how Shinto and Buddhism could be reconciled. The universe, he said, is made up of two distinct yet related parts: the Womb World and the Diamond World. The Womb World is material and female; the Diamond World is spiritual and male. Shintoist worship of the sun goddess recognizes the importance of the Womb World and Buddhism reveres the Great Master of the Heavens who rules the Diamond World.[3]

2. Honen Shonen (1133-1212), founder of the Jodo sect, was a particularly successful evangelist for the message of salvation by faith in Amida.[4] So persuasive was Honen's preaching that soldiers gave up their military careers, prostitutes became nuns, robbers confessed their sins, and even the chief official of the imperial court became one of his disciples.

Naturally, the concept of salvation by faith alone aroused criticism from other Buddhist leaders and led to disregard for the conventional moral code. Monks began to eat meat and drink wine; a few even forsook the rule of celibacy. Although many continued to revere Honen as "a living image of the Bodhisattva Maitreya," complaints grew until the emperor banished him and his followers from the capital city of Kyoto. This edict only reinforced the determination of the Jodo Buddhists who proceeded to preach the saving Amida prayer throughout the country.[5] Shortly before his death Honen was pardoned so he could return to Kyoto in triumph. By preaching salvation based on the infinite mercy of Amida he became the great Buddhist "saint" for rich and poor, high and low, men and women.

3. Eisai Zenshi and Dogen Zenshi. Eisai Zenshi (1141-1215) founded the Japanese sect of Rinzai Zen, after spending five years

---

[3] *Ibid*, pp. 16-18.

[4] H.H. Coates and Ryugaku Ishizuka, *Honen the Buddhist Saint*, Kyoto, 1925.

[5] For another Pure Land leader, see Alfred Bloom, *Shinran's Gospel of Pure Grace*, Univ. of Arizona Press, Tucson, 1965.

studying in China. Besides introducing tea drinking to Japan, he was famous for his devotion to the practical side of Buddhism. Like his Ch'an masters he minimized the value of Buddhist ritual. Dogen Zenshi (1198-1253), a Tendai Buddhist priest, became Eisai's disciple when he heard him say: "All Buddhas past and present do not know Buddha's nature, but foxes and badgers do." Both believed that the real Buddha-nature of all things is spontaneously known by living creatures which are not caught in the trap set by human words. After Eisai's death, Dogen travelled to China for four years of further practice in Zen meditation. When a Chinese master explained that "meditation means separation from body and heart," Dogen experienced the bliss of enlightenment. Returning to Japan, the monk began to advocate sitting in meditation as the means of revealing one's Buddha-nature. For a decade he taught near Kyoto and for his last ten years he resided in a beautiful mountain retreat.[6]

Brief History of Nipponese Buddhism

Although Buddhism was first brought to Japan by Chinese or Koreans who settled in the islands and was given support at court by prince regent Shotoku at the beginning of the seventh century, it was not until the Nara period (710-781) that Buddhism provided ideological guidance for the entire nation. In 741 a state-supported Buddhist temple was set up in each province and ten years later Todaiji at Nara became the national cathedral. Considering himself the head of the Buddhist church, the emperor appointed the chief abbot and the clergy were subjected to government control. Alongside "official" Buddhism, however, there appeared a sizeable number of mountain recluses, travelling faith healers and shamanic diviners (the *ubasoku)* who offered charms and incantations in the name of Buddha, the supreme miracle worker.[7]

---

[6] Daisetz Teitaro Suzuki has been the foremost internationally-recognized authority on Japanese Zen. Cf. his trilogy *Introduction to Zen Buddhism, The Training of a Zen Monk* and *Manual of Zen Buddhism,* Grove Press, N.Y., 1960.

[7] J.M. Kitagawa, *Religion in Japanese History,* Columbia University Press, N.Y., 1966, pp. 38-45. Also Daigan and Alicia Matsunaga, *Foundation of Japanese Buddhism,* Buddhist Books International, Tokyo-Los Angeles, 1974, pp. 9-23, 133-137.

In 794 the capital was moved to Kyoto. From the ninth through the twelfth centuries (the Heian period) Buddhism became thoroughly Japanese in contrast to its earlier status as a Chinese import; Shinto divinities (the *kami*) were said to be manifestations of Buddhas and bodhisattvas in Japanese form. The Tendai and Shingon Buddhist sects became the most prominent, their chief monasteries being located at Mount Hiei and Mount Koya. By the middle of the Heian period, however, many were turning to the Amida cult. Pleasure-loving aristocrats prayed to Amida Buddha to prolong their life of luxury in paradise while the downtrodden masses prayed to Bodhisattva *Jizo* who could save them from hell.[8] Whereas during the Nara period, many looked to Maitreya for comfort, some now emphasized faith in Sakyamuni as the *Lotus Sutra* taught, or the Great Sun Buddha (the Cosmic Buddha) of the Shingon sect, while an even larger number invoked the saving name of Amida. In a famous book *The Essentials of Salvation* produced by Genshin in 985 A.D. can be found a classic expression of Amida's Pure Land Buddhism.

Japan's medieval period covered the thirteenth through the sixteenth centuries. Anthropologist Ruth Benedict described the contrasts in Japanese culture with the phrase: the chrysanthemum and the sword. Beginning with the first great military leader who established his feudal regime at Kamakura in 1192 Japan was for centuries controlled by men of the sword known as *shoguns* (warrior rulers). This rise to power of rough, boisterous militarists who held in contempt the effete imperial court entailed vast changes in Japanese religious life. Aristocratic Buddhism had come to possess a lacy refinement symbolized by miniature landscape gardens and delicate tea-sipping ceremonies.

To counteract the growing influence of the Amida cult, some monks advocated a ritualistic recitation of the name of Sakyamuni. Other monks revived enthusiasm for Maitreya, the coming Buddha. Buddhist doctrines were simplified, and emphasis was placed on the strict observance of monastic disciplines. Finally, the rich

---

[8] Kitagawa, *Ibid*, pp. 82-84. *Jizo* was called *Ti-tsang* by the Chinese. He had vowed not to accept the peace of Nirvana until the last soul in hell had been redeemed.

monasteries were encouraged to engage in philanthropic activities. Yet none of these efforts could halt the spread of militant and divisive Buddhist sectarianism. At the very time Catholic Europe was being disrupted by the Protestant Reformation, Japanese Buddhism was transformed by Pure Land enthusiasts, Nichiren zealots and the "single-minded" devotees of the Shinran sect.

Honen, the founder of the Pure Land Sect (1133-1212), taught that since enlightenment is too difficult for the vast majority of men to achieve they should simply pray to Amida to be reborn in the celestial Western Paradise. As a commentary on the *Meditation Sutra* advises, "Whether walking or standing, sitting or lying, only repeat the name of Amida with all your heart. . . . This is the very work which unfailingly issues in salvation."[9]

Shinran (1173-1262) originated the True Pure Land School. Believing that man is utterly helpless and hopelessly depraved, he preached that salvation could be achieved solely through reliance upon Amida's grace. Because Amida has compassion upon us, he will save us. Although all men are by nature shameless, by the unmerited gift of Amida's holy name they can be saved. In complete opposition to Theravada self-reliance, Shinran preached that salvation comes only through the "other power" of Amida Buddha.[10]

By emphasizing the value of complete commitment, later followers of Shinran created a compact society of zealous enthusiasts whose aims were both political and religious. Almost fanatically, these "single-direction" Buddhists—as they called themselves—waged war on rival sects and the government. In the late 15th and the 16th centuries, True Pure Land believers engaged in more than twenty rebellions against the military government of the shoguns.

Nichiren (1222-82) was another charismatic leader whose activities gave birth to a militant sect. Angrily denouncing the older Buddhist schools and criticizing the government, he pre-

---

[9] A Chinese text by Shan-tao, quoted by Kitagawa, *Ibid*, p. 112, footnote 58.

[10] Kitagawa, *Ibid*, pp. 114-117. Also A. Bloom, *Shinran's Gospel of Pure Grace*, pp. 27-85.

dicted the imminent End of the Age (*mappo*)—a time of irreligion, political disasters and natural calamities. His dire predictions seemed to be confirmed by the demand of the Mongol khan for tribute in 1268 and the arrival of the Mongol fleet in 1274 and 1281. As for his attitude toward other Buddhist groups, Nichiren declared that those who recite the name of Amida would burn in hell, the Zen sect is satanic, the Shingon are ruining the country and the Ritsu are traitors. Not surprisingly, Nichiren barely escaped assassination and the shogun sentenced him to a two-year exile on a distant island.

For thirty years he called upon the Japanese to accept and practice the teachings of the *Lotus Sutra*. Against those who prayed to Amida, he advocated reciting the saving formula: "Adoration be to the Sutra of the Lotus of the Sacred Truth" *(Namu Myoho Renge Kyo)*. Because ex-Emperors Go-Toba and Juntoku neglected the *Lotus Sutra,* according to Nichiren, they had to suffer death in exile. But if Japan would practice that sutra, it would become an ideal nation, the great Buddha-land. In spite of his foes, Nichiren won large numbers of followers, many of whom enthusiastically took up arms to fight for his cause. In 1532, two and a half centuries after the prophet's death, Nichiren Buddhism was the strongest group in the imperial capital of Kyoto; four years later an army of angry monks from Mt. Hiei destroyed twenty-one Nichiren temples and massacred 58,000 of Nichiren's disciples.[11]

Rinzai Zen and Soto Zen were two new sects which also appeared in medieval Japan, brought from China but altered somewhat. Zen was favored by the powerful military caste and often supported by the shoguns. Zen monks introduced Neo-Confucian philosophy, patronized art, inspired the *Noh* play and spread the tea drinking cult. Even in times of political unrest Zen temples preserved and enriched Japan's cultural life.[12]

The Tokugawa period in Japanese history began in the 17th century and lasted until Admiral Perry forced the country to open

---

[11] M. Anesaki, *Nichiren, The Buddhist Prophet,* Smith, Gloucester, 1966.

[12] Cf. D.T. Suzuki, *Zen and Japanese Buddhism,* C.E. Tuttle, Tokyo and Rutland Vt., 1958 and *Zen and Japanese Culture,* Pantheon Books, N.Y., 1959.

its doors to the West. Three great shoguns dominate the age: Oda Nobunaga (1534-82), Toyotomi Hideyoshi (1537-98) and Tokugawa Iyeyasu (1542-1616). The last completed the unification of the country, established his seat of government at Tokyo (then called Edo) in 1603, and installed a feudal regime which lasted until Emperor Meiji took power in 1867.

These shoguns were determined to unify Japan which meant they had to break the power of the tightly-knit Buddhist sects. In 1571 Oda Nobunaga's army attacked Mt. Hiei, burned numerous buildings and massacred most of the monks. Then the shogun turned against the True Pure Land sect, killing tens of thousands. Finally, he crushed the Shingon monks by mass executions at Mt. Koya.

Under Shogun Hidetada Buddhism once more became the established religion, yet the priests were treated as mere servants of the government. At the same time, however, Confucianism became the preferred educational philosophy, which tended to make the intellectuals either indifferent or hostile to the Buddhist cause. Besides, there was a revival of Shinto, which was the native faith, and therefore a better foundation for patriotic zeal and national glory, some said.

Following the Tokugawa age (1600-1868), Japan experienced the return to direct rule by the emperor, the rapid westernization of the country, a flood of Christian missionaries, the enthusiastic promulgation of State Shinto and four decades of imperialistic expansion which ended with the unconditional surrender of the militarist government at the end of World War II.[13] From the Meiji regime to the rule of General Douglas MacArthur, Japanese Buddhism faced one hardship after another. Shinto propagandists claimed that the emperor had been handed supernatural authority from the sun goddess, Amaterasu—and not Buddha. Modernists contended that Buddhist temples, monks and such popular forms of piety as Pure Land sectarianism were obstacles to progress.

---

[13] For an interpretation of Meiji Japan given in lectures at Harvard, the College of France and Pacific School of Religion in Berkeley, California, see M. Anesaki, *History of Japanese Religion,* C.E. Tuttle Co., Rutland, Vermont, 1963, pp. 329-409.

Christian missionaries implied that theirs was the true religion because their God had blessed the British empire, German science and American business. In 1870 the Shinto faith became the state religion; many Buddhist temples were closed and all temple lands were confiscated. The emperor abolished Buddhist services at the palace and replaced them with worship of the Shinto sun goddess.[14] Yet, despite such an array of powerful foes, Buddhism survived.

Defenders of the Buddhist cause employed various methods to cope with the new situation. Some adopted Christian techniques—like Buddhist Sunday Schools or a Buddhist version of the YMCA. Others engaged in a scholarly and philosophic study of Buddhism in the light of western ideas. Still more priests actively collaborated with the nationalists and militarists, believing that the future of Buddhism depended upon an anti-western policy which hopefully would eradicate the Christian missionaries.[15] None of these endeavors however could restore the Buddhist establishment of the medieval period.

After World War II some problems disappeared—the threat of State Shinto, for example—but new ones took their place. A large number of Buddhist priests have been compelled to take on secular jobs to augment their income. Rampant sectarianism has robbed the main temples of their traditional authority and greatly weakened the financial stability of the various denominations. In 1940 there were 28 Buddhist denominations; by 1951 there were 170. Since then, interdenominational agencies have been created in order to carry on joint programs.[16]

According to one leading Japanese scholar, post-war Buddhism had to rid itself of 1) subservience to the government and excessive nationalism, 2) magical incantations and superstitious practices inherited from the past, 3) preoccupation with funeral

---

[14] Kitagawa, *Ibid,* pp. 202-203.

[15] See H. Nakamura, "Controversy between Buddhism and Christianity," *Ibid,* pp. 111-149.

[16] For one example, see J.S. Weeks, "Rissho Kosei-Kai: a Cooperative Buddhist Sect" in R.J. Miller, ed., *Religious Ferment in Asia,* Univ. of Kansas, Lawrence, 1974, pp. 157-167.

rites and memorial services for the dead at the expense of providing guidance for the living, 4) lack of doctrinal integrity, and 5) stress on formal observance without equal concern for inner spiritual disciplines.[17] In addition to these internal maladies, Japanese Buddhism in the post-war world has confronted Christianity and the rapidly growing "New Religions"—as well as Communism—in a nation where traditional values are threatened by the temptation to pursue materialistic and hedonistic goals.[18]

The Nichiren Revival

Although many of the Buddhist schools have continued to influence Japanese life and thought, particularly noteworthy is the powerful renaissance of Nichiren Buddhism. As mentioned in previous pages, Nichiren (1222-1282) originated his distinctive sect during the troubled times of the Kamakura period when he preached that he was the only person who could save Japan from ruin. As a virile, enthusiastic and zealous group, disciples of Nichiren played a major role during a crucial turning point in Japanese history and their successors are determined to carry out a similar mission in the contemporary world.

Original Nichirenism was an apocalyptic faith based on the belief that the world was approaching the End-time. According to Nichiren, Buddhism would pass through three stages. For five hundred years men would teach and practice faithfully the Way of Sakyamuni. Then, during a second period of equal length, Buddhism would become diluted and corrupted by alien influences— Hindu notions and rites in India, Taoist and Confucianist ideas in China and Shintoist tendencies in Japan. Finally would come the Latter Days of error and vice so all-pervasive that nothing but a new and pure form of Buddhism could save the world from

---

[17] Shoko Watanabe, *Nihon no Bukkyo* (Buddhism in Japan), Tokyo, 1960, pp. 69-139.

[18] In spite of the militarist government's support of Shinto and considerable anti-Buddhist propaganda, the religion had 71,326 temples, 7,753 churches, 40,000,000 believers and six universities in 1940. For a defense of Buddhism during this war period by Prof. Yoshitaru Yabuki of Tokyo Imperial University, see D.C. Holtom, *Modern Japan and Shinto Nationalism,* University of Chicago Press, 1947, pp. 133-137.

destruction. Nichiren believed that his teaching based on the *Lotus Sutra* was the message for such a time and that he was the Bodhisattva who could set up the ideal Buddha-land on earth. Proclaiming his messianic role, Nichiren declared, "I will be the pillar of Japan; I will be the eyes of Japan; I will be the great vessel of Japan."[19]

Although the 13th century monk failed to inaugurate the Messianic Age, his disciples continued to believe that what he had taught was true and that sooner or later his prophecies would come to pass. However, the fanaticism, combativeness and sectarianism which characterized Nichiren himself were inherited by his followers, who soon fought among themselves with as much zeal as they attacked everybody else. One of the six chief disciples of Nichiren—Nikko—disagreed with the others, left the main temple at Mt. Minobu, and set up a new temple across the river at the foot of Mt. Fuji. Nikko's sect claimed to be the true followers of Nichiren and called themselves Nichiren Shoshu ("the orthodox") to distinguish themselves from the Nichiren-shu of Mt. Minobu. When World War II ended, the latter, nevertheless, had over ten million followers and more than 5,000 temples while the former had only 300,000 believers and about 200 temples.[20] In addition, there were six other distinct Nichiren sects in 1945 and over forty by 1960.

The Nichiren revival has taken many forms, only four of which will be treated here. Kubo Kakutaro (1890-1944), a carpenter, and a woman companion named Kotami Kimi (b. 1901) founded the Association of the Friends of the Spirit *(Reiyukai)* in 1925. After World War I, Japan suffered economic panic, mass unemployment, rampant inflation and bloody rice riots.Then came the catastrophic Tokyo earthquake of 1923. Confused, frightened and often despairing, many Japanese were ready to believe Nichiren's dire prophecy that man had entered the age of apocalyptic destruction. Kubo warned that Japan could be saved only through

---

[19] Quoted in H. Thomsen, *The New Religions of Japan,* Charles E. Tuttle Co., Rutland, Vermont, 1963, p. 88.

[20] Thomsen, *Ibid,* p. 84.

dutiful worship of the ancestors, daily recitation of the *Lotus Sutra,* an altar in the home of every believer and reverent meditation on the Nichiren mandala. In the center of this mandala is the sacred invocation *Namu Myoho Renge Kyo* ("Hail to the Wonderful Truth of the Lotus Sutra"); around it are the names of various Buddhas, Bodhisattvas and Shinto deities. Neglect of the traditional ancestor worship causes all kinds of diseases and national calamities, but proper respect for the dead expressed by means of concentration upon the mandala will enable Japan to realize its glorious destiny as the ideal Buddha-land, it was said.

Unlike most Nichiren sects, Reiyukai tolerates other religions. In accordance with Nichiren's strong emphasis upon social responsibility, the Friends of the Spirit donate equipment to rehabilitation centers for the physically handicapped and funds for nurseries. They wage campaigns against drug abuse, provide books in braille for the blind, and give generously of their time on behalf of Community Chest and Red Cross activities. With several million members, Reiyukai was particularly important in restoring Japanese faith in the destiny of their nation prior to World War II and gave birth to at least eight new religions of which Rissho Kosei Kai has been the most successful.[21]

Niwano Nikkyo (b. 1906) and a woman helper Naganuma Myoko (1899-1957) founded the Society for the Establishment of Righteousness and Friendly Intercourse *(Rissho Kosei Kai)* in 1938. Niwano was a milk dealer in Tokyo who met Naganuma while delivering milk and persuaded her that she would be healed of a sickness if she joined Reiyukai. She was cured, and the two became good friends. The couple subsequently set up their own religion, not because of a doctrinal disagreement with Reiyukai, but rather because they wanted more freedom to exercise their own qualities of leadership. After about a decade of very modest success, Rissho Kosei Kai experienced an extremely rapid rate of growth, with membership multiplying from 1,000 to more than two million in two decades.[22]

---

[21] *Ibid,* pp. 109-116.
[22] *Ibid,* p. 254, footnote #3.

Like the other sects, this one follows the main tenets of Nichiren, recognizes the Shinto sun goddess, and regards all other Nichiren denominations as distortions of the true faith. Unlike other Nichiren groups who think of the mandala as an all-powerful concentration of saving grace, in Rissho Kosei Kai one recites "Namu Myoho Renge Kyo" only as an act of faith and gratitude.

As the sect teaches, "Our goal is the attainment of a perfect personality, that is Buddhahood, through practice of the way of a Bodhisattva."[23] Its membership system is built around the family: to join the sect an applicant must submit the names of his parents, his wife's parents and a list of deceased members of the family. A person does not exist as an isolated individual but as a representative of a family unit which includes the living and the dead. Rissho Kosei Kai claims to serve its members from the cradle to the grave with nurseries, middle schools, high schools, a hospital, old people's homes, band concerts, choral groups, baseball and judo teams, youth pilgrimages, festivals, even cemeteries. Most important are the daily religious services and the daily group counselling sessions where members can obtain practical advice about raising children or any other everyday problem. At the main temple in Tokyo a counselling session usually involves two hundred groups of ten to twenty participants.[24]

Among the Nichiren groups none has equalled *Soka Gakkai,* the Society for the Creation of Value. Tsunesaburo Makiguchi (1871-1944) was an elementary school teacher in Tokyo who formed a study group of sixty members in 1937. Emphasizing the need for a reform of Japanese education based on beauty, goodness and benefit, Soka Gakkai attracted only 3,000 members prior to World War II. Because it seemed to run counter to the official policy of the Education Ministry and because it looked to Buddhism rather than State Shinto for inspiration, Soka Gakkai encountered serious government opposition. To escape official suppression, it voted to affiliate with Nichiren Sho ("the orthodox"). Then Nichiren Sho as well as Soka Gakkai underwent persecution.

---
[23] *A Guide to Rissho Kosei Kai,* Rissho Kosei Kai headquarters, Tokyo, 1959, p. 2.
[24] Thomsen, *Ibid,* pp. 120-121.

Makiguchi lost his job as an elementary school principal, his magazine was suppressed, and he—with other Soka Gakkai leaders—was imprisoned. After a year and a half of confinement, Makiguchi died of malnutrition at the age of 74.

His successor Josei Toda (1900-1958) had also been imprisoned. He possessed administrative ability, an aggressive spirit and a charismatic personality. A monthly magazine, a weekly paper, a new edition of the collected works of Nichiren and Nikko, a series of commentaries on Nichiren's writings and Makiguchi's book *Kachiron* (Theory of Value) became Toda's tools for carrying out his mission. By 1951 he could dedicate the Great Lecture Hall at Taisekiji, the center of Nichiren Sho Buddhism, and announce that Soka Gakkai had won 750,000 family units to its cause. A month later, Toda was dead. But one sign of the magnitude of his achievements is that both Prime Minister Kishi and the Minister of Education appeared at the funeral.

Daisaku Ikeda (then only 32)[25] became Soka Gakkai's third president in 1960. The sect publishes a magazine for young people sold at newsstands, a daily newspaper, numerous books and pamphlets. Besides speaking often to audiences of 100,000 people, Ikeda has written books entitled *Lectures on Buddhism, The Human Revolution, Culture and Religion, Politics and Religion* and *Science and Religion*. Convinced that Soka Gakkai provides the ideology for a "third civilization" superior to communism and capitalism, Ikeda encouraged his followers to set up a "Clean Government" *(Komeito)* political party which has successfully elected delegates to both houses of the Diet, prefectural assemblies, ward and city councils as well as thousands of town and village councils. In spite of determined opposition from politicians, labor unions, Christian missionaries, communist agitators and Buddhist leaders from rival sects, Ikeda's program won over six million families to the Soka Gakkai cause in a seven year period.[26] Built upon a semi-military structure, strict discipline and

---

[25] Born 1928.
[26] Noah S. Brannen, *Soka Gakkai,* John Knox Press, Richmond, 1968, p. 79. Although this book contains much valuable material, it was written by a Christian missionary and some of its value judgments are those of a hostile critic.

zealous evangelization, Soka Gakkai is determined to gain control of the Diet, make Nichiren Sho the state religion and have the temple at Taisekiji with its mandala made by Nichiren become Japan's national shrine, as the Shinto shrine at Ise was in an earlier time. Nor does Soka Gakkai limit its goals to Japan. Already numerous missions have been established in other lands so that the third civilization based in Japan will create a world-wide messianic age of truth, prosperity and peace, it is believed.

Soka Gakkai zealously repudiates all rival religions. Employing a method called *shakufuku,* it believes in "breaking and subduing the evil spirits" of Christianity, Shinto and all the other Buddhist groups. *Shakufuku Kyoten,* a manual prepared by Yoshihei Kohira in 1958, teaches every convert to attack all competing faiths. Typical in this regard is the Soka Gakkai denunciation of Christian faith and ethics.

According to Nichiren Sho, when Christians say they believe Jesus rose from the dead and physically ascended into heaven, they deny the law of gravity, so their faith is unscientific. The miracles attributed to Jesus could have been invented by later Christians and inserted in the Bible, so the scriptures are historically unreliable. Ninety per cent of the New Testament represents the dogmas of the disciples rather than the pure teaching of Jesus. Furthermore, as all Buddhists believe, since there could be no uncaused First Cause, there is no Creator God. Perhaps most significant, Nichiren proved the validity of his teachings by escaping from his would-be executioners, whereas Jesus showed the ineffectiveness or powerlessness of his message by dying on the cross.

Soka Gakkai's criticism of the Christian ethic of unrestricted love is equally thorough. Men naturally love the good and abhor evil. Unlimited love is hence unnatural, impractical and impossible. No one can "love his enemies," even if he thinks he should or says he does so. The Sermon on the Mount violates common sense.

Also Christians err when they think their love will atone for the sins of others. Sins cannot be erased; our forgiveness does not nullify the effect of sins. No matter what we say or believe, the moral law of karma continues to operate: men must reap what they sow, in this life or in new lives to come.

Having dismissed the reliability of the Christian scriptures, the truth of the Creator doctrine and the usefulness of the moral teachings of Jesus, Soka Gakkai ridicules the notion of original sin. According to the Christian message, they say, man is afflicted with a sin which affects all without exception, a sin nobody can escape. Hence, declares Soka Gakkai, all humans are born criminals: naturally disrespectful, disobedient, rebellious and selfish. Such an idea greatly exaggerates the human situation. A true religion should inspire man, give him confidence, encourage him, praise his vitality instead of degrading him to the status of a common criminal, as Christians do.[27] Worshipping a convicted felon, followers of Jesus therefore teach that every man is born tainted by sin so gross that he is justly sentenced to everlasting punishment. By contrast, for all Buddhists the most important fact about every individual is that he has the capability to become a Buddha; without exception men possess the Buddha-nature or at least the seeds of Buddhahood.

Far more important than the questionable practice of *shakufuku* is the Soka Gakkai theory of value. In his book *Kachiron,* Makiguchi professed to correct western concepts about the relationship between truth, goodness and beauty. Soka Gakkai represents a fusion of Oriental mysticism and utilitarian ethical theory. The Occident mistakenly considers truth to be a value. Truth in fact merely reveals what is. Value, however, always implies a subject-object relationship. Truth is a concern of epistemology rather than ethics. Truth says, Here is a man, a horse, a rock; Value says, The man is good (or evil), the horse is beautiful, the rock is hard. Truth does not depend upon value judgments and is therefore unchanging; value grows out of human relationships so is subject to alteration.

Man creates values and in this faculty he demonstrates his greatness. Happiness comes from the pursuit and possession of

---

[27] Thomsen, *Ibid,* p. 103. Other Buddhists would say that behind the Adam and Eve "myth" is a recognition of the four-fold truth taught by Gautama: from birth, man is subject to passions, cravings, self-centeredness and suffering.

values. Whereas truth is objective, value is subjective. Distinctions must, nevertheless, be made between various values. Beauty is an emotional value, based on sense experience and relative to only a part of man's life. "Benefit"—a concept which Makiguchi put in place of truth—is a personal value relative to an individual's total life which contributes to the maintenance and advancement of his existence. Goodness refers to group values, those which buttress and develop the unity of society. We should judge right and wrong therefore, not on the basis of truth or personal pleasure, but on the basis of social value. Man cannot rely on the dictates of his individual conscience, his personal intuitions or his private pleasures. Instead he should recognize and respect the standard of goodness derived from society's need for cohesiveness. Goodness should be understood as a necessary and useful response to the demand for togetherness.[28]

While most of the converts to Reiyukai, Rissho Kosei Kai and Soka Gakkai come from the Japanese masses, Nichiren has also provided inspiration for a select but influential group of intellectuals. Chogyu Takayama (d. 1902) was a notable example of how Nichiren could attract a gifted writer during the Meiji period. Takayama was originally part of the ultra-nationalistic *Nippon Shugi* circle, a literary and philosophic group which exalted total dedication to the Japanese State and the imperial heritage. In their opinion, Japan exemplified three virtues—energetic activity, esteem for the present and observance of purity. To preserve those qualities and restore the empire to its rightful glory, the "Japanists," as they called themselves, advocated purging their country of alien influences—meaning, Chinese Buddhism, European Christianity and western, primarily American, individualism.

---

[28] N.S. Brannen, *Ibid*, pp. 133-139. Brannen claims there are inconsistencies between Makiguchi's theory and Soka Gakkai religious practice. He fails to see how the social theory of value fits nicely into Nichiren Sho if one identifies goodness with whatever Soka Gakkai proposes as goals. A social theory of value is an exceedingly useful ideology for any tightly-knit group because by definition goodness is identified with the group's collective aims. However, does a social theory of value explain goals which transcend those of the group, sometimes to improve the group, sometimes to judge it?

Rather quickly recognizing the defects of nationalism, Takayama moved to the opposite extreme. Whereas he had earlier asserted the supreme authority of the State, now he stressed the unlimited rights of the individual. In a widely-read essay entitled "The Beautiful Life" (1901), Takayama defined a man's true destiny as a life free from restrictive social conventions—purely spontaneous self-expression. Life requires complete sincerity and sincerity cannot be practiced if one worries about what society may think or what external advantages may be derived from certain actions. To be good, he insisted, was to live like the flowers of the field which simply respond to the natural warmth of the sun. To friends and critics, Takayama sounded like Plato, Rosseau, Lao-tsu and Nietzsche.[29]

Finally, the Japanese intellectual turned to Nichiren. Because he possessed a tender heart, Takayama could not long believe in Nietzsche's strong-willed and domineering superman. Because he recognized the partial validity of the Japanist cause, he could not remain satisfied with mere individualism, pure egoism, as he termed it. In Nichiren, however, Takayama found the answer to his need for hero-worship, patriotism, idealism, romanticism and enthusiasm. Although he died within a year after his conversion to Nichirenism, Takayama's influence became a major factor in the modern development of the Japanese religious spirit.[30]

Buddhist Teachings Today

Although most Japanese are Buddhists or have a Buddhist religious background, what they believe today cannot be discovered by simply reading the sutras or studying the teachings of famous monks from the past. Buddhism has undergone considera-

---

[29] During the Meiji period, German science, philosophy, educational practices and Prussian militarism became fashionable. Nietzsche's cult of the superman is one example of Teutonic influence among the architects of the new Japan. Nietzsche was thought of as a modern European exponent of the Samurai spirit.

[30] M. Anesaki, *History of Japanese Religion,* pp. 367, 370, 375-379. For a comparable case, see how the philosopher-theologian Nicolai Berdyaev was inspired by Dostoievski's concepts of the messianic mission of the Slavic people, the third Rome, "holy" Russia, and Christ, *The Idiot,* who transcends conventional reason, bourgeois respectability and middle class morality.

ble modification in Japan during the thirteen centuries since it came from Korea and, as could be expected, there is presently great variety of interpretation among priests and professors.[31]

The Meaning of Daily Life

At a time when Japanese teenagers and young adults question traditional ethical norms like filial piety and patriotism, Buddhists point to the validity of certain abiding ideals. The highest objective of life is to become a Buddha. Or in a more practical sense, supreme happiness comes from devoted service to one's parents, loving support of one's family and honorable work. Man is born to live with others: I live for others and they live for me. Individual pleasure and success from one's youth to old age are not man's real goal; our fortunes are linked with the happiness of all men, all history, all living beings; therefore we are involved in infinite time. Hence, it is important to recognize mutual personal dignity and promote mutual respect. Men can become truly happy when they rediscover the need for cooperation and communal living. Denying the goal of mere individual pursuit of material comforts, Buddhists put their fundamental faith in a collective world view, believing that the whole biological world constitutes an immense living organism of infinitely precious worth. On the basis of that "reverence for life" philosophy, they protest the international armaments race, warn of the dangers of nuclear war and campaign for world peace, in addition to repudiating the materialism and hedonism which have become so prevalent in post-war Japan because of western influence.

Karma and Sin

Because the doctrine of karma has sometimes been misinterpreted to denote predestination or to reinforce a passive attitude toward the world situation, contemporary Buddhists try to correct such false ideas about happiness and misfortune. One cannot

---

[31] This section is largely based on Yoshio Tamura, *Living Buddhism in Japan,* a summary of conversations with ten Buddhist leaders, priests, abbots and university professors. (International Institute for the Study of Religions, Tokyo, 1960).

believe in a simplistic way that good causes produce good effects and evil causes result in misfortunes, they say. Some effects of our deeds are felt immediately while others are not experienced for hundreds of years. In any case, original Buddhism did not preach resignation. To accept one's fate rather than striving to improve one's position was a teaching of Japan's feudal age and a perversion of the Buddhist message. Unlike some Christians, Buddhists do not attribute everything that happens to the will of an omnipotent God. In their opinion, man plays the chief role in shaping his own destiny.

The proper meaning of karma cannot be grasped by isolating the individual from his fellowmen. Causality does not operate only on the personal level. Although man is determined by himself alone and never subjected to a will other than his own, there is also a common karma or shared responsibility. The world is woven with an interrelated karma. An individual is part of a larger society whose benefits he enjoys and whose burden of sins he carries.

For Buddhists, common karma also means that all living beings are related. Whereas Christianity says that non-human life was created for the sake of man, Buddhism teaches that it is wrong to think that the whole world exists for the benefit of mankind. This exclusive concern for ourselves—declare the Buddhists—is a grave mistake and the weak point in modern civilization. For them, even plants possess Buddha-nature and can attain Buddhahood.

What do Buddhists teach concerning the nature of sin? On this topic, there is considerable difference of opinion. Some say that sin is a Christian concept which has no place in Buddhist thought. Since Christians define sin as turning one's back on God or rebelling against Him and Buddhists do not believe in the Creator, what can sin mean for a Buddhist? One observation is that Christians worry about sin but Buddhists worry about suffering. Other Buddhists assert that ignorance rather than immorality is the fundamental evil. Because men are unaware of the true cause of decay, suffering, disease and death, their life is polluted. A third group of Buddhists today stress the disastrous effects of man's collective karma. In our complicated social situation, evil must be considered from the social viewpoint. Sin is not primarily a personal matter. A sinner is unaware of the fact that we are interdependent. To sin is to think (and act) without relating to others.

However, some Buddhist priests assert that men should transcend good and evil in any ordinary sense. Even if one falls ill or suffers misfortune, he can still say, "It is a good day, every day." Sinfulness and blessedness have no substantial reality. This being the case, there exists only an ultimate non-duality of good and evil. When one is truly enlightened, he realizes that neither error nor sin is real. If a Buddhist understands the truth, sins evaporate like dew or melt like frost in the bright face of the sun.

Death and the Pure Land Paradise

Lay Buddhists pray for their ancestors and provide them with offerings. They believe that especially wicked persons are sentenced to hell until they pay for their sins but that those who rely on the saving grace of Amida Buddha will hereafter attain happiness in the Pure Land Paradise. Yet educated priests and some more enlightened laymen feel that such concepts as the immortality of the soul or the existence of hells and bliss in the Pure Land are only "expedients" for those who cannot grasp the profound truths of the Buddha.

According to certain Nichiren Buddhists, the Pure Land, which is said to be the ideal place where we shall rest after death, exists in no other world than on this earth. When our eyes are truly open, this world is felt to be Paradise. We know ourselves only in the present. The Pure Land therefore must be here and now. Eternal life means living continuously and living simultaneously in the three worlds of the past, present and future. Paradise has to exist in the present, for this alone is what man can experience, the past being merely a name for the present which once was, and the future simply the present which can be. The Pure Land refers to our bliss in the eternal Now.

The Continuing Inspiration of Buddha

Aside from the doctrines and ceremonies of the faith, there is always the appealing figure of Buddha. Even an occasional Christian theologian will come to pay tribute to Sakyamuni. One of these has made the observation that in Kyoto there is an impressive copper image of Buddha, a national treasure from the late 7th century, which speaks to the Japanese people through centuries of tranquillity and times of despair. It is the statue's hands which convey a striking message. There is a web, like those of a duck, between the fingers. Japanese believe this web signifies the intention of Buddha to scoop all into salvation. No one will fall between his saving fingers into the realm of darkness. Buddha's hands, so well-proportioned, so attractive and so kindly, do not reject men but seek and invite people. The hands are soft and open, with beautiful curves. Buddha will not discriminate, as men do, because his compassion is unlimited. According to a contemporary Japanese Christian theologian, Buddha's image at Kyoto depicts the mysterious power of God's all-embracing mercy.[32]

Today, as for more than 2500 years in the past, Gautama sheds a warm and friendly light in a dark world.

Buddhism in Tomorrow's Japan

As the renaissance of Nichiren sectarianism amply demonstrates, Buddhism can suit the modern temper. Nearly all the so-called "New Religions" *(shinko shukyo)* which have mushroomed since World War II come out of older faiths like Shinto, Buddhism or Christianity yet each has reshaped the religious tradition to meet contemporary needs. Students of the New Religions point out certain important characteristics which are usually held in common. They are easy to enter, understand and follow. They are based on an optimistic view of life. They are determined to establish the Kingdom of God on earth, here and now. They emphasize the oneness of religion and life. And, without exception, they rely on a strong leader.

Those faiths which are making an appeal to the Japanese masses give man a sense of importance and personal dignity. They

---

[32] Kosuke Koyama in *One World*, monthly magazine of the World Council of Churches, Geneva, June, 1976, p. 22.

ordinarily teach a doctrine of inclusiveness in regard to other religions. For more than a thousand years Japanese have accepted a synthesis of Shinto and Buddhism and this practice has done much to shape the religious environment. A new factor is that Christian ideas and ideals are being added to the mixture, as Japan seeks an all-encompassing faith for modern man.[33]

---

[33] Thomsen, *Ibid,* pp. 20-29.

MAHAYANA BIBLIOGRAPHY

Ernst Benz, *Buddhism or Communism,* Doubleday and Co., N.Y., 1965.
John Blofeld, *The Jewel in the Lotus,* Buddhist Society, London, 1948.
    The Zen Teaching of Hui Hai, Rider & Co., London, 1962.
E.A. Burtt, *Teachings of the Compassionate Buddha,* Mentor Book, N.Y., 1955.
K. Ch'en, *Buddhism in China,* Princeton University Press, Princeton, N.J., 1964.
C.A. Clark, *Religions of Old Korea,* Christian Literature Society, Seoul, 1961 reprint.
Dalai Lama, *My Land and My People,* McGraw Hill, N.Y., 1962.
S. Dutt, *The Buddha and Five After Centuries,* Luzac and Co., London, 1957.
Fung Yu-Lan, *History of Chinese Philosophy,* Princeton University Press, Princeton, N.J., 1953.
J.S. Gale, *History of the Korean People,* Christian Literature Society, Seoul, 1972 reprint.
L. Carrington Goodrich, *Short History of the Chinese People,* Harper and Brothers, N.Y., 1959.
Jerome B. Grieder, *Hu Shih and the Chinese Renaissance,* Harvard University Press, Cambridge, 1970.
Hao Chang, *Liang Ch'i-ch'ao and Intellectual Transition in China, 1890-1907,* Rainbow-Bridge Book Co., Taipei, 1971.
Christmas Humphreys, *Buddhism,* Pelican Book, Harmondsworth, England, 1969.
    The Wisdom of Buddhism, Harper and Row, N.Y., 1960.
Masao Abe, "Buddhist Nirvana: its significance in contemporary thought and life", S.J. Samartha, ed., *Living Faiths and Ultimate Goals,* Orbis Books, Maryknoll, N.Y., 1974.
William M. McGovern, *An Introduction to Mahayana Buddhism,* (1922), N.Y., A.M.S. Press, 1971 reprint.
Ping-Chia Kuo, *China,* Oxford University Press, London, 1963.
K. Venkata Ramanan, *Nagarjuna's Philosophy,* C.E. Tuttle, Rutland, Vermont, 1966.
K. Reichelt, *Religion in Chinese Garment,* Philosophical Library, N.Y., 1951.
    The Transformed Abbot, Lutterworth Press, London, 1954.
Amaury de Riencourt, *The Soul of China,* Coward-McCann, N.Y., 1958.
D.T. Suzuki, *Manual of Zen Buddhism,* Grove Press, N.Y., 1960.
    On Indian Mahayana Buddhism, Harper and Row, N.Y., 1968.
    Outlines of Mahayana Buddhism, Luzac and Co., London, 1907.
Francis C.M. Wei, *The Spirit of Chinese Culture,* Charles Scribner's Sons, N.Y., 1947.
Holmes Welch, "Christian Stereotypes and Buddhist Realities", *The Buddhist Revival in China,* Harvard University Press, Cambridge, 1968.
A.F. Wright, *Buddhism in Chinese History,* Stanford Univ. Press, Stanford, Calif., 1959.
E. Zurcher, *The Buddhist Conquest of China,* E.J. Brill, Leiden, 1959.

Korean Buddhism

Chong Ik Gi, *Life and Thought of Wonhyo* (in Korean).
Chun Shin-Yong, ed., *Buddhist Culture in Korea,* International Cultural Foundation, Seoul, 1974.
Allen D. Clark, *Religions of Old Korea,* Christian Literature Society, Seoul, 1961.
Han Woo-keun, *History of Korea,* Eul-You Pub., Seoul, 1970.
Hong il Sik, *Yukdang Studies,* Il Sin Sa, Seoul, 1959.
Ilyon, *Samguk Yusa,* Tae-Hung Ha and G.K. Mintz trans., Yonsei University Press, Seoul, 1972.
Manual of Won Buddhism, Iri City, Korea, 1974.
R. Rutt, *History of the Korean People,* Royal Asiatic Society, Seoul, 1972.
Tae Hung Ha, *Korea—Forty Three Centuries,* Yonsei University Press, Seoul, 1962.
Tongsik Ryu, *Christian Faith Encounters the Religions of Korea,* Christian Literature Society, Seoul, 1965.
Tong Sik Yu, *Korean Religions and Christianity,* Christian Literature Society, Seoul, 1973 (in Korean).

Japanese Buddhism

M. Anesaki, *History of Japanese Religion,* C.E. Tuttle Co., Rutland, Vermont, 1963.
          Nichiren, The Buddhist Prophet, Smith, Gloucester, 1966.
Robert C. Armstrong, *An Introduction to Japanese Buddhist Sects,* Hunter Rose Co., Canada (privately printed), 1950.
Alfred Bloom, *Shinran's Gospel of Pure Grace,* Univ. of Arizona Press, Tucson, 1965.
Noah S. Brannen, *Soka Gakkai,* John Knox Press, Richmond, Va., 1968.
H.H. Coates and Ryugaku Ishizuka, *Honen the Buddhist Saint,* Kyoto, 1925.
A Guide to Rissho Kosei Kai, Rissho Kosei Kai headquarters, Tokyo, 1959.
Lafcadio Hearn, *Japan's Religions,* University Books, New Hyde Park, N.Y., 1966.
D.C. Holtom, *Modern Japan and Shinto Nationalism,* University of Chicago Press, 1947.
J.M. Kitagawa, *Religion in Japanese History,* Columbia University Press, N.Y., 1966.
Ryukichi Kurata, *The Harvest of Leisure,* (Tsure-Zure Gusa), J. Murray, London, 1931.
Daigan and Alicia Matsunaga, *Foundation of Japanese Buddhism,* Buddhist Books International, Tokyo-Los Angeles, 1974.
Hajime Nakamura, *History of the Development of Japanese Thought,* Japan Cultural Society, Tokyo, 1969.
Soyen Shaku, *Zen for Americans,* Open Court, LaSalle, Illinois, 1974.

Toratoro Shimomura, et. al., *Philosophical Studies of Japan,* Society for Promotion of Science, Tokyo, 1966.

Daisetz Teitaro Suzuki, *Introduction to Zen Buddhism,* Grove Press, N.Y., 1960.

The Training of a Zen Monk, Grove Press, N.Y., 1960.

Manual of Zen Buddhism, Grove Press, N.Y., 1960.

Zen and Japanese Buddhism, C.E. Tuttle, Tokyo and Rutland, Vt., 1958.

Zen and Japanese Culture, Pantheon Books, N.Y., 1959.

Yoshio Tamura, *Living Buddhism in Japan,* International Institute for the Study of Religions, Tokyo, 1960.

H. Thomsen, *The New Religions of Japan,* C.E. Tuttle Co., Rutland, Vermont, 1963.

Shoko Watanabe, *Nihon no Bukkyo* (Buddhism in Japan), Tokyo, 1960.

J.S. Weeks, "Rissho Kosei-Kai: a Cooperative Buddhist Sect" in R.J. Miller, ed., *Religious Ferment in Asia,* Univ. of Kansas, Lawrence, 1974.

Taoism

In our Taoism, the expression "to produce emptiness" contains the whole work of completing life and essence. All three religions (Taoism, Confucianism, Buddhism) agree in the one proposition, the finding of the spiritual Elixir in order to pass from death to life. In what does this spiritual Elixir consist? The deepest secret in our teaching...is confined to the work of making the heart empty. Therewith the heart is set at rest.

Lü Tung-pin (b. 755 A.D.)[1]
The Secret of the Golden Flower

---

1. R. Wilhelm, trans., The Secret of the Golden Flower, Harcourt, Brace & Company, N.Y., 1938, p. 66.

I. LAO-TZU, THE TAOIST SAGE
The Most Exalted Old Master

LAO-TZU (604 ?-531 B.C.) was the great sage of Taoism, the oldest of the three religions of ancient China. Concerning the date of his birth, suppositions vary from the sixth to the third century. According to Taoist tradition, Lao-tzu was born in Honan province in central China, worked as the keeper of the archives at the court of the Chou dynasty and was an older contemporary of Confucius.[1]

On account of his official position and great learning, the elderly philosopher was visited by Confucius, then only thirty-two years old. Quite unimpressed by the younger scholar and his teachings, Lao-tzu concluded their discussion saying, "I have heard it said that a clever merchant, though possessed of great hoards of wealth, will act as though his coffers were empty; and that the princely man, though of perfect moral excellence, maintains the air of a simpleton. Abandon your arrogant ways and countless desires, your suave demeanor and unbridled ambition, for they do not promote your welfare. That is all I have to say to you." Shaking his head, Confucius went away, remarking to his disciples, "I understand how birds can fly, how fishes can swim, and how four-footed beasts can run.... But when it comes to the dragon, I am unable to conceive how he can soar into the sky riding upon the wind and clouds. Today I have seen Lao-tzu and can only liken him to a dragon."[2] Lao-tzu must have appeared to Confucius like a speculative dreamer and Confucius must have seemed to Lao-tzu like a busybody,

---

[1] Who Lao-tzu was and what he wrote have been a debatable matter in Chinese studies for more than half a century. Was Lao-tzu an historical figure or a legendary one? Did he meet Confucius? Is the *Tao-Te-Ching* his writing? There is no agreement about such problems. At least thirteen different hypotheses have been offered. In the above account, we assume that Lao-tzu actually lived, met Confucius and is responsible for at least the core of the *Tao-Te-Ching*. See Wing-tsit Chan, *The Way of Lao-tzu*, Bobbs-Merrill Co., Indianapolis, 1963, pp. 35-59 for details of the debate. According to him, after 1950 the scepticism regarding Lao-tzu and his book diminished. For another view see the writings of Fung Yu-lan (i.e. *History of Chinese Philosophy*).

[2] Chan, *Ibid*, pp. 50-53.

meddling in other people's affairs.[3]

Later, recognizing the decay of his country and disgusted with the Chou emperor, Lao-tzu decided to pursue virtue in a more congenial setting. Riding a water buffalo he sought to leave the kingdom and headed toward Tibet. However, upon arriving at the border he was stopped by the local governor. Realizing that Lao-tzu's departure was a great loss to China, the official requested that the sage leave behind a record of his teachings to benefit the civilization he was deserting. In three days, Lao-tzu returned with a compact book of 5,000 words, the *Tao-Te-Ching*, handed it to the governor, left China and was never heard from again.

The book we know as the *Tao-Te-Ching* is Lao-tzu's original writing plus additions made by later editors whose names are unknown. This book, "a testament to man's at-home-ness in the universe",[4] has been entitled by various translators: the *Book of Reason and Virtue*, the *Path of Virtue*, *Book of the Principle and Application*, the *Canon of Reason and Virtue*, and even *Thoughts on the Nature and Manifestations of God*.[5] This basic text of Taoism can be read in an hour or studied over a lifetime. Wing-tsit Chan notes: "No one can hope to understand Chinese philosophy, religion, government, art, medicine or even cooking without a real appreciation of the profound philosophy taught in this little book."[6]

Teachings of Lao-tzu
Tao

Tao literally means the road, the Way. In the history of Chinese philosophy there have been three major concepts of Tao: Confucius and Mencius defined Tao as the norm for ethics, the moral standard by which man judges his behavior; Lao-tzu and his disciples considered Tao as the source or basic principle of all things in the universe and therefore treated it as the Abso-

---

[3] R. Hume, *The World's Living Religions,* Scribner's Sons, N.Y., 1924, p. 130.
[4] Holmes Welch, *Taoism, The Parting of the Way,* Beacon Press, Boston, 1957, p.4
[5] Hume, *Ibid,* p. 134.
[6] Wing-tsit Chan, *Ibid,* p. 3.

lute; later Sung dynasty Confucianist scholars combined these two theories, emphasizing the more theoretical aspects, and identified Tao with the basic metaphysical concept *Li* (reason or principle). In studying the *Tao-Te-Ching*, it is necessary to keep from confusing these three distinct meanings of the term.

According to Professor Fung Yu-lan, Lao-tzu took the word *Tao*, previously restricted to human affairs as the proper way of conduct, and gave it a metaphysical meaning. For the universe to have come into being there must exist an all-embracing first principle (Tao). Each existing thing has its own individual principle but Tao brings the principles of all these into single agreement. Tao represents the all-inclusive principle whereby all separate things are produced.[7] As Lao tzu wrote, "Tao is formless yet complete, existing before heaven and earth, without sound, changeless, all-pervading and unfailing, the mother of everything under heaven. We do not know its name, but we term it Tao. Forced to give an appellation ot it, I should say it was Great."[8]

In another passage Lao-tzu explains what he means by the greatness or ultimacy of Tao. "Man's standard is Earth. Earth's standard is Heaven. Heaven's standard is Tao."[9] This means Tao is great because it is the first principle through which all things come into being. It is great because Tao's actions are the actions of all things. And it is great because only through Tao are all things possible.

Because Tao is intangible, invisible, incommensurable, Lao-tzu says that it is therefore nameless. It cannot be a thing like a tree, a chair, a man, or "the ten thousand things" which make up our world of sensory experience. Tao is a "shape without shape, a thing without form." "The Tao that may be called Tao is not the invariable Tao." When we try to imagine the reality of the Tao we necessarily begin to limit it, but in actual-

---

[7] Fung Yu-lan, *History of Chinese Philosophy*, Princeton University Press, Princeton, N.J., 1952, volume I, p. 177.

[8] *Tao-Te-Ching*, chap. XXV.

[9] *Ibid*, chap. XXV.

ity Tao is limitless. When we give it a name the way we name ordinary objects we make the Tao like them, but in fact it has no restrictions, no boundaries. Tao therefore transcends our faculties of sensory experience and is beyond our rational analysis. Tao is "the Mystery of Mysteries."[10]

Since visible objects have being, Lao-tzu describes Tao as Non-being (*wu*). This, however, only means "Non-being" as opposed to the "Being" of material things. For the *Tao-Te-Ching*, Non-being in reference to Tao does not signify a mere zero, nothingness, an absence of Being. Tao is shadowy and dim yet within it are entities. Heaven and earth spring from Tao. Hence it is both Non-being and Being, the former because it is indescribable, the latter because it is the source of all existence. Non-being refers to the essence of Tao, Being to its function. "The ten thousand things are produced from Being; Being is the product of Non-being."[11]

As the first cause, Tao is the source of everything that exists. "Tao produced Oneness. Oneness produced duality. Duality evolved into trinity, and trinity evolved into the ten thousand things. The ten thousand things support the *yin* and embrace the *yang*. It is on the blending of the breaths of yin and yang that their harmony depends."[12] Various explanations have been given for this important verse,[13] but all scholars agree that it teaches that multiplicity is not the fundamental fact of existence but a secondary and derivative characteristic of reality. Also, that all existing objects (the ten thousand things to be found in our world) are held in balance because of the harmonious polarity of the male and female cosmic principles. Thus, Taoism goes beyond the fact of multiplicity and beyond the duality of the yin-yang philosophy by asserting the primacy of the one Tao.

---

[10] *Ibid*, chap. I.
[11] *Ibid*, chap. XL.
[12] *Tao-Te-Ching,* chap. XLII (Fung Yu-lan translation).
[13] Cf. R.B. Blakney, *The Way of Life,* Mentor Book, N.Y., 1955, p. 95 and Y.C. Yang, *China's Religious Heritage,* Abingdon-Cokesbury, N.Y., 1948, pp. 150-151.

Te (Virtue)

Te has been defined as character, virtue, influence, moral force. Literally, the Chinese ideograph means "to go straight to the heart." *Te* therefore involves inner righteousness, a harmony of a man's outward effect and the inner effect of his self. In this sense, there is a definite moral flavor to the term and so *Te* has been compared to the law of karma.[14]

Yet the Chinese concept goes far deeper. *Te* refers to the inner dynamic constitution of every existing being—the basic magnetic force which makes a creature what it is and gives it power. *Te* is the vibrant concentration of energy which characterizes the vitality of a man. *Te* denotes the psychic magnetism of the human personality—a man's charisma, so to speak. Because of *Te* an individual has a distinctive personality and can exert influence over others.[15] "*Te* is what individual objects obtain from Tao and thereby become what they are.... Te is Tao dwelling in objects. Tao gave them birth. Te reared them."[16]

Wu wei (actionless activity)

Since all men are by nature gifted with *Te* because their original nature comes from the Tao—and preeminently endowed with Te is the sage—a person is virtuous when he merely lets his inner radiance shine forth. In contrast to the warlords of ancient China who relied solely upon military force, the legalists who believed in legislating goodness, and the Confucian teachers who gave advice about how to reform the government, the *Tao-Te-Ching* favors "doing without doing, acting without acting"—*wu wei*. If a man is still, quiet, passive and receptive, the Tao will act through him. Because he is filled with Te, a sage influences the world by his very presence. He does not need to teach or get involved in programs for human betterment or busy himself with trying to change his society. Just by being himself he will enlighten his fellowmen.

---

[14] A. Waley, *The Way and Its Power*, Grove Press, N.Y., 1958, p. 120.

[15] Blakney, *Ibid*, pp. 38-39.

[16] Fung Yu-lan, *Ibid*, p. 180.

Wu wei does not necessarily imply avoiding all action. What Lao-tzu opposed was the reformer's attempts to change nature. What he laughed at was the statesman's efforts to improve the Tao. When Confucius told Lao-tzu how he wanted to reform society on the basis of "goodness and duty," the old sage advised him to study how nature works, how heaven and earth maintain their course, how the sun and moon give light, and how the trees grow. If you follow the path that the Way of Nature (Tao) sets, said Lao-tzu, you will no longer need to go round laboriously advertising goodness and duty, like a town-crier with his drum, seeking for news of a lost child. In Lao-tzu's opinion, reformers like Confucius were trying "to disjoint men's natures."[17]

According to the *Tao-Te-Ching*, many kinds of action are natural, spontaneous, and therefore innocent. Eating and drinking, making love, ploughing a field, planting rice—such acts are natural and in conformity with the Tao. Hostile, aggressive acts run counter to the Tao and should hence be avoided. When men try to force others to be good, when they impose duties, when they seek to dominate or subjugate their fellows, they are defying the natural order and inevitably upset the harmony decreed by the Tao. As Lao-tzu complained about Confucius, in the name of bettering men all he does is break their bones.

In terms of the ancient yin-yang philosophy, Lao-tzu stressed the overlooked and ignored virtues of the yin. When the rulers, the warlords and the statesmen were overemphasizing the masculine principle (yang), especially its reliance upon mastery, control and domination, the *Tao-Te-Ching* reasserted the equally valuable virtues of the feminine principle (yin).[18] Quite specifically Lao-tzu extolled "the mystic female."[19] Repeatedly he urged men to imitate the valley, to be like the water, to be open and receptive rather than possessive and domineering.

---

[17] An anecdote from Chuang-tzu, quoted by A. Waley, *Three Ways of Thought in Ancient China,* Doubleday, Garden City, N.Y., 1939, pp. 13-14.

[18] R.B. Blakney, *Ibid,* p. 25.

[19] *Tao-Te-Ching,* chap. VI.

> What is of all things most yielding (water)
> Can overwhelm that which is of all things most hard (rock).
> Being substanceless it can enter even where there is no space;
> But that is how I know the value of action that is actionless (wu wei).
> But that there can be teaching without words,
> Value in action that is actionless,
> Few indeed can understand.[20]

Because Lao-tzu lived in the declining years of the Chou dynasty and the *Tao-Te-Ching* is believed to have achieved its present form during the Warring States period (403-221 B.C.) Taoism was intended to provide advice to rulers of a new China. In Lao-tzu's opinion, the doctrine of *wu wei* is a practical political philosophy. Through *wu wei*, the sage can become the model for the perfect ruler, the ideal leader. Lao-tzu would have the people act on the ruler, not the ruler on the people. The wise ruler "takes the people's opinions and feelings as his own."[21] He attracts them by what he is, not so much by what he does. "In this way everything under Heaven will be glad to be pushed by him and will not find his guidance irksome."[22] He must let his mind "penetrate every corner of the land" but "never interfere." He must "rear" the people, "feed them" but "not lay claim upon them, control them but never lean upon them, be chief among them but do not manage them."[23] The ruler should "require hatred with virtue," because that is the best way to get what he wants. In all his actions he should demonstrate how "the soft overcomes the hard and the weak the strong,"[24] as water permeates the earth and wears away even solid stone.

---

[20] *Ibid*, chap. XLIII, Waley translation.
[21] *Tao-Te-Ching*, XLIX (Waley trans.).
[22] *Ibid*, LXVI.
[23] *Ibid*, X.
[24] *Ibid*, XXXVI.

Original Nature: the Uncarved Block

Lao-tzu believed that in ancient times, sages abounded and man lived in paradise. Men possessed an original nature which was pure, totally free from hostility and aggression. This he compared to an "uncarved block" (*P'u*), a piece of wood which exhibits its intrinsic, unmarred natural beauty. When men were unadorned, unmutilated by social regulations and free of the paint of conventional morality, Confucius' 3300 rules of social etiquette were not necessary. Ancient man—whose example is set up as the ideal—did not belong to a complex social structure.[25] Living in small settlements which consisted in all likelihood of but a single family, man had few desires: "to be contented with his food, pleased with his clothing, satisfied with his home, taking pleasure in his rustic tasks."[26] Since there were almost no social pressures, there could be no aggression against the individual: no repressive morality, no onerous duties to the community, no oppressive punishments. Because the society was not aggressive in its demands, it did not provoke hostility or aggressiveness on the part of its members. By eating, a man satisfied his physical needs; he "filled his belly and weakened his ambitions." For him money and power, learning and reputation did not even exist. Completely satisfied, man was so content that, even though "the neighboring settlement might be so near he could hear the cocks crowing and the dogs barking, he would grow old and die without ever having been there."[27]

If an earthly paradise existed in the past, Lao-tzu believed it was also always a possibility for the present. As man was originally created by Tao pure and good, like an uncarved block of wood, so are children always born simple, unmarred and virtuous. As Lao-tzu asked, "in controlling your vital force to achieve gentleness, can you become like the newborn child?"[28] The sociologist Max Weber notes, for Lao-tzu the essential goodness of human nature was the self-evident point of depar-

---

[25] Cf. J.J. Rousseau's concept of "the noble savage."
[26] *Tao-Te-Ching*, LXXX (Waley).
[27] H. Welch, *Taoism, The Parting of the Way*, p. 36.
[28] *Tao-Te-Ching*, X (Waley).

ture.[29] Man is born good; only society can mar and distort his original nature. Hence, the individual who can recover this primordial state—symbolized by the uncarved block and the newborn child—has learned *wu wei*, the secret of active inaction.

Lao-tzu's formula for uncovering our original nature—thus, making the Way (Tao) for an ideal kingdom on earth—is to reduce the desires foisted upon us by a fallen society: desires for money, power and status. Riches, hard to obtain, get in the way of their owner.[30] Favor and disgrace drive men out of their minds. When a ruler's subjects get fame, they become distracted. When they lose influence, they turn distraught.[31] If a man depends upon what others think of him and the position he temporarily holds in society, he can hardly be expected to keep a balanced mind or be able to express his original nature.

However, Lao-tzu seems to go beyond this to suggest that we should not esteem duty, law, or knowledge of right and wrong. These too, in his opinion, are useless trappings of a fallen society. He would therefore eliminate from his projected ideal state all that does not come straight from our individual understanding of the Tao. As he put it, "Banish wisdom, discard knowledge, and the people will be benefited a hundred fold: banish human kindness, discard morality, and the people will be dutiful and compassionate."[32] While many of his critics have accused Lao-tzu of being an anarchist, probably all he really opposed was the pseudo-wisdom of the learned mandarin class, the legislated morality of the government and the "benevolence" of those who subjugate the people for their own good, as they put it. Relying on the intrinsic goodness of all men, Lao-tzu protested against an oppressive State, a repressive system of ethics and the meddling activities of so-called "do-gooders" in the established bureaucracy. Once man was liber-

---

[29] M. Weber, *The Religion of China*, Free Press, Glencoe, Ill., 1951, p. 187.
[30] *Tao-Te-Ching*, XII.
[31] *Ibid*, XIII.
[32] *Tao-Te-Ching*, XIX (Waley).

ated from the artificial and unnecessary restrictions of society, he would be free to express his original kindness, compassion, purity and goodness.

Government by Tao

The doctrine of *wu wei* was in part a reaction to China's age of troubles. The period of the Warring States was a time in which armies marched all over the land and wars were frequent. The Chou dynasty civilization was in shambles. Looking about, Lao-tzu beheld reprisal following reprisal, so asked himself, Can this ever be stopped?[33] The *Tao-Te-Ching* was written for leaders who had to cope with injustice, tyranny, pillage and slaughter. Speaking to the government authorities, Lao-tzu asked, "When the people do not fear death (because they had seen so much of it), how can one frighten them with death?"[34] The leaders must rule a large country as if they were "cooking small fish."[35] As an ancient Taoist commentary points out, when cooking small fish, the intestines are not taken out and the scales are not scraped off. One does not dare to scratch them for fear that they might go to pieces. Similarly, when governing a country if one starts meddling around, then the subjects become confused.[36]

Throughout Chinese history, Taoism has often been the philosophy of a disaffected minority from the upper classes and the suppressed peasants, a protest embodied in the secret societies which plotted revolts against oppressive rulers. The ideal form of government, as Lao-tzu envisions it, is a system of *laissez faire*. By interfering in the people's affairs as little as possible, "they will transform spontaneously and the world will be at peace of its own accord."[37]

Chuang-tzu, Lao-tzu's most prominent disciple, explained

---

[33] Welch, *Ibid*, p. 19.

[34] *Tao-Te-Ching*, chap. LXXIV (Waley).

[35] *Ibid*, chap. LX.

[36] *Ho-Shang-Kung's Commentary on Lao-tse*, Artibus Asiae, Ascona, Switzerland, 1950, p. 222.

[37] Wing-tsit Chan, *Ibid*, p. 15.

the proper principles of the ruler and ruled in terms of the facts of nature. In nature, considered apart from man, there are degrees of honor. The "dome of Heaven," for example, is of greater dignity than the "pavement of Earth." So, likewise, in the case of man there are exalted positions and humbler ones, a class of rulers and a class of the ruled. In a family there is the head of the household and its members. The ruled are those who perform the inescapable taskwork; the rulers are those who direct this activity. However, according to the Taoists, rulers can only expect success if they rule "lightly from afar, so lightly that the reins of government might be threads of gossamer in their hands."[38]

It is important to note that Lao-tzu was not against government per se, but only bad government. Like Confucius, like all Chinese, he took for granted the positive value of government. For the Taoist, the worth of a civilization ultimately depends to a considerable degree upon the worth of the ruler.[39] Lao-tzu does not believe in escaping from the world. Nowhere in his writings is displayed any active antagonism to the world or religiously-motivated flight from society.[40]

Taoism, like Confucianism, looked forward to a golden age when harmony and tranquility would prevail, a perfect and ideal state in which everybody would be happy. The great difference is that Confucianism magnified man's role in constructing such a perfect social order, while Taoists minimized man's role by comparison with the vastness and majesty of nature. More specifically, Lao-tzu's ideal State was to be found in returning to the uncorrupted state of nature; whereas Confucianism sought to build the good society by continually improving upon man's original barbarism through the gradual development of civilization.[41] Confucius was an apostle of culture, Lao-tzu

---

[38] Edward Herbert, *A Taoist Notebook,* John Murray, Ltd., London, 1955, pp. 27-28.
[39] Max Weber, *Ibid,* p. 185.
[40] *Ibid,* p. 186.
[41] Yang, *Ibid,* pp. 157-158.

was an advocate of naturalism.[42] The former wanted to reform the world through moral education; the latter by contrast urged men to return to the Origin, the Tao.

II. CHUANG-TZU

Following Lao-tzu was his even more brilliant disciple, Chuang-tzu (369-286 B.C.), a contemporary of the Confucian philosopher Mencius. Often called China's greatest philosopher, Chuang-tzu took the basic ideas of the Taoists, refined them and expressed their abiding truth in a series of dialogues whose literary form is equal to that of Plato.

Chuang-tzu agreed with Lao-tzu in his concept of the Tao as an all-embracing reality. For him there is not a single thing without Tao. When asked to specify where Tao could be found, the sage replied that it was located in the ant, the grass, the earthenware tile.[1] Just as water can be found in many places—the sea, a lake or an ordinary ditch—so the Tao is the one substance which can be found everywhere under different names.

In Chuang-tzu's opinion, nature is a process of ceaseless change. Everything is in perpetual movement—like a galloping horse. Nothing remains constant, hence, one must recognize that the evolution of nature, symbolized by the endless circle, is the basic fact of existence.[2]

As part of a larger universe, men can attain happiness by following their specific innate natures. Liberate your instincts and follow the Tao in a life of unadorned and spontaneous simplicity, Chuang-tzu advised. Each individual has his own special likings. No one should be forced to fit a pattern set by others. To be in harmony with Nature is the secret of obtaining happiness but each person must express his uniqueness rather than be forcibly made to conform. Chuang-tzu therefore con-

---

[42] J.J.L. Duyvendak, *The Way and Its Virtue,* John Murray, Ltd., London, 1954, p. 11.

[1] Burton Watson, ed., *Complete Works of Chuang Tzu,* Columbia University Press, N.Y., 1970, pp. 240-241.

[2] Fung Yu-lan, *Ibid,* pp. 221-245.

demned all fixed standards which men should obey. As he put it, while fish are made to live in water, men will die if submerged in it for any length of time. When they are free to express themselves in a spontaneous fashion there will be no need for oppressive government or repressive social institutions.

To oppose the Confucian administrators, Chuang-tzu told the story of the Marquis of Lu and a bird he had captured. Determined to help the bird, the nobleman gave it wine to drink, played classical music for its entertainment and sacrificed an ox for it to eat. Naturally, in spite of all this loving concern for its welfare, the bird was dead within three days. The Marquis treated the bird as one would treat himself, and not as a bird would treat a bird. Similarly, the Confucian reformers try to make all men conform to their standards of "human-heartedness" and "righteousness."[3] Though undoubtedly actuated by love for the people, they ignore the different constitutions which nature has given to man. For the State to make people good is like putting a halter on a horse or a string through an ox's nose; these things may seem like benefits to the masters but they serve no useful purpose for the horse and the ox. As Chuang-tzu asked, why attempt to lengthen a duck's legs because you think them short or cut off part of a crane's legs because to you they look too long? In nature the long is never too much and the short is never too little.[4]

Chuang-tzu taught the value of complete liberty and equality. There should be no artificial restraints put on individuals. Men differ and their differences must be respected. Who can say what is the right way to live, when eels thrive in damp places and monkeys like to dwell in trees? What is *proper* food in a world where men eat meat, deer eat grass, owls feed on mice, and insects enjoy eating dead snakes? Or how can we be so sure of our standards of beauty? Men may praise two women as the most attractive creatures; but at the sight of them, fish dive deep into the water, birds soar high in the sky, and deer hurry away.

---

[3] Chuang-tzu, *Collected Works*, XVIII.
[4] *Ibid*, VII.

Of these four, who truly recognizes the beautiful? By what right can man say his notion of beauty is superior to that of the deer or the bird? According to Chuang-tzu, all our rules of goodness and paths of right and wrong have become hopelessly snarled or jumbled because we fail to recognize the natural differences among individuals.[5]

Right and wrong are purely relative. From the standpoint of Tao, nothing is valuable or worthless in itself. Hence, one should not be bigoted in his opinions or one-sided in his conduct. From the perspective of Tao, everything is equal to everything else. So, as Chuang-tzu advises, we should be dispassionate, impartial, recognizing the equality of all things and holding all things in our embrace. Let us forget the artificial, arbitrary, merely conventional distinctions between right and wrong; harmonize all differences within the boundary of nature and trust in the spontaneous process of natural evolution. Let us find enjoyment in the realm of the infinite which transcends all such limited social distinctions![6]

Although the central theme of Chuang-tzu's writings can be summed up in the single word "freedom,"[7] the Taoist sage was also interested in showing men how to be contented. According to Chuang-tzu, those who quietly follow the course of Nature will not be affected by either sorrow or joy. The wise man knows how to control his emotions by means of reason.[8] First he learns to disregard worldly matters; then he understands how to ignore external things. Finally, when he becomes fully enlightened he can stop worrying about his own vision of the One (Tao). As he perfects himself, the sage can maintain his tranquillity, no matter how great the disturbances which occur around him. For this philosopher, it is important that men accept the fact of change. We cannot hold on to anything forever. By trying to do so we subject ourselves to the experience of unhappi-

---

[5] *Ibid*, II.
[6] *Ibid*, II.
[7] Burton Watson, introductory essay to *Complete Works of Chuang Tzu*, p. 3.
[8] Fung Yu-lan compares Chuang-tzu to Spinoza in this matter.

ness. Chuang-tzu points out that when a young girl was captured by invading soldiers she wept for the loss of her former way of life. But soon she was brought to the palace of the king, lived the life of a princess and regretted that she had ever cried over her capture. Why lament the inevitable fact of change? How can our fortune be improved without change? "What an incomparable bliss it is to undergo these ceaseless transformations!"[9]

Besides accepting the inevitability of change, the sage identifies with everything in the universe. Since the universal Tao has no beginning or end, by uniting with it a man will participate in immortality. The universe is eternal, and so are we, when we realize our union with it. One reaches eternity through an experience of mystical enlightenment in which one sees the unity of all things. Thus, the individual becomes one with the All. When a man awakens to the all-embracing Tao, he says, "Heaven and Earth came into being with me together, and with me all things are one."[10]

Chuang-tzu calls the highest goal "the fast of the mind" or "sitting in forgetfulness." By disregarding worldly matters and not being disturbed by external things, the *True Man* sleeps without dreaming and wakes up without worries. He neither loves life too much nor fears death. He receives with delight anything that comes to him. He lives calmly, feeling no resistance. Death is only the natural result of life; to rebel against it or feel bitter about it will merely strain the emotions to no effect.

When a friend was surprised to discover Chuang-tzu singing soon after his wife died, the Taoist philosopher replied that originally his wife had been lifeless, had no form and lacked all substance. For a time she had substance, form and life. Now, she had merely changed again—exactly as spring, summer, autumn and winter take place in the natural world. Why be upset? Why mourn? For one to weep and wail while she sleeps would be to show oneself ignorant of fate.[11]

---

[9] Chuang-tzu, *Ibid*, VI.
[10] Fung Yu-lan, *Ibid*, p. 241.
[11] Chuang-tzu, *Ibid*, XVIII.

From realizing oneness with the universe the sage achieves absolute freedom. If life and death are only two aspects of the natural process and the distinction between good and evil is only relative, man frees himself from dependence upon anything. He no longer tries to rely on transient riches, fame, power, or even love, as a foundation for happiness. The perfect man is like a free spirit. Were the great lakes to burn up, he would not feel hot. Were the rivers to freeze solid, he would not be cold. Were the mountains to be split by thunderstorms, he would not be frightened. As a pure spirit, he would simply ride the clouds, as it were, and wander beyond the seas. If neither life nor death can affect the True Man, of course, he does not worry about the difference between what benefits him and what is harmful.[12]

Some of Chuang-tzu's ideas vaguely resemble those of the Chinese hermits who tried to escape from the world. However, the Taoist philosopher was no advocate of the solitary life of the recluse. Chuang-tzu denied that one could be free of all entanglements. Instead of fleeing society, the Taoist should do what he must, without praise or blame. He should be ready to change with the times, act spontaneously, using harmony as a measure. Above all else, the True Man devotes himself to "using things as things, and not being used as a thing by things."[13]

III. VARIETIES OF EARLY TAOISM

Historically, Taoism refers to a religion composed of several very heterogeneous elements. According to the Taoists themselves their faith goes back far earlier than Lao-tzu's time to the reign of the legendary "Yellow Emperor" who ruled China in the very distant past. While this claim is not literally true, it rightly indicates that the roots of Taoism may be found as early as the Shang period (circa 1300 B.C.).[1] Although Lao-tzu was the founder and great sage of Taoist philosophy, impor-

---

[12] *Ibid*, II.

[13] Fung Yu-lan, *Ibid*, p. 245; cf. Chuang-tzu, chap. XX.

[1] Werner Eichhorn, *Taoism*, in R.C. Zaehner, ed., *Concise Encyclopedia of Living Faiths*, Beacon Press, Boston, 1967, p. 385.

tant elements in the Taoist cult predate his work by many centuries.

In addition to the *Tao-Te-Ching* which was made scripture, Taoism was interested in the pseudo-science of alchemy, exotic herb medicines, breathing exercises, a cult of wine and poetry, revolutionary secret societies, incantations and amulets, the search for the famed Isles of the Blest, and the establishment of a theocratic state in China.

The Hygiene School

Since all Chinese believed that living as long as possible is a much desired blessing, some Taoists devoted themselves to the search for medicines which would guarantee longevity. These priests became peddlers of herb tonics which were supposed to rejuvenate the elderly, cure dangerous diseases and bestow occult powers. To assure longevity these herb doctors also recommended special breathing exercises and gymnastics. Taoists taught that if a person practiced certain breathing techniques, exercised properly, followed a special diet and reinforced his natural powers with appropriate drugs, he could become an "immortal."

Yin-yang Philosophy and the Five Elements School

From early times there were attempts to explain the phenomena of the universe in terms of two cosmic forces which represent female (yin) and male (yang), darkness and light, soft and hard, inactivity and activity. Everything in the world was supposed to result from the interaction, conflict or harmony of the yin and yang principles. As early as 780 B.C., a disastrous earthquake was attributed to the domination of the yin by the yang.[2] Since there was also a widespread assumption that there is a mutual interaction between the ways of nature and the conduct of man, the ruler's acts were supposed to affect the state of the physical world. Hence, it was important for men to know

---

[2] Fung Yu-lan, *Ibid,* p. 32.

how to harmonize the yang and yin principles.

In the *Tao-Te-Ching*, scholars have discovered traces of an ancient Chinese belief that "the gate of the dark female" is the origin of all things. Men then worshipped an earth or water goddess (the Mystic Female) who gives birth to the visible creation. During the pre-Christian era Taoists gave preference to the yin, represented by the element water. Because of this, rest was considered prior to motion, and tranquillity to action. According to traditional Chinese thought, silence, humility and profound peace are the characteristics of the earth and water, as opposed to the active, aggressive qualities of the sun, the heavens and the yang. After the time of Lao-tzu, however, the exclusive rights of the cosmic earth mother were balanced with their opposites in the yin-yang philosophy.[3]

Often connected to the yin-yang concept but originally separate from it was another naturalistic explanation of the universe known as the *five elements* theory. According to its advocates, the five agents—metal, wood, water, fire and earth—operating with complete regularity, motivate and govern all growth and change in the physical world. The five elements are not to be thought of as physical substances like the wood we can see or water we drink but are cosmic forces which dominate certain periods of time according to a fixed plan. These agents control our world in the order in which they were believed to "beget" each other: wood produces fire, fire produces earth, earth produces metal, metal produces water. Wood controls the season of spring, the color green and the direction east. Fire is assigned to summer, the color red, and the direction south. Metal dominates autumn, its color is white, and its direction is west. Water controls winter, the color black, and the direction north. Since there are only four seasons, earth was placed in the center, aiding the other elements, and given the color yellow.

According to the five elements theory, numerous correspondences in the natural world can be derived by analogy. All facets of the spiritual world and physical world can be thus clas-

---

[3] W. Eichhorn, *Ibid*, p. 386.

sified in terms of their relationship to the five basic agents. Some of these patterns of interrelatedness are seen in the following table:

Wood	Fire	Earth
Spring	Summer	......
Benevolence	Wisdom	Faith
Number 8	7	5
East	South	Center
Jupiter	Mars	Saturn
sheep	fowl	ox
spleen	lungs	heart
scaly creatures	feathered ones	naked beings
wheat	beans	millet (type A)
sour taste	bitter	sweet

Metal	Water
Autumn	Winter
Righteousness	Decorum
9	6
West	North
Venus	Mercury
dog	pig
liver	kidneys
hairy	shell-covered
hemp	millet (B)
acrid	salty[4]

Although it is easy to criticize some of the details of the five elements theory, the important fact is that Taoist philosophers were concerned to find an overall pattern by which all the different aspects of creation could be related and

---

[4] De Bary, *Sources of Chinese Tradition,* Columbia Univ. Press, N.Y., 1960, p. 215, abridged.

explained. On the whole Taoism, far more than its rivals, promoted scientific investigation, because of its reverence for the natural world and its belief that the one Tao was the ultimate reality.

Later Taoist Philosophers
Huai-nan Tzu (d. 122 B.C.)

Liu An, the Prince of Huai-nan, was considered the most eminent Taoist philosopher of his time. Known mainly for his diligence in reiterating and elaborating the ideas of Lao-tzu and Chuang-tzu, he also served as the wealthy patron of thousands of scholars and prepared the way for the neo-Taoist school of the third and fourth centuries A.D. He and his scholarly friends produced a lengthy work on metaphysics, astronomy, government, military strategy, etc., which was simply entitled *Huai-nan Tzu*.[5]

There is not much which is distinctive in Liu An's philosophy. His concept of the Tao is like that of Lao-tzu and Chuang-tzu. As for his general cosmology, it resembles the standard doctrine of the later Confucianists. Nevertheless, one idea is worthy of note. According to *Huai-nan Tzu*, Heaven, earth, infinite space and infinite time are the body of a single person, and the space within the six cardinal points of the compass is the form of one man. Because man is the microcosm of the universal macrocosm, the sage can recognize his oneness with all things and attain harmony with the Absolute.[6]

Yang Hsiung (53 B.C.-18 A.D.)

Yang Hsiung, a Taoist metaphysician of some note, although a poor man whose public career was an undistinguished one, shows how Taoism reacted to and improved the dominant Confucian philosophy. Mencius (371-289 B.C.) had stated flatly that man's nature was basically good, whereas Hsun Tzu (298-238 B.C.) had contended that human nature was evil and had to

---

[5] Huai-nan Tzu, *Tao, the Great Luminant,* Kelly and Walsh, Shanghai, 1934.
[6] Cf. W. Chan, *A Source Book in Chinese Philosophy,* Princeton Univ. Press, Princeton, 1963, p. 308.

be corrected. Yang Hsiung, in typical Taoist opposition to simplistic Confucian teachings, declared that man's nature is a mixture of good and evil. Those who cultivate the moral aspect will become virtuous and those who let the lower aspect dominate will become evil. Each individual rides a horse which can carry him in any direction. His *ch'i* (vital force) has no set goal. Therefore the superior man must study hard and act with earnestness. His actions should be based on careful planning.[7] Avoiding the extreme positions set forth by Mencius and Hsun Tzu, Yang Hsiung represented a real advance in the Chinese philosophers' understanding of human nature.

At a time when many of his fellow-Taoists were saying that some men had actually found the secret of living forever, Yang Hsiung denounced such interest in so-called "Immortals." Some Taoists talk so much about the existence of those who are supposed to be able to conquer death that many believe there must be some truth to the notion, he said. When asked if he himself believed in the existence of Immortals, Yang Hsiung replied that we should stop talking about such matters but rather concentrate on practical questions like loyalty or filial piety.[8] In this respect the philosopher concurred with the general attitude of Confucius in regard to the supernatural, yet was also in agreement with Lao-tzu and Chuang-tzu who advocated indifference to the problem of life or death.

In metaphysics, Yang Hsiung referred to Tao as "the Supremely Profound Principle" and "the Great Mystery" *(T'ai-hsuan)*. Like his predecessors he said that it deeply penetrates all things but has no visible physical form. It operates yin and yang, gives birth to motion in the universe, and originates all things. By looking up man can see the form of the heavens; by looking down he sees the condition of the earth; by looking within he will understand his nature and destiny.

However, to this Taoist metaphysic, Yang Hsiung added the

---

[7] Yang-Hsiung, *Fa-yen* (Model Sayings) 3:1, *Le catechisme philosophique de Yang-Hiong-tse,* Editions de l'Occident, Brussels, 1960.

[8] *Fa-yen* 12:4-5.

Confucian ethic. While one should follow the principles of the world without trying to alter them, to be human means to attend to the affairs of this life, to be in society and to love universally. Man's business in life is to get hold of the Way, act like a human being and practice righteousness. To look and to love is to be human; to determine and to decide is courage. To act impartially is to control things and to use them for the sake of all men.[9]

Wang Ch'ung (27-100 A.D.?)

Another Taoist metaphysician, Wang Ch'ung, has enjoyed unusual popularity among contemporary thinkers because of his skepticism, his revolt against the authority of the past and his attacks on superstition. Actually, he should be seen primarily as a philosopher who adopted and amplified the skeptical aspect of Chuang-tzu's teachings. At a time when Confucian philosophy was often being misinterpreted to reinforce popular belief in occult phenomena, prophecies and mysterious portents, Wang Ch'ung used Taoist ideas to raise the pitch of naturalism and rationalism to a height never before reached in Chinese history.

Of particular concern to religious people is his attack on the concept of cosmic purpose. Against those who found a basic teleological factor in the universe, Wang Ch'ung insisted that all things are spontaneously produced when the material forces (ch'i) of Heaven and earth come together. We do not live in a universe designed for man. Heaven does not procure grain in order to feed man or create silk and hemp in order to clothe him. Heaven is not a farmer for the sake of man. Things are simply spontaneously created; there exist no lucky influences from Heaven. Heaven has no purpose, no mind or will, declared Wang Ch'ung, even if people would like to think so.

To those who believed that because Heaven is engaged in action its activities must resemble the purposive activities of man, Wang Ch'ung replies that Heaven merely generates and distributes material energy. It has no desire to produce things.

---

[9] *Classic of the Supremely Profound Principle,* chap. IX; for a brief extract, see W. Chan, *A Source Book in Chinese Philosophy,* p. 291.

Heaven and earth are like a furnace, spontaneously giving forth heat. Heaven does not create calamities to warn us of our sins. Natural oddities and natural disasters simply represent the spontaneous products of aimless material forces.[10] Wang Ch'ung tries to prove his point about the purposelessness of the cosmic process by contrasting the awesome majesty of Heaven with the insignificance of man. "How can our deeds activate Heaven?," he asks. Man is subject to the cosmic material force but his petty deeds cannot alter it. The wind can sway the branches of a tree but the branches cannot cause the wind.[11]

With equal vigor Wang Ch'ung tried to demolish the common Chinese belief in life after death. In his opinion the dead do not become spirits, do not possess consciousness and cannot hurt the living.[12] Wang Ch'ung's argument, however, fell on deaf ears, because the Confucianists remained convinced of the reality of the spirits, because the Taoists believed a way could be found to assure physical immortality, and because Buddhism arrived with a doctrine of the immortal spirit within every man. His attack on spirits is significant because it shows how philosophic Taoism could be rationalistic as well as mystical about matters which most religious people consider to be of ultimate importance.

The Lieh Tzu

As we have seen, Taoism taught the equality of all things, indifference to life and death, freedom to follow one's own nature without regard for social proprieties or official morality, and the need simply to accept one's fate. Lieh-tzu was a famous Taoist of the fifth century B.C., whose writings have been lost. However, under his name, someone in the third century A.D. circulated a book which turned Taoism into a call for complete abandonment of efforts to improve society or to cultivate the self. One section of the *Lieh Tzu*, supposedly containing the

---

[10] *Lun-heng*, XIII. Alfred Forke, trans., Luzac, London, 1907-11, 2 volumes.
[11] *Ibid*, XLIII.
[12] *Ibid*, LXII.

teaching of another ancient Taoist philosopher Yang Chu (440-360 B.C.?), expounds a purely hedonistic ethic. According to most Chinese scholars, the Taoist canonical book *Lieh Tzu* comes from an era of political and moral chaos when intellectuals despaired of society so therefore extolled private indulgence in sensuous pleasures.

In opposition to the scholars and government officials who encouraged men to try to eradicate the evils of their age, the cynical author of *Lieh Tzu* pointed out the uselessness of such endeavors. Drawing illustrations from traditional Chinese history he showed that all man's striving was of no effect. What good is there in becoming wise? Peng-tzu, the Chinese Methuselah, lived to be eight hundred without being as learned as the sage-emperors; while a virtuous disciple of Confucius died at age eighteen. Wicked king Chou stayed on his throne, but his three good viscounts were exiled, imprisoned or executed. If effort is so valuable, asked Lieh-tzu, why is a sage unrecognized and a scoundrel made powerful, why are worthy men kept from high positions and the stupid given honors, why are the good so often poor but the wicked rich?

Even fate or destiny offers no real explanation for what happens to men. Fate does not control men. The longevity or brevity of a man's life, his obscurity or prominence, his riches or poverty are inexplicable. They happen, but the reason why is beyond our capacity to fathom. For Lieh-tzu the skeptic, we are confronted by questions to which there are no answers. In a time of social collapse, nothing has any rhyme or reason. As the Taoist would say, the Tao has no name.

Yang Chu bases his devotion to selfish pleasure-seeking on a philosophy of despair. Look at man, he urges. Infancy and feeble old age account for almost half an individual's allotted lifespan. His nights are wasted in sleep and half his waking hours are spent with things which are unimportant. Pain and sickness, sorrow and suffering, the death of loved ones, worry and fear occupy half the time we are not busy with trivia. Is there not at least a moment in which we have the right to enjoy ourselves?

What pleasure is there? According to Yang Chu, life is for beauty and abundance: "For music and sex, that is all." Even these pleasures however are prohibited by threats of punishment, checked by laws, pushed from us by our desire for fame. Thus, we lose the great happiness of the present because we cannot give free reign to our impulses for even a single moment. Whether men are worthy or stupid, honorable or despised, in death they all rot, disintegrate and disappear. Let us therefore hasten to enjoy the present; why bother about what comes after death?[13]

According to Mencius, Yang Chu's philosophy could be summed up in the motto: each one for himself. This meant that nothing is more important than one's personal happiness. Yang Chu vowed that he would not sacrifice a single hair from his head even to benefit the whole world. Realizing the difficulty of rescuing society from its troubles, he and others like him took no part in political affairs.

Although the author of the *Lieh Tzu* called it "the Pure Classic of the Perfect Virtue of Simplicity and Vacuity," its readers and admirers used it to justify a life of unbridled sensuality. Young men from the upper classes created what they called the Light Conversation school of Taoism which avoided politics, ridiculed traditional morality, indulged in every form of unconventional behavior and pretended to be free.[14]

Neo-Taoism

During the last fifty years of the Han dynasty (200 B.C.-220 A.D.), China was politically divided, subjected to repeated floods and droughts, ravaged by continuous warfare, and miserably governed by corrupt officials. Disgusted by what was taking place, many scholars turned away from government service and tried to find consolation in transcendent values. Because of

---

[13] A.C. Graham, trans., *The Book of Lieh Tzu,* John Murray, Ltd., London, 1960, vii.
[14] W. Chan, *Source Book,* pp. 315-316.

the disordered world in which they lived, they could not be satisfied with Confucian orthodoxy or the Taoist occultism of the masses. Neither the sterile scholasticism of the former nor the astrology, alchemy and divination of the latter were inspiring. All the anti-Confucian philosophers soon became fashionable, among them Lao-tzu and Chuang-tzu. With Confucius in disrepute, who could be more stimulating than his arch-critics?

Chinese thinkers during the Wei-Chin dynasties (220-420 A.D.) looked for some common ground on which to base their arguments. They found this in *Li* (Principle) which gradually became a central concept in Chinese philosophy. In the second place, as a result of renewed study of the Taoist classics, Wei-Chin scholars interpreted *Wu* (non-being) not as the opposite of being but rather as pure, undifferentiated and ultimate reality. Three former imperial ministers played the major roles in the formulation of Neo-Taoism: Wang Pi (226-249 A.D.), Ho Yen (?-249 A.D.) and Kuo Hsiang (?-312 A.D.). Although Wang Pi died before he was twenty-five, he wrote important commentaries on Lao-tzu and the *I Ching*, the Confucian classic most easily interpreted in Taoist terms. Whereas earlier Taoism had concerned itself with the all-embracing and immanent Tao manifested in the visible world, Wang Pi stressed the transcendent Tao, the ultimate reality, the original non-being. It is pure being, the primal yet indescribable reality. In it substance and function are one. Where Lao-tzu used the word "fate" or spoke of "*destiny* decreed by Heaven," Wang Pi used the term Principle (Li). When neo-Confucian philosophy made its appearance (late eighth century), its adherents borrowed from Wang Pi by emphasizing "the Principle of Nature" (T'ien-li). In an age of disunity and trouble, Wang Pi sought a unified system based on a single reality, *pen-wu*.[15] His work became enormously influential.

Ho Yen, the second great exponent of Neo-Taoism, stressed the transcendence of non-being rather than its value as a unify-

---

[15] W. Chan, *Source Book,* pp. 316-317, 318-324.

ing principle. Tao has no predicates or attributes so cannot be given a name. When one looks at it, it has no form; when one listens to it, it has no sound. It possesses nothing and yet strangely possesses everything. Because of Tao, no matter how far apart similar things are, they respond to each other; and no matter how near different things are, they do not violate each other. At a time when scholars were so involved in naming, classifying, arranging and regulating everything—with disastrous consequences—Ho Yen reminded his contemporaries that the ultimate and most important reality is transcendent.

Nevertheless, Wang Pi and Ho Yen combined Taoist metaphysics with Confucian ethics. For them Lao-tzu was the great sage in matters of ontology but Confucius provided a superior guide in questions of social or individual morality. Possibly it was because Wang Pi and Ho Yen recognized the individualistic anarchism which could be derived from the *Tao-Te-Ching* that they asserted the continuing validity of the Confucian family-centered ethic.

Kuo Hsiang, the third apostle of Neo-Taoism, wrote a commentary on the collected essays of Chuang-tzu. As Wang Pi went beyond Lao-tzu by introducing the concept of Principle, Kuo Hsiang dropped Chuang-tzu's term "Tao" in favor of *Tzu-jan* (Nature). Heaven is not considered something behind, above or beyond the process of Nature but is merely a synonym for Nature as a whole. Because every thing has its specific principle there is no need for an over-all original reality to combine and govern them. In contrast to Wang Pi, Kuo stresses being, the many, and the fundamental immanence of principle. Each being has its own principle therefore each is self-sufficient.

Kuo Hsiang also was a fatalist. The principles of things were correct from the outset and remain so: our nature and destiny are only what they should be. By letting nature take its course, men can be perfect. We must know our nature, accept it, trust it, express it and be satisfied with it. Allow the foot to walk according to its capacity and let the hand grasp with all its strength, he urged. Kuo claims that to be in accord with all things necessarily implies the fullest possible exercise of one's talents and capabilities. As he put it, one roams about all over the transcendental world in order to enlarge the mundane world.[16]

From the days of Lao-tzu and Yang Chu to the full flowering of Taoist philosophy in the writings of Wang Pi, Ho Yen and Kuo Hsiang about seven hundred years of study, scholarship and speculation took place. Lao-tzu and Chuang-tzu were not like meteors which suddenly appear, briefly light up the dark skies and quickly vanish. Instead, they should be seen as initiators of an intellectual, moral and mystical period twice as long as the Protestant movement from Luther to the present. During this lengthy period there was time to examine every aspect of Taoism, see the relevance of the Tao to such diverse problems as ontology and social ethics, as well as investigate and refine the meaning of specific concepts like *Li, Wu* and *T'ien.*

Taoism never existed in a vacuum. From the meeting of Lao-tzu and Confucius onward, it had critics and rivals. For most of the early period the Taoists faced opposition from the Confucian scholars and government officials. By the time Neo-Taoism appeared, equally vigorous activity by Buddhist monks weakened the hold Taoism had on the Chinese.

Soon Taoism relied almost exclusively upon diviners, alchemists, faith healers and other masters of the occult to gain adherents. Since Confucian scholars preferred to concentrate on social ethics and practical statesmanship, Chinese concern for communion with the spiritual world was left to the Taoist psychics and herb doctors or the Buddhist priests. Some of the best emperors—and the worst—became devotees of the occult. After 1016 A.D. Taoists looked to "celestial masters" at the Dragon and Tiger mountain for psychic advice, charms and prognostications of the future. Philosophic Taoism became folk Taoism.[17]

---

[16] W. Chan, *Ibid*, p. 333.

[17] For material on subsequent folk Taoism, the reader should consult Holmes Welch, *Taoism, The Parting of the Way.*

IV. TAOISM IN THE MODERN AGE

As China entered the modern age, Taoism already seemed to be fated for eventual extinction. According to Professor Wing-tsit Chan, by 1950 there was nothing in it to promise, let alone insure, its survival. Since folk religion (which is what Taoism had become) is ridiculed by the intellectuals, condemned by the Christians and suppressed by the Communists, it is easy to prophesy its early demise. What future can a religion have which is largely superstitious, lacking in capable leadership, unconcerned with educational, medical or philanthropic service, without strong organizations and primarily devoted to banishing evil spirits? Both Chinese Communists and their Nationalist opponents believe that prosperity, good health and happiness will come not by relying on spirits but through secular education, family planning, economic growth and material improvements.[1]

However, Taoism has always been open to new ideas and has easily taken on new forms. For several centuries the old folk religion has evolved into a variety of new religious societies like the Tsai-li Society (the Religion of Principle).[2] Founded during the last days of the Ming dynasty by Yang T'sun-jen, a member of the mandarin class, and his disciple Yin Yeng-sheng, this society calls itself the Principle-Abiding Sect because the members follow the Principle of the ancient sages who transmitted the doctrine of Heaven and Earth. Principle *(Li)* on the human level refers to discipline of the mind and body, rectifying the heart, returning to the Root, and reawakening the spirit. Tsai-li members abstain from smoking, using snuff and drinking intoxicating beverages. Adherents are specifically urged to be hard-working and thrifty. Besides worshipping the Buddhist goddess of mercy (Kuan-yin) and the coming Buddha Maitreya, members have altars to the two founders of their sect. The Tsai-li Society attracted large numbers of the farmers and artisans in north and west China as well as many residents of the cities in

---

[1] W. Chan, *Religious Trends in Modern China*, Columbia University Press, N.Y., 1953, p. 146.

[2] Also called *Li Chiao* and *Li Men*, "Li" meaning Principle.

the Yellow River valley.

Related to this group is the older White Lotus Society, founded originally as a Buddhist sect, which produced a variety of Taoist offshoots. Of these, the Big Sword Society was organized during the reign of the last Manchu emperor (1875-1908). Originally it was strongly pro-government and anti-Christian. Big Sword members worship Heaven and Earth, the sun and moon, the Black Tiger who protects the human body, as well as two other guardians of mankind, the heavenly tortoise and snake.

Another White Lotus group, The Way of Following the One (Kuei-i Tao), has not been involved in politics. Founded by Li T'ing'yu about 1630, it stressed the value of devotional practices like using the rosary, reciting sacred verses and bowing four thousand times every day with the head touching the ground. Believing in avoiding the vices associated with the desire for wealth and fame, those who follow the One emphasize a self-reliant life based on hard work, practice vegetarianism and try to be kind to every living thing. Worship is given to the Mother of No-birth, the creator and preserver of all life, the one God whom Buddhists, Taoists and Confucianists recognize under different names. Combining the three traditional faiths of China, the Kuei-i Tao borrows Taoist techniques for relating to the spirit world, the Buddhist doctrine of salvation from universal suffering, and Confucian ethics. To follow the One, a person should practice eight virtues: sincerity, rectification of the heart, carefulness in speech, personal integrity, seriousness in handling business affairs, urging others to be good, respect for elders and affection for the young. To avoid harm to himself and others, one should not seek fame or wealth, desire illicit sexual gratification, be gluttonous, feel jealous or commit falsehood. In line with the strong ethical emphasis of the sect, members center their religious life in the home rather than in temples.[3]

After World War I, the Tao Yuan (Society of the Way) appeared, and within a single decade it had gained more than

---

[3] W. Chan, *Ibid,* pp. 161-162.

30,000 members. Based on a revelation received from a planchette or ouija board, it called upon men to worship one God—the Great Unity, the Ultimate Sage and Primeval Ancestor. At its altar, praise is paid to Confucius, Lao-tzu, Buddha, Muhammad and Christ. Among the key doctrines is the ideal of community between Heaven and man to be achieved through spiritualism. Also stressed is the need for world brotherhood. Members practice meditation, cultivate the spiritual life, believe in the use of planchettes to communicate with the spirit world and experiment with spirit photography. At the same time the Tao Yuan operated hospitals, emphasized social service, established credit bureaus for its poorer members and carried on extensive Red Cross work. In fact, the charitable side of its activities caused the Tao Yuan to be renamed the Red Swastika Society, much as the Red Cross is called the Red Crescent in Islamic nations.[4]

Another sect, The Way of Pervading Unity (I-kuan Tao) grew out of the remains of the once powerful Boxers (the Society of Righteous Fists). About 1928 Chang T'ien-jan gave new life to the movement and its influence spread through the World War II years until his death in 1947. According to this Taoist group, the One is the root of all things, the Principle which permeates all existence. The universe evolves from the realm of Principle to the realm of material energy *(ch'i)* through the active and passive force of yang and yin. We are now in the midst of the third and final catastrophe in human history, this sect maintains, but through the mercy of the Mother of No-birth—and our own efforts—the world will be saved. In I-kuan Tao, every religion is believed to provide vehicles for salvation; and in the end, all people will be saved. Images of all religions are worshipped. Buddhist as well as Taoist sacred texts are studied, memorized and recited. Members abstain from smoking, eating meat or consuming alcoholic drinks. They communicate with the spirit world by means of the planchette, value the use of mantras and carry sacred charms. During World War II, the Way

---

[4] *Ibid*, pp. 163-164.

of Pervading Unity was active in almost all of the country occupied by the Japanese soldiers; following the Communist takeover it, like other popular religions, was ruthlessly suppressed.

Since reeducation of the masses has been energetically carried out by the Maoist government, it is difficult to say how much of Taoism will survive on the mainland. During the Republican period there were at least 43,000,000 Taoists in the country, in spite of government crusades against "superstition," Christian missionary attacks and the ridicule of the Chinese intellectuals.[5] It is undoubtedly premature to predict the extinction of Taoism even in Red China; and beyond the reach of the state police are the millions of Chinese in Hong Kong, Macao, Taiwan, southeast Asia and America who are free to be Taoist if they wish. At least some of the newer Taoist sects which emphasize the spirit world, social service, a synthesis of all religions and a high standard of personal ethics, still have a worthwhile message for the modern world.

---

[5] W. Chan says that prior to 1950, the Taoist priests and "vegetarian women" were far fewer in number than the 600,000 Buddhist monks and nuns in China. This merely shows that as a religion for the masses, Taoism does not need or stress a priestly class. (Wing-tsit Chan, *Ibid,* p. 141).

BIBLIOGRAPHY

R.B. Blakney, *The Way of Life,* Mentor Book, N.Y., 1955.
Wing-tsit Chan, *Religious Trends in Modern China,* Columbia University Press, N.Y., 1953.
    A Source Book in Chinese Philosophy, Princeton University Press, Princeton, N.J., 1963.
    The Way of Lao-tzu, Bobbs-Merrill Co., Indianapolis, 1963.
William T. de Bary, *Sources of Chinese Tradition,* Columbia Univ. Press, N.Y., 1960.
J.J.L. Duyvendak, *The Way and Its Virtue,* John Murray, Ltd., London, 1954.
Alfred Forke, trans., *Lun-heng,* Luzac, London, 1907-11, 2 volumes.
Fung Yu-lan, *History of Chinese Philosophy,* Princeton University Press, Princeton, N.J., 1952.
A.C. Graham, trans., *The Book of Lieh Tzu,* John Murray, Ltd., London, 1960.
Edward Herbert, *A Taoist Notebook,* John Murray, Ltd., London, 1955.
Ho-Shang-Kung's Commentary on Lao-tse, Artibus Asiae, Ascona, Switzerland, 1950.
Huai-nan Tzu, *Tao, the Great Luminant,* Kelly and Walsh, Shanghai, 1934.
R. Hume, *The World's Living Religions,* Scribner's Sons, N.Y., 1924.
A. Waley, *Three Ways of Thought in Ancient China,* Doubleday, Garden City, N.Y., 1939.
    The Way and Its Power, Grove Press, N.Y., 1958.
Burton Watson, ed., *Complete Works of Chuang Tzu,* Columbia University Press, N.Y., 1970.
M. Weber, *The Religion of China,* Free Press, Glencoe, Ill., 1951.
Holmes Welch, *Taoism, The Parting of the Way,* Beacon Press, Boston, 1957.
Y.C. Yang, *China's Religious Heritage,* Abingdon-Cokesbury, N.Y., 1948.
R.C. Zaehner, ed., *Concise Encyclopedia of Living Faiths,* Beacon Press, Boston, 1967.

Confucianism

There have been many kings, emperors and great men in history, who enjoyed fame and honor and while they lived and came to nothing at their death, while Confucius, who was but a common scholar clad in a cotton gown, became the acknowledged Master of scholars.... All people in China who discuss the six arts, from emperors, kings and princes down, regard the Master as the final authority.

Szema Ch'ien[1]
official Han court historian
(d. circa 85 B.C.)

---

1. Lin Yutang, The Wisdom of Confucius, p. 91.

I. THE LIFE OF CONFUCIUS

CONFUCIUS (the Latinized form of the Chinese phrase K'ung-fu-tzu: "Great Master K'ung") was born about 551 B.C. in the feudal duchy of Lu, now part of Shantung province. It is generally agreed that his father died when he was very young. Confucius was brought up by his impoverished mother in very humble circumstances. For a time he worked as keeper of the government storehouses and later he was in charge of the town's herds of oxen and sheep. Whatever education Confucius obtained came from his work as a young apprentice clerk.

Even though he wanted to be appointed a high court official, in a corrupt society there was no ruler who would provide him an opportunity to straighten out the government by implementing his political ideals. Deprived of the prime minister's post he sought, Confucius turned to teaching. Three thousand young men became his pupils. What may have begun as an informal debating society made up of Confucius and his friends gradually developed into a notable school for diplomats and courtiers. Several of his students rose to positions of considerable influence. One, for example, became steward and chief advisor to the Chi family who controlled the state of Lu.

Traditions of questionable validity claim that Confucius himself became a high official. More likely, he was merely given some sort of minor government pension and was otherwise supported by gifts from a few affluent disciples. However, according to the traditional biography, Confucius was appointed Metropolitan Magistrate of Lu, got promoted to Secretary of Public Works and eventually became Grand Minister of Justice before being forced to resign by jealous aristocrats. Many modern historians, Chinese and Western, doubt the historicity of these stories.[1]

When he was about fifty years old, friends did get Confucius some sort of official post. Probably he even had a high sounding title like "Member of the Council of State." Although he may have

---

[1] The oldest biography of Confucius, that by Szema Ch'ien, can be found in Lin Yutang, *The Wisdom of Confucius,* Random House, N.Y., 1943, pp. 48-91.

expected to become the Duke of Lu's chief advisor, those in power were willing to give him a title and a salary provided he had no authority. After ten years, Confucius realized that the ruler would not follow his advice, so he left the Lu court to look elsewhere for recognition.

At the end of thirteen years of fruitless wanderings, Confucius went back to his native state. The situation had not improved. When the Duke of Lu or his chief advisors asked for Confucius' support on matters of dubious merit he refused and when he gave advice they usually rejected it. As a result, the would-be statesman spent much of his time collecting and editing old books or teaching. At age seventy-three Confucius died, apparently a failure. However, the disciples could not forget what he meant to them; and because of them, Confucius has ever since been considered China's greatest sage.[2]

Emperor Wu, the second ruler in the Han dynasty (140-87 B.C.), gave state recognition to Confucianism. Although later emperors vacillated at times in their devotion to the teachings of Master K'ung, some embracing Taoism or Buddhism, on the whole the study of the Confucian Classics served as the basis of Chinese education until the appearance of the Republic in 1911. Confucius had been the first person in China to devote his life, almost exclusively, to teaching; and he established the institution of literati who dominated Chinese society until the 20th century.[3] For this alone—the ideal of the gentleman-scholar—he put an indelible mark on subsequent history in China, Korea and Japan.[4]

Confucius' preference for conservatism and almost romantic attachment to the past should not blind us to his originality. He initiated four of the characteristic features of subsequent Chinese

---

[2] Cf. H.G. Creel, *Confucius and the Chinese Way,* Harper & Bros., N.Y., 1960, pp. 25-56. Creel is especially concerned with separating the historical Master K'ung from the myths which were created about him by admirers.

[3] Wing-tsit Chan, *Source Book in Chinese Philosophy,* Princeton University Press, Princeton, 1963, p. 17.

[4] For Confucian influence in Japan, see J.W. Hall, "The Confucian Teacher in Tokugawa Japan" in Nivison and Wright, *Confucianism in Action,* Stanford University Press, Stanford, Calif., 1959, pp. 268-301.

civilization. First, he created the role of the private teacher. Previously officials relied on nothing but on-the-job training. Secondly, he developed the contents, methods and ideals of Chinese education. Insisting upon broad liberal arts learning as a prerequisite for public service, he produced well-rounded and cultured gentlemen rather than technicians or politicians. Thirdly, Confucius accepted students from a variety of social backgrounds. No longer would mere noble birth guarantee entry into public office. Master K'ung permanently destroyed the closed society by disregarding the traditional privileges of the princelings and aristocrats.[5] Superior men, in his opinion, were made and not born, made by their wisdom, education, idealism and social graces. Confucius thus invented a mechanism for encouraging social mobility and justifying the ideal of an open society.[6] Fourthly, Confucius stressed the moral nature of education and politics. From beginning to end he was a moralist. For him there was no such thing as pure research, value-free scholarship or learning for its own sake. Above all else, Confucius was a man of integrity who demanded that his disciples become trustworthy advisors of the government. At its best Confucianism therefore gave China a loyal and honest bureaucracy.

II. THE CHINESE CLASSICS

The written cultural heritage of ancient China can be found in the six Classics: the Book of History (*Shu Ching*), the Book of Poetry (*Shih Ching*), the Book of Changes (*I Ching*), the Book of Rites (*Li Chi*), the Book of Music (*Yueh Ching*, nearly all of which has been lost), and the Spring and Autumn Annals (*Ch'un Ch'iu*). Because Confucius called himself "a transmitter and not a creator, a believer in and lover of antiquity,"[7] his name has been attached to

---

[5]Frederick W. Mote, *Intellectual Foundations of China,* Columbia University Press, N.Y., 1971, pp. 37-41.

[6]Contrast the view of Hu Shih who condemned Confucius as a political absolutist and reactionary, J.B. Grieder, *Hu Shih and the Chinese Renaissance,* Harvard University Press, Cambridge, 1970. Hu Shih (1891-1963) was a journalist, professor, diplomat and internationally famous philosopher, a disciple of John Dewey and the inventor of the slogan "Down with Confucius and company!"

[7]*The Analects* (Lun Yu), VII:1; Legge translation, vol. I, p. 195.

these six collections but the exact nature of his connection with them has long been a matter of debate. Confucius could have merely transmitted the six classics which were generally accepted in his time. However, he could have arranged and compiled a vast amount of ancient materials in six books. Or he could have considerably edited the already existing classics. Or he may have compiled, edited and circulated the core of the classics to which numerous additions were made at a later time. Finally, though this view has few defenders, Confucius could have written the entire set of classics in order to promote his ideal of benevolent government directed by superior men. A noted scholar, K'ang Yu-wei (1858-1927), contended that only when one recognizes that the six classics were actually composed by Confucius to encourage reform in his day can one understand why Confucius should be called the Great Master, the model for all sages and the founder of a doctrine encompassing all enduring truths.[8]

In the *Shu Ching* one finds a collection of political documents from seventeen centuries and four historical periods: the Yu Shun age, Hsia dynasty, Shang dynasty and Chou dynasty (2200-628 B.C.). Many of these documents are considered forgeries and probably none of the authentic ones are earlier than the Western Chou period (11th-6th century B.C.).[9] The *Shih Ching,* China's oldest anthology of poems, contains 305 folk songs. Tradition says Confucius selected these from three thousand poems and he personally set them to music. However, numerous textual emendations were made as time passed. The *Li Chi* is a book of rules about aristocratic etiquette and a code of rituals. According to the majority of scholars, very little of the present text of the *Li Chi* goes back to Confucius' time.[10] *The Spring and Autumn Annals* (Ch'un Ch'iu), a compendium of brief historical records, was compiled by Confucius from materials he found in the archives of the state of

---

[8]K'ang Yu-wei, *The One World Philosophy* (L.G. Thompson, translator), Allen & Unwin, London, 1958. Also, Ch'u Chai and Winberg Chai, *Confucianism,* Barron's Educational Series, Woodbury, N.Y., 1973, pp. 157-168.

[9]Chai and Chai, *Ibid,* p. 10.

[10]*Ibid,* pp. 15-17.

Lu. More important are three commentaries on these *Annals* from the Han dynasty, especially the *Tso Chuan*, which purportedly give the philosophical significance of the historical items.[11]

The *I Ching* was originally a book of divination, based on eight simple trigrams consisting of all possible combinations of three straight lines and three broken ones. Out of the Supreme Ultimate (*Tai Chi*) are produced the *Yang* and *Yin* from which arise four symbols which combine in various ways to create eight trigrams. These were rearranged in sixty-four hexagrams. Together the hexagrams symbolize all that has happened or will take place in the universe; each also represents one or more natural phenomena. Ten appendices were added to the original fortune teller's manual, transforming it into a masterpiece of profound speculative philosophy.[12] As for Confucius' connection with the book, that presents a regular briar patch of problems through which no generally accepted path has yet been discovered. Traditionally it was believed that Confucius arranged the book, added the commentary and wrote the appendices. Few now find it possible to accept that ancient view. Some contemporary scholars feel that the bare divination texts go back to 12th century B.C. Chou traditions, but that additions were made to them from time to time. If so, the *I Ching* has become "a bottomless well" from which Chinese thought has continued to draw provocative insights.[13]

In regard to the six Classics as a whole, most modern scholars assert that Confucius used them to create a model for an ideal society based on ancient practices and precedents. As he stated, "If a man preserves and cherishes old knowledge so as to acquire

---

[11] See James Legge, *The Chinese Classics*, University of Hong Kong Press, Hong Kong 1960, vol. V. For a critical evaluation of the *Annals* as literature and history, cf. pp. 1-16, 38-53. Legge's translation includes the Tso commentary in footnotes.

[12] See R. Wilhelm, trans., *The I Ching*, Princeton University Press, Princeton, N.J., 1967.

[13] On Chinese cosmology, cf. Joseph Needham, "Human Laws and Laws of Nature in China and the West," *Journal of History of Ideas*, XII, pp. 3-30, 194-230 and Frederick W. Mote, *Intellectual Foundations of China*, pp. 15-28. A similar opinion is found in Joseph Needham and Wang Ling, *Science and Civilization in China*, Cambridge University Press, Cambridge, 1954-69, six volumes.

new, he can be a teacher of others."[14] Believing in the wisdom of the past and loving the ancients, he nevertheless brought Chinese civilization to full flower as a result of his original writing and creative editing. Because of his labors the six scriptures became priceless intellectual treasures of the Chinese world. In the *I Ching* he expounded a profound metaphysical view of the universe which united the way of Heaven and the way of man. Through teachings in the Classics of *Rites, Music* and *Poetry,* he laid the base for political education: government by propriety and rule by virtue. Then, he formulated a philosophy of history in the *Shu Ching* and *Spring and Autumn Annals.* By means of these Classics Confucius established the normative pattern for imperial China in political philosophy, ethics and education.

III. THE CONFUCIAN ETHIC

What Confucius taught is to be found in three books: The *Analects* (Lun Yu), *The Great Learning* (Ta Hsüeh), and *The Doctrine of the Mean* (Chung Yung). These are generally accepted as "the orthodox doctrine of the Chinese people,"[1] the *Analects* having been compiled by the immediate followers of Confucius, *The Great Learning* by Tseng Ts'an, one of his chief disciples,[2] and the *Mean* by the Sage's own grandson, Tzu-ssu.

Confucius transformed the customary feudal code of rites and etiquette into a universal system of ethics. After 2500 years the fundamental concepts are still up-to-date. Because of what Confucius taught so persuasively and exemplified in his own life so forcibly, the Chinese have possessed an ethical creed far transcending the limits of any one age or social order.[3] Confucius held up the

---

[14] *Analects,* Bk. II:11. Ezra Pound interprets this epigram to mean that if men keep alive the old and recognize novelty they can eventually teach *(Confucius,* New Directions Book, N.Y., 1951, p. 199). Other modern scholars claim it means all new learning is already found in the old (Legge, *Ibid,* vol. I, p. 149).

[1] Liu Wu-Chi, *A Short History of Confucian Philosophy,* Penguin Books, Harmondsworth, 1955, p.34.

[2] *Ta Hsüeh* is sometimes said to have been written by Tzu-ssu.

[3] Liu Wu-Chi, *Ibid,* p. 25.

ideal of moral perfection as the ultimate goal of the superior man and that has managed to survive momentous political, economic and cultural changes.

As a statesman, he insisted upon the need for benevolent government. A ruler should govern his people like a father cares for his children. Ruler and ruled must be bound together by unbreakable ties of paternal love and filial respect if the nation is to remain strong and healthy. Of course, military strength is needed to safeguard the nation's sovereignty and sufficient food is required to sustain the inhabitants of a state, yet most crucial in Confucius' view is the people's confidence in their government. When the people lose respect for their ruler, thinking him an enemy rather than a kindly parent, the mandate of Heaven will be withdrawn from him and the government forfeits its right to expect obedience. Paternalism may have serious defects in the eyes of modern democrats, but for Confucius the alternative to patriarchal government was ruthless tyranny by unprincipled autocrats. With illustrations drawn from stories of mythical sage-kings of the distant past, Confucianists taught dukes and emperors to treat their subjects like fathers caring for their children.

In *The Great Learning,* Confucian political philosophy is expounded in terms of three guiding principles and eight general rules. The Heavenly Way means that proper government should 1) manifest illustrious virtue, 2) show love for the people, and 3) rest in the highest good. To fulfill his duties, an official must 1) investigate many things, 2) extend his knowledge, 3) be guided by sincere thoughts, 4) "rectify" his heart, 5) cultivate his personality, 6) regulate his own family, 7) govern his state well, and 8) bring peace to the world. As a famous text says, "To know what comes first and what comes last is to be near the Tao. The ancients who wished clearly to manifest illustrious virtue throughout the world would first govern their own states well. Wishing to govern their states well they would first regulate their families. Wishing to regulate their families, they would first cultivate their own persons. Wishing to cultivate their own persons, they would first rectify their hearts. Wishing to rectify their hearts, they would first seek sincerity in their thoughts. Wishing for sincerity in their thoughts, they would first extend their knowledge. The extension of knowledge lay in the investigation of things."[4]

For Confucius, the art of politics was based on the importance of rule by virtue yet he also stressed the value of a social hierarchy. As he put it, the ruler should be a ruler, a father should be a father, a son should be a son.[5] With the maintenance of a carefully defined social order, the prince is able to do his duty well, paternal rights are guaranteed, family relationships are secure and individuals act responsibly. However, rule by virtue is realized through rites and music rather than reliance upon military force.

Because government cannot be effectively exercised by the king alone, he should seek out wise and virtuous men to serve as his counselors. When someone asked how to rule benevolently, Confucius said to love men because loving them will make them peaceful. A wise ruler should be generous with his subjects and not simply take from them, he declared.

Beyond the obvious unity of politics and ethics, it is important to recognize the principle of polarity which characterizes Confucian social thought. The political and the personal, outer and inner, ideal and action, public office and individual self-culture all exist in a relationship of polarity.[6] These are not contrasted but connected. What happens at one level of human experience affects all other levels. The Confucian ethic starts with a practical social problem and digs down ever and ever deeper until it reaches the very bottom—an investigation of the structure of all things. What begins as a political matter is gradually seen to be a family problem, a personal concern, a question of attitude and finally ontological awareness—an understanding of the nature of being itself. Confucianism is not merely an ethical system but rather a moral

---

[4] *Ta Hsüeh,* 2:3b-4. Chai and Chai, ed., *The Humanist Way in Ancient China,* Bantam Press, N.Y., 1965, pp. 294-295.

[5] *Analects,* Bk XII, chap. 11: "There is government, when the prince is prince, and the minister is minister; when the father is father, and the son is son." (Legge translation)

[6] Cf. Benjamin Schwartz, "Some Polarities in Confucian Thought," D.S. Nivison and A.F. Wright, *Confucianism in Action,* pp. 50-62.

code rooted in metaphysics.[7]

Until China encountered the West during the 19th century, Confucianists agreed unanimously that the family provides the ridge pole of civilization. For good or ill, since that time, some beleaguered defenders of Confucius have dropped the centrality of the family in favor of the allegedly superior authority of the individual or the State. Nevertheless, it is beyond question that Master K'ung himself believed in the pivotal role of the family. Since the *Analects* contain no lengthy commentary on this subject, one should turn to *The Classic of Filial Piety* (Hsiao Ching), long considered a work of Confucius' disciple Tseng Tzu, for a definitive exposition of the Confucian family-centered philosophy.[8]

According to the *Hsiao Ching,* Confucius taught that filial piety is the basis of virtue and source of all culture. To prove this he pointed out that our physical bodies are gifts from our parents. Because we owe our existence to parents, respect for them grows naturally out of biological existence. When we love our parents and serve them gratefully, our moral sense is born. "The body and the limbs, the hair and the skin, are given to one by one's parents, and to them no injury should come; this is where filial piety begins. To establish oneself and practice the Tao is to immortalize one's name and thereby to glorify one's parents; this is where filial piety ends. Thus, filial piety commences with service to parents; it proceeds with service to the sovereign; it is completed by the establishment of one's own personality."[9]

From this single virtue of filial piety all others can be derived by extension, say the Confucianists. Because we respect our parents, we hold in high esteem the ruler who is the father of the entire country. As the emperor is the surrogate father of the whole nation, his officials are like our elder brothers to whom we owe obedience and respect. Also, since the nation has one father, all citizens

---

[7] As we shall see, Confucianism was never just humanist in the sense of being a pragmatic exercise in moral judgments. From Confucius' teachings themselves was born interest in the objective "investigation of things" and intuitive "rectification of the mind."

[8] Many doubt the traditional authorship but even if the *Hsiao Ching* is a later compilation, it became a standard elementary textbook from the Han period onward.

[9] *Hsiao Ching,* I (Chai and Chai, *The Humanist Way in Ancient China,* pp. 326-327).

become members of a single family and should be treated fraternally. Man's earliest social groups, primitive clans, were made up of people united by blood ties; but Confucianism goes far beyond loyalty to one's actual relatives. Purely physical kinship is transcended by the concept of a wider relationship. However, Confucius does not appeal to a supernatural sanction. His filial piety ideal is grounded on the natural bond between man and man rather than the affection of the Father God for His human children.

It should be noted that the Chinese word for religion, *chiao,* literally means "support for filial piety." This then is the most elemental religious as well as social concept of Chinese civilization. As taught in Confucianism, filial piety starts as a domestic virtue but diffuses its beneficial influence throughout society. Not only was it the chief cornerstone of the social structure which embraced everything from the home to the imperial court, it also provided the ideology for ancestor worship which was the main feature of Chinese religion throughout the imperial period.

Starting with filial piety, Confucian ethics analyzed all human behavior in terms of five key relationships: that of father and son, husband and wife, elder brother and younger brother, friend and friend, ruler and subject. To quote the *Hsiao Ching,* "The Tao of father and son is rooted in the Heaven-endowed nature, and develops into the equity between sovereign and ministers."[10] And again, "Filial piety is the basic principle of Heaven, the ultimate standard of earth, and the norm of conduct for the people. Men ought to abide by the guiding principle of Heaven and earth as the pattern of their lives, so that by the brightness of Heaven and the benefits of earth they would be able to keep all in the world in harmony and in unison."[11]

In modern China, as elsewhere, harmonious relationships of society have been broken. Is paternalism the answer to all our problems? Confucius was not unaware of the disruptive influences which create family breakups, the generation gap, marital discord, group rivalries and national disorder. Are the father, husband,

---
[10]*Hsiao Ching,* IX.
[11]*Ibid,* VII.

elder brother and ruler to be obeyed without question? Most of the time Confucius advocated obedience to one's superiors, regardless of circumstances. When asked by a disciple what filial piety meant, the Master replied, "Never disobey."[12] But occasionally his position was less rigid. He once admitted that "in serving his parents, a son may gently remonstrate with them. If they refuse to listen to his argument he should remain reverent and obedient. Even if he is belabored, he should not complain."[13] In the *Classic of Filial Piety*, the author recognizes the danger in unquestioning obedience and quotes Confucius to prove that a son has a duty to admonish his father. If a father has a son to admonish him, he will not commit gross wrongs. In the case of gross evils, the son should never fail to warn his father against them. How otherwise can a son be called truly filial?[14] Nevertheless, on the whole Confucius underscored the importance of strict loyalty to the father—and the ruler.

Confucius defined the truly good man as *chun-tzu*, the superior man, a noble among commoners, a genuine aristocrat. Likewise, he described those who failed to attain this ideal as nothing but peasants, barbarians, *hsiao-jen*. In so doing, the Sage transformed conventional feudal classifications into ethical ones. When those around him divided mankind into distinct social castes based on birth—the upper class and everybody else—Confucius insisted on a moral standard of excellence.

Many sayings in the *Analects* explain the qualifications to be found in *chun-tzu*. He is broad-minded and not small-minded, conciliating but not flattering, dignified but not arrogant. According to Confucius, nine things occupy the thought of *chun-tzu*. When looking, he sees clearly; when hearing he hears distinctly. He has a kind expression, a respectful manner and is sincere in what he says. Because the superior man is serious about his work, he asks questions when in doubt rather than pretending to know everything. If he is tempted to get angry, he pauses to think of the

---
[12]*Analects*, II:5.
[13]*Ibid*, IV:18.
[14]*Hsiao Ching*, XV.

consequences of his display of temper. Most importantly *chun-tzu* prefers righteousness to personal profit.[15] If this advice seems rather trite and platitudinous, we must remember that Confucius spoke on the basis of firsthand experience with the Chinese governing class. Instead of being lifeless moral commonplaces his remarks were blunt criticisms of this duke, that prince, a specific minister of public works or court functionary. Therefore, his seemingly bland maxims represent an ever-valid attack on the sins of the bureaucrats in every age.

Confucius listed the special evils which corrupt the privileged bureaucratic class. When men are young, they have to guard against lust. Once they have grown up, when their blood and vital powers are strong, they must be careful not to get involved in strife. In old age, men are in danger of succumbing to greed.[16] For the young official the gravest danger was to use his government position to satisfy his desire for sensual pleasure. For the man who had achieved a respected post in the court, the fatal temptation was to endanger his status by meddling in palace politics. Worse, in Confucius' opinion, was the elderly courtier's desire to amass a fortune before the time came for retirement. As the philosopher must have learned from his own unfortunate career as a government official, the money-hungry bureaucrat was the major threat to the establishment of national well-being.

Although Confucius' code for the responsible civil servant was a major contribution to human thought, far greater was his concept of *jen*. *Jen* is one of those little words which are so rich in meaning for Chinese culture that it is difficult to find an adequate English equivalent. *Jen* is the central thesis of the whole Confucian system. Translators have interpreted it to mean "true virtue," "benevolence," "mutual respect," "reciprocal love," "goodwill"—and perhaps best of all, "human-heartedness." *Jen* combines filial piety and fraternal love. As the bond of social solidarity for all men and the connection between the generations, *jen* provides a rational basis for all the lesser, derivative virtues like

---
[15]*Analects*, XVI:10
[16]*Ibid*, XVI:7.

courage, propriety, altruism and righteousness.

According to Confucius, the ancients were not satisfied with material comforts. For them, the way for a man to be truly human must be found in ethics. The Chinese ideogram *jen* is composed of the character "man" and the character "two." Since men are social beings, *jen* means love for others. *Jen* grows out of the natural affection one has for his parents and kinsmen. What Confucius did was extend this feeling beyond the immediate family. To be one with Heaven is to treat everybody with human-heartedness, to help them to live and grow. For Confucius, *jen* was the basis for a philosophy of benevolent humanism and the foundation for a group ethic applicable to all mankind. Bestowed upon men by Heaven, *jen* provides a practical instrument for the relative betterment of the social order, until individuals attain self-perfection and an ideal world is achieved. Unlike philosophies which emphasize the exercise of power, the goal of Chinese humanism is to move people's hearts with virtue.

The Confucian ethic originated with Master K'ung's intense desire for political and social participation. He waited for a wise ruler who could use him, because he wanted to be involved in the creation of a better world. He himself possessed a strong sense of mission as the superior man. Using his learning, virtue and *jen,* he wanted to put into practice his political ideals.

Specifically, the aim of superior men is to make old people comfortable, help friends trust each other and raise well-bred children. Concern for the elderly shows one's respect for the past; devotion to friendship reveals one's interest in the present; attention to the young indicates one's hope for the future. Cultivating one's own virtues and giving benefit to others represents the Tao of *chun-tzu*. Through active involvement in the social process, the superior man can bring happiness and comfort to all.

According to the Confucian ethic, the mandarin becomes learned and cultured in order to implement his love for humanity. By loving and caring for the young, he will inculcate in them great respect for the merits of their ancestors and reverence for man's cultural heritage. Filial love means for Confucius that the present generation should treasure the values of the past and add to human civilization the unique contributions of their own time in order to prepare for the Great Commonwealth to come. This was Master K'ung's philosophy of history and his hope for an ideal world.[17]

As Confucius insisted, if a *chun-tzu* departs from *jen,* he is unworthy of being called a superior man. Not even for the space of one meal should a *chun-tzu* act contrary to *jen.*[18] Summing up what he meant, Confucius invented what has been called the Silver Rule: "What you do not wish to yourself, do not do to others."[19] According to the *Chung Yung* this Heavenly Way of the superior man means 1) "to serve my father as I would have my son serve me," 2) "to serve my sovereign as I would have my minister serve me," 3) "to serve my elder brother as I would have my younger brother serve me," 4) "to set an example in behaving to a friend as I would have him behave to me."[20]

IV. CHINESE PIETY

Many writers, Chinese and Western, claim that Confucianism is not a religion but merely a system of ethics. According to a recent Chinese scholar, Confucianism is a practical moral system without any trace of the metaphysical and supernatural. A contemporary American scholar agrees noting that Confucius expounded a consistent humanism, believed in no flight into the beyond and had no concept of a Creator who made man in his own image. Confucianism, it is said, begins and ends with man.[2] Because this interpretation of the purely moralistic, humanistic, and anti-mystical Confucius is widespread, it is necessary to insist upon the

---

[17]Cf. Ki-Kun Chang, "The Absolute Value in Society and Restoration to the Way of Heaven" in proceedings of the fourth International Conference on the Unity of the Sciences, ICF, Inc., N.Y., 1975, vol. I, pp. 387-395.
[18]*Analects,* IV:5.
[19]*Ibid,* XII:2.
[20]*The Doctrine of the Mean*, XIII:4.
[1]Liu Wu-Chi, *A Short History of Confucian Philosophy,* p. 11.
[2]Charles Corwin, *East to Eden?,* Wm. B. Eerdmans, Grand Rapids, Mich., 1972, pp. 53, 65.

religious dimension of Confucianism.

Confucianism does lack several of the important characteristics of most religions. It never possessed a specialized priesthood. It wrote no creeds. Its scriptures were never considered "revelations." Nevertheless, Confucianism is concerned with the ultimate meaning of human life and destiny, and has manifested a deep sense of dependence upon a supreme spiritual power. In addition, it has fostered an intimate relationship with the world of spirit, created elaborate rituals and relied on the efficacy of prayer. For these reasons, Confucianism should be classified as a religion rather than simply an ethico-political philosophy of self-betterment.[3]

Confucius' teachings reveal his intense religious feelings. According to him, the superior man is calm and quiet, waiting for the mandate of Heaven. He does not grumble against men nor murmur against Heaven. In order to know men, one cannot dispense with a knowledge of Heaven.

The good life is connected with man's relationship to Heaven. As sincerity is the way of Heaven, the attainment of sincerity is the way of men. Illustrious virtue comes from contemplating and studying the decrees of Heaven. Only by possessing the most complete sincerity that can exist under Heaven can man fully develop his nature.

Confucianism teaches that the cosmic order is benevolent and that the social order should imitate Heaven's uprightness. Heaven and Earth are the parents of all creatures, of which man is the most highly endowed. Bright and high Heaven enlightens and rules our world. Heaven has compassion on all the people; Heaven will give effect to what they desire. For the help of the masses, Heaven made rulers and instructors that these might aid God and secure the peace of the entire kingdom. If the rulers do not reverence Heaven above, they inflict calamities on the people below. If a sovereign pos-

---

[3]D. Howard Smith, *Chinese Religions,* Weidenfeld and Nicolson, London, 1968, pp. 32-33. For additional information, see C.K. Yang, "The Functional Relationship between Confucian Thought and Institutions, in J.K. Fairbank, ed., *Chinese Thought and Institutions,* University of Chicago Press, Chicago, 1957, pp. 269-290.

sesses all the sagely qualities which can exist under Heaven he becomes the equal of Heaven. By assisting the transforming and nourishing powers of Heaven and Earth, the sage joins them to form a trinity.[4]

The religious spirit of Confucianism is clearly expressed in an ode of King Ching to be found in the *Shih King:*

> Let me be reverent, let me be reverent,
> The way of Heaven is evident,
> And its appointment is not easily preserved.
> Let me not say that It is high aloft above me.
> It ascends and descends about our doings;
> It daily inspects us wherever we are.[5]

Another way to demonstrate Confucian piety is to look at one of the classics, the *Li Chi* ("Treatises on the Rules of Propriety or Ceremonial Usages"). [6] *Li* has been translated variously as "rites," "etiquette," "good manners," "decorum," "customs," "social usages" and "propriety." In the ancient Chinese dictionary, *Li* is defined as an act by which one serves the spirits. Originally, *Li* referred to a vessel used in performing sacrificial rites. Confucius made *Li* one of his key concepts, implying that the awe and respect with which man worships should cover every aspect of his behavior.

Although polytheism had been part of the Chinese religious heritage, monotheism—worship of Shang-ti, Lord of Heaven—was well established long before the Chou dynasty period which Confucius took as his model for the good society. At that time, religion involved sacrifices to Shang-ti outside the home and worship of one's ancestors by every family.[7] Ancestor worship

---

[4] A. Doeblin, *The Living Thoughts of Confucius,* David McKay Co., N.Y., 1960, pp. 55, 68, 70, 73, 74, 77, 152-153, 156, 161.

[5] *Ibid,* p. 165.

[6] See J. Legge, translator, *The Li Ki,* Sacred Books of the East, Oxford University Press, London, 1926, vol. XXVII and XXVIII.

[7] E.W.F. Tomlin says the Chinese family formed its own church, because reverence for ancestors was a cult stronger than devotion to any god. *The Oriental Philosophers,* Harper & Row, N.Y., 1963, p. 251.

was though to be as indispensable as veneration of the Lord of Heaven. Only by showing respect for the dead and obedience to Shang-ti could one live a good life.

Li is therefore most important, according to Confucian theory. If one does not practice *Li,* he cannot worship properly the God of Heaven. Likewise, if mankind does not obey the law of propriety (i.e., good manners, in the deepest sense), the ruler and his subjects, fathers and sons, old and young, men and women will be unable to maintain their rightful status in society. Without *Li,* there will no longer be a social distinction between a man and his wife, parents and children or elder and younger brothers. For this reason—concern for a stable and structured society—the superior man and sage treasure *Li.*

As for the public official, he recognizes the value of propriety so that the social order he is called upon to govern will not be disturbed, disorganized or disrupted. For him too, *Li* means following the Way of Heaven. His is the responsibility to obey the commands of Heaven and act according to the mandate of Heaven. As ceremonial rites are based on the need for a proper relationship with Shang-ti and the ancestral spirits, so respect for the rights and welfare of one's subjects is derived from reverence for the Heavenly Way.

Throughout its history, Confucianism has been inextricably attached to ritualistic worship. In the imperial age the emperor served as the high priest at sacrifices conducted during spring, autumn and winter solstice festivals. Most impressive were those at the magnificent Temple of Heaven in Peking, held annually on December 22 until 1911. To these traditional rites were gradually added religious ceremonies honoring Confucius. Worship of Master K'ung became part of the state religion of China.[8] In 195 B.C. the emperor offered animal sacrifice at the tomb of the Sage. In 57 A.D. sacrifices to him were begun at all imperial and provincial colleges. After the year 287, Confucius was worshipped four times

---

[8]Cf. J.K. Shryock, *Origin and Development of the State Cult of Confucianism,* The Century Co., N.Y., 1932 and D.H. Smith, "The State Cult of Confucianism," op. cit., pp. 140-147.

a year and in 555 A.D. temples to him were built at the capital city of every Chinese prefecture. By 1086 he was honored with the title of emperor and in 1906 the Manchu ruler declared that Confucius was equal to the deities Heaven and Earth.[9]

V. APOSTLES OF CONFUCIANISM
Mencius (b. circa 369 B.C.—d. soon after 300 B.C.)

In the long history of Chinese philosophy, Master Meng (Latinized as Mencius) attained a position next in importance to Confucius. Gradually, Mencius became honored as the Second Sage and his writings were added to the Confucian scriptures. He studied under a disciple of one of K'ung's students, so was a third generation Confucian. History has preserved no record of his birth or death, and what little we know about his life must be deduced from casual references in his works. He seems to have been a well-known exponent of government by benevolence *(jen)* and undertook journeys to the courts of various Chinese petty rulers on behalf of that Confucian ideal. However, for hundreds of years Mencius' thought was merely one of many conflicting interpretations of Chinese wisdom, simply one of "the hundred schools" of philosophy in the nation's period of intellectual ferment. His collected essays were not made part of the curriculum for Chinese officials until the Sung dynasty in the 12th century A.D.[1] The book *Mencius,* a volume made up of seven distinct parts, contains Meng's own writings plus additions by his disciples.

Mencius once told the story of what happened to a mountain to illustrate his conception of the human predicament. It was covered with lovely trees but people living nearby cut the woods down and the place lost its beauty. Hence, men think the mountain was always bare. Similarly the natural state of man was far differ-

---

[9]R.E. Hume, *The World's Living Religions,* Charles Scribner's Sons, N.Y., 1924, pp. 114-115. Cf. Julia Ching, "The Problem of Self-transcendence in Confucianism and Christianity," *Ching Feng* (Hong Kong), vol. XIX, no. 2, 1976, pp. 81-97.

[1]A. Waley, *Three Ways of Thought in Ancient China,* Doubleday Anchor Book, Garden City, N.Y., 1956, pp. 105-111.

ent from what we see now. Originally man possessed feelings of decency and kindness. If they are now frequently absent it is because they have been tampered with, cut down and burned away. What chance has human nature, like the mountain, had to keep its original beauty?

More than anything else, Mencius stressed the innate goodness of man. In this he went beyond Confucius and counter to the opinion of Hsün Tzu, one of the prominent later Confucian reformers. Against realists, legalists and pessimists Mencius championed man's basic goodness. For him *jen* meant compassion, a feeling of responsibility for the sufferings of others. Hence, he praised the human-heartedness of the legendary hero Yü who said that if anyone drowned he felt as if he himself had drowned him. Mencius believed that good feelings and a capacity for goodness are the natural birthright of everyone. The problem is not how to get them but how to keep them.[2]

However, Mencius did not rely on man's natural good sentiments alone, which would have made him a disciple of Lao-tzu rather than Confucius. *Jen* should be coupled with *yi* (righteousness). *Yi* means the moral imperative, the sense of duty, an unconditional and absolute standard. As Mencius phrased it, "*Jen* is man's heart, and *yi* is man's path."[3]

Yi is also described as "shame and dislike."[4] For Confucianists, good is at least in part avoiding "loss of face." Nothing is worse than to lose the respect of one's superiors and equals.[5]

As an advisor to many officials and several Chinese petty kings, Mencius advocated "government by goodness." In some cases his suggestions were practical while in others he was primarily concerned with pointing out the ideal. He encouraged rulers to reduce or abolish unpopular taxes, limit conscripted labor to times of the year when agriculture was slack, eradicate inhuman forms of

---

[2] A. Waley, *Ibid*, pp. 83-85. See especially Mencius' debates with Kao Tzu who taught that human nature by itself is indifferent to good or bad. *Meng Tzu* VI A-11.

[3] *Ibid*, VI A-11.

[4] *Ibid*, VI A-6

[5] Hence, anthropologists contrast "guilt-centered" and "shame-centered" societies.

punishment, provide public aid to the aged and establish schools centered on moral instruction.[6] Like Master K'ung, Mencius condemned the dominance of the profit principle at the royal court. Speaking to the king of Wei, he said: Why must your Majesty speak of profit instead of right and goodness? If the king seeks profit for his kingdom, his ministers will seek profit for their families and ordinary subjects will seek only profit for themselves. With equal enthusiasm Mencius criticized the common reliance upon warfare as a means of achieving national success. To King Hsiang, he said that if there were one ruler who did not delight in slaughtering men, he could unite the whole world. Such a king would attract men, as water flows downhill, in a flood no one could hold back.[7]

Like Confucius, Mencius taught that public officials have the chief responsibility in creating a new and better social order. The superior man's function is like that of the wind. When the wind blows, the grass cannot do anything except bend.[8] When rulers doubted that "a government by goodness" could be established, Mencius offered a simple prescription for establishing a righteous society. The ruler has but to push his natural softness of heart *(jen)* far enough and he would become the protector of all. In the past sages excelled ordinary men because they continually extended their innate tenderness. For rulers to think that world government can be achieved by armed might is as foolish as thinking that they can get fish from a tree, said Mencius. To King Hsuan of Ch'i, he promised that if the monarch were on that very day to set up a government founded upon *jen,* at once all the officials under Heaven would want to be enrolled in his court, all the farmers would want to plough his fields, all the tradesmen would want to bring their goods to his market, all travellers would want to use his roads and all who had a grievance would want to lay their com-

---

[6]For Mencius humane government was dependent upon political economy. When most men are only trying to save themselves from death, what time do they have to cultivate morality and good manners? he asked. Cf. Chai and Chai, *Confucianism,* pp. 62-63.

[7]Waley, *Ibid,* p. 91.

[8]*Ibid,* p. 94.

plaint before him. Everybody would be so determined to come to him that no power on earth could stop them.[9] Needless to say, China has yet to find the True King who conquers the world by goodness, as Mencius believed was possible.[10]

Although he aspired to become a great statesman, he was far too wise to be crushed when no king made him prime minister. Eloquently he pictured the role of the sage: "He who dwells in the broad house of the universe, stands firm on the right place of the universe, and walks in the great way of the universe; he, who, if successful, walks along with the people, and if unsuccessful, walks in the way all alone; he whom wealth and honor cannot corrupt, poverty and obscurity cannot move, threats and violence cannot subdue—he it is who may be called a great man."[11]

Hsün Tzu, the Confucian Pessimist (circa 323-238 B.C.)

Whereas Mencius was an idealistic and tender-hearted Confucianist, Hsün Tzu expounded a different but equally influential version of the Master's teachings.[12] In thirty-two exquisitely written logical essays, he accepted Confucius' ideas about the need for *chun-tzu* and the importance of social institutions to achieve progress but added to them valuable insights derived from other schools of thought. Hsün Tzu originated what has been called "tough-minded" Confucianism.

As a result of the tragic political and economic state of China in his day, Hsün Tzu found it impossible to accept Mencius' notion of man's innate goodness. All about him he saw proof that human nature is evil. To demonstrate this, he carefully separated man's ability to reason from the egocentric desires which make up his intrinsic constitution as a human being. Men are born evil because they have a basic desire for personal gain which results in strife. They are envious and hateful. Such evils lead to cruelty and injury

---

[9] Waley, *Ibid*, pp. 105-111.

[10] For additional reading, see James R. Ware, trans., *The Sayings of Mencius*, New American Library, N.Y., 1960.

[11] *Meng Tzu* III B-2.

[12] For his life, see Chai and Chai, *Confucianism*, pp. 66-68. For his writings, see Burton Watson, trans., *Hsün Tzu Basic Writings*, Columbia University Press, N.Y., 1963.

inflicted upon others. Man is also born with sensual desires which uncontrolled produce social confusion and civic disorder. With these basic drives in human nature, what else can one expect but the disappearance of loyalty, courtesy, trust and righteousness?

Hsün Tzu agreed with the Taoists that Heaven is indifferent to human standards of right and wrong. Unlike Mencius, he did not expect Heaven to uphold morality. Heaven is not an ethical order or a personal guarantor of righteousness; Heaven is merely the impersonal law of nature.

While Mencius perceived the goal of education to be "nothing but the search for the lost heart,"[13] Hsün Tzu considered "acquired training" to be more vital than man's original nature. The original nature comes from Heaven whereas acquired training rests with man. What we are born with is at best crude material which has to be refined and polished by culture. By itself human nature lacks beauty. It is up to man to beautify it. Education means improving oneself and restraining natural impulses toward evil. Human nature has to be "rectified," as Confucius taught—just as a knife needs to be sharpened.

Unlike Mencius who believed education served to bring out the good which is in man, Hsün Tzu asserted that rigorous moral training is necessary to transform human nature, radically altering it by counteracting natural evil desires. Wisdom and value come from without, as an individual is reshaped by laws, a code of etiquette and inspiring ceremonies.[14]

If men's desires are allowed free expression, chaos will result. Regulations become necessary to keep our impulses from disrupting the social order. This is the negative function of laws; the positive is that traditions, rules and rituals *(Li)* refine and ennoble human emotions. Through *Li,* love and hate, our two basic responses, can be tempered. Therefore *Li* is the culmination of culture.[15]

---

[13]*Meng Tzu* VI 11:4.

[14]Chai and Chai, *Confucianism,* pp. 69-77.

[15]The ancient historian Ssu-ma Ch'ien observed that Hsün Tzu's writings were attacks on the superstitious belief in magic, omens and portents that dominated his age. Wm. T. de Bary, *Sources of Chinese Tradition,* Columbia University Press, N.Y., 1960, p. 113. For examples, cf. pp. 114-118.

Heaven, earth and man are three separate things, each of which has a distinctive purpose. Heaven controls the seasons; earth provides man with necessary material resources. Man's function, no less necessary, is to set up and maintain good government. Man's job is to employ his intelligence and talents so as to use Heaven's orderliness and earth's wealth to his advantage. To neglect human effort by relying on Heaven is to miss the true nature of things, according to Hsün Tzu. Don't praise Heaven; domesticate it, he urged.

Chu Hsi (1130-1200)

During the Han and Tang dynasties, Confucianism had been concerned with the immediate practical problems of human society. By the twelfth century, followers of K'ung became interested in metaphysics, probably because of Taoism and Buddhism which were then prevalent. *Tao* was henceforth the main topic for discussion among the literati. Speculation about the true nature of things (ontology) took precedence over matters of ethics. For example, Ch'eng Hao (1032-1085) complained that simple memorization and recitation of the Classics had become mere playing with Confucianism without seeing its true meaning. Consequently, he stressed the need for a deep and systematic study of metaphysics. Since most Confucianists of his day had so overemphasized minor points, the original significance of K'ung's thought had become blurred, he believed. Feeling the necessity for reasserting Confucian orthodoxy, scholars like Chou-Tun-yi (1017-1075), Ch'eng Hao, Cheng-i (1033-1107) and Chang Tsai (1020-1076) initiated a metaphysical interpretation of Confucianism which was carried to completion by Chu Hsi. These learned mandarins founded the school of Neo-Confucianism. As a writer of numerous books, definitive commentaries on all the Classics and distillations of the best thinking of his predecessors, Master Chu systematized Sung dynasty Confucianism and finalized the authoritative interpretation of Chinese orthodoxy which was generally accepted for the next seven hundred years.[16]

---

[16]See C.M. Schirokauer, "Chu Hsi's Political Career" in A.F. Wright and D. Twitchett, *Confucian Personalities,* Stanford University Press, Stanford, Calif., 1962, pp. 162-188.

Chu Hsi became the chief exponent of a school of Confucian rationalism known as the Philosophy of Principle *(Li)*. Principle means that there is an immutable and immaterial element inhering in all existing objects. As he walked, Chu said to his disciples that the bricks of the steps beneath his feet have within them the Principle that pertains to bricks; and sitting down, he observed that a bamboo chair has within it the Principle which makes it what it is.[17] In ethics, Principle is man's true nature, his mind and his essential goodness.

According to Chu, in the universe there has never been any material force without Principle, or Principle without material force. Principle exists above the realm of corporeality and material force exists within the physical realm. Although these two fundamental aspects of reality can be distinguished they cannot be separated. Chu Hsi insists on the basic polarity of Principle and material force. *Li* is prior to material force logically, in origin and in value, but it exists right in material force. Without matter, Principle would have nothing to adhere to. Using the five elements theory, Chu describes material force as metal, wood, water, fire and earth. *Li* by contrast is *jen,* righteousness, propriety and wisdom. There is only one Principle for Heaven, earth and the ten thousand things; however, in man each individual has his own particular Principle.[18]

Neo-Confucianism was designed to refute Taoism and Buddhism—both of which threatened to outshine Confucius' teachings. To overcome their ideological foes, the Neo-Confucianists turned to metaphysics, especially those of the *I Ching*. They also adopted Taoist and Buddhist concepts to defend Confucian wisdom. This greatly deepened and enriched their position. For Chu, as for the Taoists, *Li* is not personal, a creator God or an indwelling one. When specifically asked if Principle referred to "a Master doing all this up in the blue sky,"[19] he stated that Heaven

---

[17] Fung Yu-lan, *The History of Chinese Philosophy,* Princeton University Press, Princeton, N.J., 1953, vol. II, pp. 535-536.

[18] Wing-tsit Chan, "The Great Synthesis in Chu Hsi," *Source Book in Chinese Philosophy,* pp. 588-653.

[19] Quoted in de Bary, *Sources of Chinese Tradition,* p. 537.

has no personal consciousness. Borrowing a Taoist expression, Chu spoke of the Principle as "the Supreme Ultimate," *T'ai-chi*. The Supreme Ultimate is to be found in Heaven, earth and each of the myriad of existing things. Because *Li* is a single reality, every separate thing possesses the Supreme Ultimate in its entirety, just as one moon casts its beams upon numerous lakes and rivers.

Principle is invisible, manifesting itself indirectly by means of the activity of yin and yang. *T'ai-chi* has no mind apart from the separate minds and will of men, animals, birds, grass and trees. Heaven and earth have their cosmic mind in all things, yet of themselves they have no mind. Presumably Chou means by this to avoid anthropomorphism. *T'ai-chi* has no separate, limited, specific and partial mind because the cosmic mind is all-inclusive, unattached and therefore impartial. *T'ai-chi* is the Principle beyond the limitations of being or non-being.

Neo-Confucianism, at least in some of its forms, has two additional characteristics worth mentioning. Once scholars began speculating on the meaning of the *I Ching*, they became enamoured of "the study of emblems and numbers." Since the Chinese language is made up of ideograms (little pictures) rather than letters, it was natural to think that diagrams could be worked out to solve the subtlest metaphysical problems. In the *I Ching* eight basic trigrams interpret every object and event in the world of space and time. Equally important was a "diagram of the Supreme Ultimate" created by Chou Tun-yi (1017-75) and employed by many of his successors.[20] Diagrams as well as words were relied on by the Neo-Confucianists to explain what they believed.

Also noteworthy was the Chinese fascination for the metaphysical and mystical significance of numbers. Some of the most prominent Neo-Confucian scholars were adepts of numerology. Shao Yung (1011-77) was one of these.[21] If a thinker can understand the "mysterious, dark learning"[22] in numbers, he can

---

[20]Fung Yu-lan, *History of Chinese Philosophy*, vol. II, p. 436.

[21]Cf. Fung Yu-lan, *Ibid*, pp. 451-476.

[22]The typical Chinese expression for the occult.

comprehend the nature and destiny of all things. For example, according to Shao Yung the secret of cosmology—Heaven's relationship to earth—can be found in the way 1 divides to make 2, 2 divides to make 4, 4 to make 8, 8 to make 16, 16 to make 32 and 32 to make 64—the total number of hexagrams in the *I Ching*. Ten is another mystical number (because ten divides to become a hundred, a hundred to become a thousand and a thousand to become ten thousand—the symbol of the myriad of existing things.) Of the first ten basic numbers, 1, 3, 5, 7 and 9 are of Heaven and 2, 4, 6, 8 and 10 are of earth. One represents "the Supreme Ultimate." For Shao Yung the number 4 was the key to unlock the mysteries of the universe, because Heaven has four forms (greater and lesser yang, greater and lesser yin), there are four sense organs, four kinds of rulers, four ways of transforming the world, four different types of Mandates of Heaven, etc.[23]

Chu Hsi's Neo-Confucianism determined the course of subsequent Chinese thought by adding four books to the Confucian Five Classics: the *Analects, Doctrine of the Mean, Great Learning* and the collected writings of Mencius. These nine books were henceforth accepted as Confucian scripture and in time were made the foundation for the education of all Chinese officials. Until 1911 and the fall of the Manchu empire, Chu Hsi's theory was the standard for Confucian orthodoxy. Except for a rather brief period when a rival school of metaphysical idealism was popular, Confucianism meant the School of Principle definitively expounded in the writings of Chu: his man-centered, rationalistic and unmystical philosophy was considered normative.[24]

Toward the end of the Koryo dynasty, Chu Hsi's views were introduced into Korea and later in Japan. Among scholars of the Yi

---

[23] Chan, *Source Book,* p. 481. Shao Yung was strongly influenced by Taoism and in his own day he was a famous fortune teller. For these reasons, rationalist-minded Chu Hsi omits his writings from his anthology of early Sung philosophy. Most other Neo-Confucian scholars describe Shao Yung as one of the Five Masters of the early Sung period. (Chan, *Ibid,* p. 482).
[24] Cf. W.T. de Bary, "A Reappraisal of Neo-Confucianism" in A.F. Wright, *Studies in Chinese Thought,* University of Chicago Press, Chicago, 1953, pp. 81-111.

dynasty, this type of Neo-Confucianism was predominant. Thinkers like Yi Hwang (Toe-gye) and Yi E (Yoolgok) in the 16th century further developed Chu Hsi's system. In China and Korea, though the School of Principle degenerated resulting in bitter political factionalism and social stagnation;[25] however, in Japan Chu Hsi's ideas were used to overthrow the corrupt rule of the feudal shoguns and enhance the position of the emperor Meiji, thereby contributing greatly to the country's progress.

Wang Yang-ming (1472-1529)

Wang Yang-ming's monistic idealism shows a very different type of Neo-Confucianism from that taught by Chu Hsi. Yet the School of Mind, as it was called, has been almost as influential in Chinese thought as the School of Principle. Like Chu, Wang was a practical man of affairs as well as a philosopher, serving at various times in the Ministry of Justice, Ministry of Civil Service and Board of Censors. In addition he was an imperial governor, an army commander and the Minister of Military Affairs. Besides his success as an official, Wang was well-known as a teacher and praised as one of the world's great thinkers.[26] In the long history of China, it is very rare to find one who was a great scholar as well as a great national hero.

Whereas Chu had emphasized the two factors *Li* and material force as the basis for every existing things, Wang was a thorough-going monist. For him, mind alone reveals the character of reality. What we call the external world is merely the object of consciousness. Common sense is mistaken to perceive the world in terms of external things, extra-mental objects or hard facts. Mind alone is real: all else is made up of the ideas which mind evaluates. Man's knowing is the core of reality. Matter is simply material for

---

[25]Cf. Chai Sik Chung, "Christianity as a Heterodoxy" as an example of the use of Chu Hsi Confucianism to refute Christian missionaries in 18th century Korea. (Yung-Hwan Jo, ed., *Korea's Response to the West,* Korea Research and Publications, Kalamazoo, Mich., 1971, pp. 57-86.

[26]On Wang's life and thought, cf. Carsun Chang, *The Development of Neo-Confucian Thought,* Bookman Associates, N.Y., 1962, volume II, pp. 30-159. Chang uses the philosopher's other name, Wang Shou-jen.

mind to work with, merely data of consciousness. For Wang, there is no dualistic separation of man and the universe, mind and the physical world, mind and body, desire and reason, or knowing and doing. In other words, Wang believed in metaphysical idealism.

Wang interpreted reason in terms of "intuitive knowledge" *(Liang-chih)*. It embraces intellect, will and emotion. Reason is both knowledge (in the ordinary sense) and moral consciousness. This faculty for intuitive knowledge is not limited to man. Reason is shared by grass, trees and stones. For Wang "the investigation of things" (a famous Confucian phrase) means the "realization of knowledge." Therefore, he summed up his philosophy in the motto: unity of knowledge and action. To see what is beautiful is to know; to like what is beautiful is to do, he explained.[27]

Wang interpreted *jen* to mean an awareness of man's unity with the entire cosmos. Love between parents and children which produces filial piety is only the beginning of benevolence. Human-heartedness should be extended to include love of all one's fellow creatures. In the Neo-Confucian School of Mind one learns to appreciate the spiritual kinship which exists among men, animals and plants. This is "the greater *jen.*"

In 1871, General Tseng Kuo-fan who had suppressed the Taiping rebellion prepared a brief collection of mottos by which his family could understand what Confucianism meant. They were:

> *Vigilance in solitude makes the mind peaceful.*
> *Concentration of mind makes the body strong.*
> *Realization of human-heartedness makes one more*
> *   loved by others.*
> *Hard work is approved by the spirits.*[28]

Confucianism grew and developed, schools appeared and controversies raged; but Mencius, Hsün Tzu, Chu Hsi, Wang Yang-ming and all those who looked to Master K'ung for inspira-

---

[27]C. Chang, *Ibid,* p. 36.
[28]*Ibid,* p. 398.

tion and guidance would have agreed with General Tseng's "four reminders" to the coming generation.

VI. CONFUCIANISM IN THE MODERN WORLD

Wang Yang-ming lived at the time of Columbus, the Renaissance, the Reformation and the creation of Europe's first great adventure in imperialism and colonialism: the Spanish empire which spanned the entire globe from South America to the Philippines. Strange as it may seem to us, the great scholar-courtier knew nothing of these events, yet what was taking place would have momentous significance for the Confucianism he loved. China had remained isolated for centuries but the fate of Confucianism in the modern world has been determined, for better or for worse, by the impact of the West. While Chinese scholars argued about the authenticity of Classical texts,[1] used Confucius to buttress the status quo and professed to be residents of the Middle Kingdom located at the center of the world, westernization soon swept aside every venerable ideal and institution with the fury of a tornado.

Looking back on this period of transition, Chinese historians write about three distinct periods in the modernization of their country. First, China grudgingly acknowledged the superiority of western scientific and technological knowledge. Next, she began reforming politically in accord with European-American patterns.[2] Finally, there was a literary and ethical revolution, led by Hu Shih, an advocate of American pragmatism, and Ch'en Tu-hsiu, founder of the Chinese Communist Party.[3] Each of these changes, implicitly or explicitly, undermined the Confucian tradition. As Chinese writers sadly, joyfully or with resignation admit, Confucianism was shaken to its very foundations. While some shouted "Down with Confucius and sons,"[4] others tried to salvage what they could of China's philosophical, ethical, cultural and religious heritage.

---

[1] The controversy over the Modern and Ancient Scripts. Cf. Chang, *Ibid*, pp. 415-417.
[2] President Sun Yat-sen and his protégé Chiang Kai-shek belong to the second group.
[3] Chang, *Ibid*, p. 410.
[4] A motto of the Hu Shih westernizers.

K'ang Yu-wei (1858-1927) was one of the most controversial modern defenders of Confucius. His three books *Inquiry into the Forged Classics of the Wang Mang Period, Study of the Reform-Idea of Confucius* and *On the Great Commonwealth* combined the most audacious radicalism with ultra-conservatism. Chinese intellectuals compared the first to a hurricane, the second to a volcano, and the third to an earthquake.[5] K'ang contended that the officially-approved texts of the Confucian Classics were forgeries made by the imperial librarian at the close of the Western Han dynasty (circa 200 A.D.). While few accept the validity of K'ang's charges, he could not have been more iconoclastic in his attack upon the scriptural foundations of Confucian orthodoxy.

K'ang also asserted that Confucius had as much right to be considered a "religion-founder" as Buddha, Jesus or Muhammad. Putting Confucianism on the same level as Christianity, Buddhism or Islam, K'ang implied that it was a religion rather than a humanistic philosophy or rational system of ethics, as some Confucianists had previously insisted in their denunciations of Buddhism, Taoism and Christianity. K'ang even tried to get Confucianism established as the state religion of China when the republic was set up, but to no avail.[6] Mixing conservative sympathies and radical criticism, he maintained that Confucius did not merely compile ancient traditions but actually composed all six Classics to expound his own views of the ideal society. Though K'ang's ideas were taken seriously for a brief period, he alienated the traditionalists by his criticism and could not retain the interest of the progressives for long. Nevertheless, as an important reformer in the last days of the Manchu empire, he aroused an enormous amount of discussion. As he put it, he was the Luther of China.

---

[5] Descriptions first used by Liang Ch'i-ch'ao and repeated widely. Cf. Hao Chang, "K'ang Yu-wei's Intellectual Role in the late Nineteenth Century," *Liang Ch'i-ch'ao and Intellectual Transition in China,* Taipei, 1971, pp. 35-57.

[6] Liu Wu-chih, a staunch Confucian modernist, denies that Master K'ung founded a religion. In his opinion, Confucianism is "anything but religion." Even if ancestor worship and filial piety were the main props of Confucianism, more important is the fact that Confucius did not claim to be a god and never taught a faith that was supernatural. *A Short History of Confucian Philosophy,* pp. 183-184.

At the very end of the 19th century, prominent Chinese intellectuals and all westerners accused Confucianism of being a reactionary force and a major stumbling block in the path of modernization and progress. Particularly for Christian missionaries, who were the main Occidental source of information about conditions in China, Confucianism meant the pigtail, opium smoking, concubinage, coolies, bound feet, warlords, the Boxers and the Dowager Empress. However, after a half century had passed, it became possible to look at Confucianism more objectively. Confucian scholars were seen to be a corrective and almost prophetic influence in imperial China. Since Confucius himself was the "uncrowned king," this implied that Chinese emperors were not Heaven's gift to man simply because they sat on the imperial throne. Confucianism placed numerous obstacles in the way of uncritical acceptance of the totalitarian state. For one thing, an emperor had to prove that he deserved the high post he held by being the father of his people. Secondly, he could not exercise his authority arbitrarily but must submit to the authority of past experience. A living emperor could always be judged by the example set by great rulers of the distant past whose actions were reported in the Confucian Classics. In the third place, the Son of Heaven was subject to ethical ideals. Even the ruler was not above the commandments to practice *jen*, filial piety, righteousness, wisdom and fidelity. Confucianism raised a standard which all office-holders, including the highest, must obey.

Chairman Mao and his adherents opposed Confucianism because they wanted to be free of such restraints. If one seeks to be a dictator he must deny the authority of the past. Confucianism was condemned by Marxists because it said that the ruler is subject to the moral law. For this reason, Mao compared himself to China's first emperor Shi-huang-ti, who unified the country; then he simply did what he pleased—burning the ancient classics, defying tradition, and executing the Confucian scholars who dared to defy him. Consequently, Maoists praised Legalists like Han Fei-tzu (d. 233 B.C.) who taught that a successful ruler can stay in power only if he rewards his friends and severely punishes all dissidents. In contrast to the moral law upheld by Confucianists, the Legalists favored "positive laws" whose sole authority was that of the earthly ruler who could promulgate and enforce them.[7] Whereas Confucianism insisted upon government by ethical principles, the Marxists practiced the rule that might makes right. If a man has the power of Shi-huang-ti or Mao, whatever he decrees must be obeyed upon pain of death.

In their irrational infatuation with European and American ideas, Chinese professors were converted to every variety of philosophic novelty: the pragmatism of John Dewey, the vitalism of Henri Bergson, the neo-realism of Bertrand Russell and the Marxism of Lenin and Stalin. In each case the primary aim was to eradicate the supposedly pernicious grip of traditional Chinese philosophy. Typical of this destructive attitude was the New Culture Movement.[8] Wu Chih-hui (1865-1953) was a young Manchu official who studied in Japan, England and France. His foreign experience turned him into an anarchist, so when he came back to China he joined the anti-Manchu rebels and soon became a confidante of Sun Yat-sen and Chiang Kai-shek. Later an elder statesman of the Kuomintang, Wu first won praise for his attack upon Confucian traditions. The modern philosopher Hu Shih, for example, was delighted when Wu said all old-style books "should be dumped in the lavatory."[9] According to Hu Shih, with one stroke of the pen Wu had ruled out God, banished the soul and punctured the metaphysical illusion that man is the most spiritual of all things. Wu denied that the idea of a soul meets any real need, insisted that man's spirit cannot be separated from matter, affirmed that science can explain everything in the universe, and claimed that men today are far superior to those in the past. With intellectuals talking like that, what chance did Confucius have in twentieth century China?

Ch'en Tu-hsiu, professor of literature at Peking National University who organized the Chinese Communist Party in 1921,

---

[7] De Bary, *Sources of Chinese Tradition*, pp. 136-158.
[8] Cf. Wing-tsit Chan, "The New Culture Movement" in de Bary, *Ibid*, pp. 813-857.
[9] De Bary, *Ibid*, p. 840.

was one of the prominent intellectuals denouncing Confucianism because of its alleged inferiority to Western thought. If China is to advance and become a modern nation it must adopt attitudes diametrically opposed to the traditional ones. In his opinion the West is successful because 1) it is individualistic, 2) warlike, 3) always pushing ahead rather than being bound to the past, 4) international, 5) utilitarian and 6) scientific. China by contrast is backward, weak and undeveloped because it has favored group harmony, peace, ancient customs, nationalism, excessive cultural refinement and superstition.

When Confucianism was being considered a possible state religion for the Chinese republic, Ch'en was among the severest critics of the proposal. He complained that Confucius advocated monarchial government but the modern world is committed to democracy. Secondly, the Confucian doctrine of "the three superiorities" (the ruler's, the father's and the husband's) is detrimental to the development of individual personality. Thirdly, Confucianism denies women their rights. How can women have a career and be free if Confucian rules are obeyed? Fourthly, Confucianism is the product of a feudal age and reinforces unjust class-distinctions. According to Ch'en, Chinese tradition reduced the minds of people to a dead uniformity at a time when survival required the acceptance of vast changes. Like Hu Shih, Ch'en concluded that Confucianism is the greatest hindrance to modernization because it is incompatible with contemporary ideals of liberty and equality.[10]

After the Communist takeover of the mainland, many refugee intellectuals began to reevaluate the Confucian heritage as the political situation worsened. For example, Dr. Carsun Chang in 1962 attempted a defense of Confucianism against its numerous critics, complaining that the intellectuals in China had shattered confidence in national traditions, squeezed the country dry of all moral convictions, and initiated a "wild rush for new ideas and

---

[10] C. Chang, *The Development of Neo-Confucian Thought*, vol. II, pp. 433-436. Before Ch'en's death he broke with communism because of its dictatorial tendencies. Hence, Maoists try to ignore his role in the creation of their Party (*Ibid*, p. 434).

expectations of a miracle"[11] that resulted in the tragedy of Communist rule. In his view, China was conquered by Mao because of a maladjustment to Western ideas and institutions, a psychology of desperation, the intellectuals' love for originality without a sense of responsibility, wild and imaginative thinking and utopian experimentation. According to Chang, a mental state of romanticism, fancy, confusion and skepticism is no match for Marxist dictatorship. By attacking Confucianism, the intellectuals had caused the youth "to run wild and join the Communists."[12]

Chang insists that the basic ethical stance of Confucianism is as valid now as ever. For him, Confucianism has a future because it understands the four dispositions which are cornerstones on which all worthwhile institutions must be built. Out of these innate dispositions—(1) feelings of commiseration, (2) shame and dislike, (3) modesty and complacence, (4) approval and disapproval—grow man's inherent benevolence, righteousness, propriety and knowledge. Chinese thought, in Chiang's opinion, is superior to Western because 1) it treats knowledge and morality as equally important whereas the West divorces them or extols knowledge for its own sake; 2) it keeps a sense of continuity with the past, emphasizing harmony and peace, as the West does not; and 3) it values comprehensiveness of understanding above the sort of originality which makes the West one-sided.[13]

As a student of the Chinese intellectual tradition, Chang doubts that communism will last. Its economic interpretation of civilization violates man's principles. It denies human rights and the value of the individual. It is too dogmatic. Marxist party dictatorship is no more tolerable than absolute monarchy. Finally, Communist totalitarianism has no way of providing a peaceful succession of leadership.[14] For these reasons, Chang predicts the

---

[11]C. Chang, *Ibid*, p. 439.
[12]*Ibid*, p. 437.
[13]*Ibid*, pp. 452-453.
[14]*Ibid*, p. 475. Cf. "A Manifesto for a re-appraisal of Sinology and reconstruction of Chinese culture" by Chang and Professors Tang Chun-i, Mou Tsung-san and Ho Fo-kuan drawn up in Taiwan in 1957 (*Ibid*, pp. 455-483). President Chiang Kai-shek encouraged a revival of Confucian studies as an antidote to Chinese Marxism. Although a Christian, he recognized that Confucianism represents an indispensable feature of Chinese culture.

ultimate doom of the Communist regime in China. Once Marxism is repudiated, China will revive its Confucian heritage.

VII. SOME CONFUCIAN GIFTS

As a result of two and a half millennia of testing, certain Confucian gifts to the storehouse of wisdom are incontestable. Foremost is the crucial role played by the sage. Confucianism paints the picture of the ideal leader as a man who is "inwardly a sage, outwardly a king." The sage represents the highest point of man's achievement. He knows Heaven, and serves Heaven. Confucianists taught that the sage is superior to the all-powerful political ruler. The sovereign rules only because of the mandate of Heaven and is a good ruler if he follows the advice of his learned advisors.

Confucianists also refused to identify the sage with someone who was merely scholarly. Being a sage depends upon virtue rather than knowledge. Man at his best possesses *jen,* which is not a matter of technical know-how or factual information. All the leader really needs is an open mind, impartial judgment and all-embracing sympathies. He is great not because of what he knows. Because of what he is, he can get all the talented men around him to do their best.[15]

Secondly, Confucianism stresses the central role of the family. Because fathers love their children, the young respect their parents and brothers care for each other, a perfect social order becomes possible. For Confucian scholars the ideal is based upon the actual and grows out of it. At various times, Chinese have relied on the government to provide happiness or believed that legislation could bring contentment, or abandoned society and retreated to the solace of nature. Yet after experimenting with such alternatives, they have recognized the all-important function of the family as the foundation for a stable, secure and peaceful society.

When the Chinese faced an assault from the West, some

---

[15]Fung Yu-lan, "A New System," *The Spirit of Chinese Philosophy,* Routledge and Kegan Paul, London, 1947, pp. 215-220.

advised the adoption of European methods in order to protect the substance of Far Eastern culture. Admittedly it was difficult to distinguish between the secondary and essential features of Chinese civilization. Is the family structure indispensable? In the past there was no question about this matter on the part of most people. As a result of the destructive revolutions in the 20th century, however, even some defenders of Confucianism have doubts. Westernizers have contended that the individual rather than the family is of fundamental value. Nationalists in China, as elsewhere, proclaim the superiority of the nation over one's particular family. Still others, like the Marxists, insist that the Confucian concepts of family loyalty and filial piety stand in the way of the classless society of the future. For Chinese Communists, the traditional family structure of the Confucian empire is an evil which must be abolished to provide a better world order. For the Maoist nothing should threaten an individual's unwavering submission to the authority of the Marxist party and state. One must repudiate his father, disavow his friend, denounce his elder brother and set aside marital obligations if they interfere with one's primary duty to the People's Republic.

Confucianism has always affirmed the primacy of ethics. As a result of the chaotic situation in 20th century China, this belief has been severely tested, yet prominent contemporary Chinese thinkers have reasserted man's basic moral imperative. Professor Fung Yu-lan of Peking, for example, published *A New Treatise on the Nature of Man* (1943) which redefined the need for goodness to revive the essential Confucian spirit. According to Fung, there are four grades in man's moral life. First, he may live a purely instinctive type of existence. Without trying to understand what he does or why, an individual may simply respond to social pressures or inner feelings. Second, he may seek private gain on the basis of egoistic "profit." Thirdly, man becomes truly "moral" when he recognizes his duty to society by subordinating his personal advantage to the common welfare. Finally there is an even higher type of living which he calls "the transcendent sphere." At his best man extends his sense of obligation beyond society to embrace the whole universe. The "transcendent" man is one devoted to the Great Whole. Fung uses religious language to explain this. By recognizing the existence of the Great Whole, man obtains "knowledge of Heaven"; by responding positively to the Great Whole one serves Heaven and identifies with Heaven. Man's duty is to elevate himself from the purely natural and utilitarian spheres of existence to the moral realm and finally to the transcendent level.[16]

However, whether Fung Yu-lan's thought, as well as the traditional Confucian ideals of the family and the sage, will hold a prominent place in the thinking of China in the foreseeable future is, at best, an uncertainty.

---

[16]Fung Yu-lan, *The Spirit of Chinese Philosophy*, preface, pp. xiii-xiv.

BIBLIOGRAPHY

Ch'u Chai and Winberg Chai, *Confucianism*, Barron's Educational Series, Woodbury, N.Y., 1973.
Chai & Chai, ed., *The Humanist Way in Ancient China*, Bantam Press, N.Y., 1965.
Wing-tsit Chan, *Source Book in Chinese Philosophy*, Princeton University Press, Princeton, N.J., 1963.
Carsun Chang, *The Development of Neo-Confucian Thought*, Bookman Associates, N.Y., 1962.
Hao Chang, "K'ang Yu-wei's Intellectual Role in the Late Nineteenth Century," *Liang Ch'i-ch'ao and Intellectual Transition in China*, Taipei, 1971.
Ki-Kun Chang, "The Absolute Value in Society and Restoration to the Way of Heaven" in proceedings of the fourth International Conference on the Unity of the Sciences, ICF, Inc., N.Y., 1975, vol. I.
Chu Hsi and Lu Tsu-Ch'ien, *Reflections on Things at Hand*, Columbia University Press, N.Y., 1967.
Charles Corwin, *East to Eden?*, Wm. B. Eerdmans, Grand Rapids, Mich., 1972.
H.G. Creel, *Confucius and the Chinese Way*, Harper & Bros., N.Y., 1960.
Wm.T. de Bary, *Sources of Chinese Tradition*, Columbia University Press, N.Y., 1960.
A. Doeblin, *The Living Thoughts of Confucius*, David McKay Co., N.Y., 1960.
Pierre Do-Dinh, *Confucius and Chinese Humanism*, Funk and Wagnalls, N.Y., 1969.
J.K. Fairbank, ed., *Chinese Thought and Institutions*, University of Chicago Press, Chicago, 1957.
Thomé H. Fang, *The Chinese View of Life*, Union Press, Hong Kong, 1956.
Fung Yu-lan, *The History of Chinese Philosophy*, Princeton University Press, Princeton, N.J., 1953.
    "A New System," *The Spirit of Chinese Philosophy*, Routledge and Kegan Paul, London, 1947.
J.B. Grieder, *Hu Shih and the Chinese Renaissance*, Harvard University Press, Cambridge, 1970.
R.E. Hume, *The World's Living Religions*, Charles Scribner's Sons, N.Y., 1924.
Yung-Hwan Jo, ed., *Korea's Response to the West*, Korea Research and Publications, Kalamazoo, Mich., 1971.
K'ang Yu-wei, *The One World Philosophy* (L.G. Thompson, translator), Allen & Unwin, London, 1958.
James Legge, *The Chinese Classics*, University of Hong Kong Press, Hong Kong, 1960.
J. Legge, translator, *The Li Ki*, Sacred Books of the East, Oxford University Press, London, 1926.
Lin Yutang, *The Wisdom of Confucius*, Random House, N.Y., 1943.
Liu Wu-Chi, *A Short History of Confucian Philosophy*, Penguin Books, Harmondsworth, England, 1955.
Frederick W. Mote, *Intellectual Foundations of China*, Columbia University Press, N.Y., 1971.

Joseph Needham and Wang Ling, *Science and Civilization in China,* Cambridge University Press, Cambridge, 1954-69, six volumes.

Nivison and Wright, *Confucianism in Action,* Stanford University Press, Stanford, Calif., 1959.

Ezra Pound, *Confucius,* New Directions Book, N.Y., 1951.

J.K. Shryock, *Origin and Development of the State Cult of Confucianism,* The Century Co., N.Y., 1932.

D.H. Smith, *Chinese Religions,* Weidenfield and Nicolson, London, 1968.

Huston Smith, "Confucianism," *The Religions of Man,* Harper and Row, N.Y., 1965.

E.W.F. Tomlin, *The Oriental Philosophers,* Harper & Row, N.Y., 1963.

A. Waley, *Three Ways of Thought in Ancient China,* Doubleday Anchor Book, Garden City, N.Y., 1956.

Wang Yang-Ming, *Instructions for Practical Living,* Columbia University Press, N.Y., 1963.

James R. Ware, trans., *The Sayings of Mencius,* New American Library, N.Y., 1960.

Burton Watson, trans., *Hsün Tzu Basic Writings,* Columbia University Press, N.Y., 1963.

R. Wilhelm, trans., *The I Ching,* Princeton University Press, Princeton, N.J., 1967.

Arthur F. Wright, ed., *The Confucian Persuasion,* Stanford University Press, Stanford, Calif., 1960.

Studies in Chinese Thought, University of Chicago Press, Chicago, 1953.

A.F. Wright and D. Twitchett, *Confucian Personalities,* Stanford University Press, Stanford, Calif., 1962.

Shamanism and Shintoism

Our country is begotten of the Divine Couple, The Divine Male and the Divine Female.
Therefore the mountains, rivers, trees and herbs have their own divine names. . . .
Thus in every cloud of dust or in each particle of the natural elements there is deity.
In what the eye can reach, what the ear can hear, what the hands and feet can feel,
We are everywhere—in amazement—met with Divinity.

—Kitabatake-Chikafusa[1]

---

1. Notes on the Twenty-One Shinto Shrines, 14th century Japanese text.

I. SHAMANISM
Shamanism Defined

THROUGHOUT THE world one finds a form of religion called shamanism. The shaman is one who specializes in a technique inducing a state of trance, during which his soul leaves his body, either ascending to heaven or descending to the underworld realm of the dead. According to Mircea Eliade, the world-famous authority on such matters, shamanism is based on archaic techniques of ectasy of which we have evidence from paleolithic times onward.[1] However, there is a clear distinction between the primary religious experience of the shaman and the ideology, mythology and rites attached to his ecstasy. The interpretations and rituals are a product of the general religious environment—Taoist, Shinto, Buddhist or Christian—and may differ decidedly. But shamans, in the strict sense, are a particular class of privileged beings, ecstatics, with certain basic experiences in common to be found in a variety of cultures.

In Eliade's opinion, it is important to differentiate between shamanic ecstasy and spirit-possession. Both the shaman and the "possessed" establish contact with the spiritual world. But the shaman controls his spirits rather than being controlled by them. He is able to communicate with the dead, the angels, demons and "nature spirits" without thereby becoming their helpless instrument. Besides being a medium, the shaman is in some sense the master of the spirit world. He has become a specialist in the human soul because, unlike ordinary men, he sees it, knows its form and can describe its destiny.

Shamans are gifted persons who stand out in their society by virtue of the fact that they possess a religious calling. In their lives are clear signs of a mystical crisis which sets them apart. This difference from ordinary men manifests itself in a temporary derangement of one's psychological equilibrium. Yet this experience of a psyche in crisis should not be confused with aberrant psychic behavior patterns and mental diseases which it may re-

---
[1] M. Eliade, *Shamanism,* Princeton University Press, Princeton, N.J., 1964.

semble superficially. As maturity approaches, the future shaman will begin to have visions, prefer to wander in solitude rather than take part in the social routine, or sing in his sleep. He may become subject to fits of frenzy, lose consciousness, withdraw into the forest, feed on the bark of trees, wound himself with a knife or fling himself into the water.[2] Sometimes the spirit of a dead shaman appears to him in a dream and orders him to be his successor. In numerous cases and in very different parts of the world, the future shaman first attracts public notice because he manifests a considerable degree of alleged mental aberration and unconventional behavior.[3]

However, anthropologists have discovered the basic contrast between the psychopathological victim and the shaman. The shaman differs from the epileptic or victim of mental illness because he can deliberately enter into trance. Like the sick man, the ecstatic is projected onto a different plane of existence where he experiences the solitude, danger and hostility of the surrounding world. But unlike the sick, he is one who has been cured. As a result, the shaman displays a remarkably keen intelligence, a perfectly supple body and almost unbounded energy. He has experienced through mystical "death and resurrection" the reality of the sacred—with far greater intensity than the rest of his community. As Eliade concludes, the shamans incarnate the sacred because they live it to the fullest.[4]

Myths of shamanic initiation vary. The beliefs of the *Yakut*—a Siberian version of shamanism—do nevertheless illustrate the basic stages in this process. According to the Yakut, each shaman has a Bird-of-Prey-Mother, a supernatural being resembling a huge bird with an iron beak, hooked claws and a long tail. This supernatural bird appears only twice: at the time of the shaman's spiritual birth and his death. When someone is ready to become a shaman, the bird suddenly shows up, pecks his body to pieces, grabs his soul, carries it to the world of the dead and hangs it on a pine

---

[2] *Ibid*, p. 16.
[3] *Ibid*, pp. 23-32.
[4] *Ibid*, p. 32.

branch. After the soul reaches maturity, the bird carries it back to earth, restores the dismembered body to life and the shaman wakes up as if he had been in deep sleep.[5] Typically, shamanic initiation involves death, a trip to the underworld and rebirth.

Shamanist Cosmology

The shaman passes from one cosmic region to another: from earth to heaven or from this world to the underworld of the dead. According to shamanic descriptions, the universe has three levels—the sky, the earth and the lower region. These three cosmic regions (and their subdivisions) can be traversed because they are linked together by a central axis. As the shamans say, they fly up or down through the same hole by which the gods descend or devils climb up. All this means is that communication is possible between terrestrial and supernatural realms. By means of the shaman, the sacred can break through to be manifested on our level.

For some Central Asian tribes, the road to the sky runs through the Pole Star.[6] In fact, shamans believe there is a *Cosmic Pillar* at the heart of the universe which facilitates travel between heaven, earth and the underworld. In archaic cultures, such a channel between different realms of the creation explains how offerings can be made to the gods. For shamans, however, this world pillar presents their means for a *personal ascent* to regions beyond ordinary reach.

Besides believing in a world pillar uniting the three levels of the universe, ancient shamanists speak of the Cosmic Mountain which connects the earth with the sky. Belief in the Cosmic Mountain is part of Babylonian, Indian and Far Eastern mythology. In the Babylonian ziggurat—an artificial holy mountain—is found a symbolic image of the cosmos, its seven storeys representing the seven planetary heavens. Even in early Christian circles the imagery of the holy mountain linking heaven with earth was used. It was said that Golgotha was the center of the world and the

---

[5] *Ibid*, p. 36.
[6] *Ibid*, p. 263.

summit of the Cosmic Mountain: the place where Adam was created and buried, as well as the spot where the Savior shed his redeeming blood.[7]

Shamanic theology has also included widespread belief in a *World Tree*. This cosmic tree—like the cosmic pillar—connects the three levels of the universe. Its branches touch the sky and its roots penetrate the underworld. The World Tree expresses the sacredness of the cosmic order, its power of fertility and its continued life. As such, it becomes the Tree of Life and Immortality. Among the people of Central Asia and among the far distant Germanic tribes, the Cosmic Tree has a bird at its top and a snake at its roots, symbolizing the divine and demonic aspects of the supernatural powers.[8]

According to archaic mythology, the World Tree depicts in addition the total unity of the cosmos—the union of the divine powers of earth and heaven. The creation of the world shows a conflict between the cosmic polar principles: the feminine symbolized by the waters and the snake, the masculine (or upper region) symbolized by the sky and the bird.[9] But the opposite and seemingly contradictory forces of yin and yang (snake and bird) are really complementary powers by which the totality of creation is produced, preserved and rejuvenated. At least in some archaic cosmologies, the Tree of Knowledge of Good and Evil is also the Tree of Immortality. By climbing it the shaman reaches heaven. This is the reason for ascending a tree in the initiation rites of shamanism among Siberian tribes and North American Indians. In a typical ceremony, the candidate uses a young birch tree, which has been stripped of its lower branches. On the trunk seven (or nine or twelve) footholds are cut. The birch symbolizes the Tree of the World, and the notches correspond to the number of heavens a man must pass through on his way to the abode of the supreme God.[10]

---

[7] *Ibid*, p. 268.

[8] *Ibid*, p. 273.

[9] *Ibid*, p. 284. The snake, an obvious phallic symbol, is both the sign of aggressive masculinity and (as in this case) the fascination of the female.

[10] "Shamanism and Cosmology," *Ibid*, pp. 259-274.

Nostalgia for Paradise

Besides claiming to be able to communicate with the spirit world, the shaman demonstrates mankind's longing to recover the happiness of the Garden of Eden. According to Eliade, primitive religion clearly reveals man's "nostalgia for Paradise," to use his phrase. We long to return to the time when heaven was so close to the earth that it could be easily reached by climbing a tree, a vine, a ladder or a nearby mountain, as various primitive myths asserted.

According to African mythology, when men lived in Paradise they felt so near to all of creation that they understood the language of animals. Living in peace with every living thing, men found food to be abundant and within easy reach, and there was thus no need for back-breaking work. In fact, so perfect was the harmony between heaven and earth that hatred, fear and death were nonexistent. The parallels between African religion and the Genesis story are obvious. Both show us primordial man (Adam and Eve) enjoying a paradisiac state of perfect freedom, contentment and beatitude. Both likewise incorporate an implicit condemnation of our present condition of frustration, animosity and alienation from God.[11]

Paradise for the archaic societies of tropical Africa or the Palestinian hill country meant four things: 1) an ideal environment in which man could easily meet the gods, 2) friendship and fellowship with animals and all creation, 3) freedom from exhausting work and 4) immortal life. Furthermore, for the Africans—as for the Hebrews—some sort of tragic Fall of man occurred in the distant past. A loss of grace deprived him of his original happiness, radically altered his original nature and created a terrible rift between heaven and earth.

The task of the shaman then is to transcend the fallen human condition and reenter the original primordial state. In primitive societies, the first step in the process is for the shaman to imitate the behavior of certain animals and endeavor to copy their language. By doing so he is supposed to meet an animal or bird, which

---

[11] Eliade, "Nostalgia for Paradise in the Primitive Traditions," *Myths, Dreams and Mysteries,* Harper and Bros., N.Y., 1960, pp. 59-72.

in turn teaches him its language, becomes his friend and reveals to him the secrets of the universe. Becoming one with the animal creation, the shaman masters a spiritual life much richer and more basic than that available to ordinary mortals. He is blessed with the occult wisdom of the furry and feathery denizens of the cosmos. He recovers man's original kinship with all the forces of nature. Not until the shaman enjoys intimacy with animals, it is felt, can he possess the freedom and bliss which are necessary prerequisites for his mystical journey. Friendship with the animals takes him out of the general condition of "fallen" men and enables him to cross the frontier separating us from Paradise.

In Malaya this shamanic communion with animals takes an extraordinary form. The shaman begins his séance by evoking the spirit of the tiger. According to a western observer, the Malay shaman in effect turns himself into that jungle creature. He runs on all fours and roars. Also like a tigress licking her cubs, the shaman licks for a long time the body of a patient who has come to be healed. Losing consciousness of his own human personality, the shaman incarnates a tiger spirit. Among the Malays, it is believed that when the shaman dies he becomes a tiger at the end of seven days.[12] Consequently, one who seeks shamanic gifts of clairvoyance, spirit healing and ecstasy seeks to be possessed by the tiger spirit, who will serve as his guardian and guide in the perilous journey beyond the earth, bestowing its blessings and granting supernatural powers.

Less extreme examples of the paradisiac kinship of man and animals have been preserved in the Judeo-Christian tradition. For example, in Isaiah's picture of the Messianic age to come, the wolf will dwell with the lamb and the poisonous snake will no longer bite.[13] Similarly, according to medieval accounts, a lion was the constant companion of St. Jerome, and St. Francis knew the language of the birds so was able to preach the gospel to them. Furthermore, in popular legends about the nativity of Jesus Christ, the animals in the manger bowed down and worshipped him as

---

[12] Eliade, *Shamanism,* pp. 344-345.
[13] *Isaiah* 11:6-9.

soon as he was born of Mary.

All over the world, learning the language of animals is believed to be equivalent to knowing the secrets of nature.[14] Being able to imitate their voices enables one to communicate with the Beyond. In the case of birds, since the bird can fly, by becoming a bird—by being "possessed" by its spirit or learning its language—one can undertake a mystical journey to the sky. By putting on a mask in the form of a bird's head or wrapping himself in an animal's fur skin, the shaman signifies his identification with the wisdom of "the wild kingdom" and the fact that he has reestablished the original situation lost at the dawn of time.[15]

Having united with the animal world and learned its language, the shaman is equipped to make the ascent to heaven. In the experience of trance, he bridges the gulf dividing the spirit world from our own level of existence. At least for a time he abolishes the changes made in the structure of the cosmos and in the human situation caused by the Fall. When a Siberian shaman climbs the sacred birch tree he reaches the ninth heaven inhabited by the supreme God. He encounters God face to face and speaks to Him directly as man once did in Paradise. Having attained this state of the highest sort of ecstasy, the shaman describes to his audience all that he sees and all that is happening in the spirit world. His mission accomplished, he collapses exhausted, and after a short time seems to wake up from a deep sleep. He immediately greets those present as though he had just come back from a long journey.[16]

---

[14] In European folklore the owl is said to be gifted with exceptional wisdom; the crow (or raven) and the bat are signs of the presence of evil supernatural spirits. In Asia the tortoise is the possessor of immortality and the fox is thought to be the abode of usually evil supernatural spirits. As for the serpent, among its many roles as a symbol it is believed to possess the power of immortality because it can shed its skin and replace it with another. These animals are believed to manifest powers which men no longer possess but are thought to have a longing to secure. Thus to unite with them is to rise above the human condition.

[15] Eliade, *Ibid*, p. 99.

[16] Eliade, *Myths, Dreams and Mysteries*, pp. 63-64. Cf. St. Paul's remark: "I know a man in Christ who, fourteen years ago, was caught up to the third heaven—whether in the body or out of the body I do not know, God knows—and he heard things that cannot be told, which a man may not utter" (II Cor. 12:1-4).

One more important fact should be noted. In the Genesis account, angels with flaming swords block the entrance to the Garden of Eden to keep ordinary men from returning to it. Among the shamans, one of their most notable powers is their mastery of fire. In their state of ecstasy and trance, they can walk upon fire, swallow live coals and handle red-hot iron without feeling burned.[17] Mastery of fire symbolizes the way the shaman has transcended the human condition. By being able to pass through fire he shows that he can reenter Paradise. He reestablishes communications between earth and heaven interrupted by the Fall—at least temporarily. At least for Eliade, a Roman Catholic, the shamanic experience of "nostalgia for Paradise" is akin to the longing for Eden which is seen in different cultural forms by Isaiah, Virgil, the Church Fathers and St. Francis of Assisi.[18]

The Social Role of the Shaman

Aside from their importance as practitioners of mystical religion, the shamans fulfill an essential social role. As Eliade points out, they are used to defend the psychic integrity of the community. Theirs is the task of combatting demons, curing diseases of all kinds and protecting the tribe from enemies who resort to black magic.

The most important of these functions is the shaman's work as a demon slayer. He serves as the indispensable champion of "Light," defending the positive forces of life, health and fertility. In the eyes of his fellow tribesmen he is one of the most useful members of society—without him they would be overwhelmed by the world of darkness. Serving as a spiritual warrior in the relentless struggle against powerful demonic forces, the shaman may use a spear, bow or sword in his rites or as emblems of his vocation. He can see the spirits, meet the gods and fight the ever-present demons of sickness and death. Ordinary men are comforted knowing they are not alone and helpless in the war against invisible enemies.

The shaman fulfills a second social function in bringing back

---

[17] Cf. Leonard Feinberg, "Fire Walking in Ceylon," N.E. Hoopes and R. Peck, ed., *Edge of Awareness,* Dell, N.Y., 1966, pp. 87-95.

[18] Eliade, *Ibid,* p. 72.

direct and reliable information from the spirit world. Through first-hand experience he is able to explain what happens after death; during his trances and afterwards he gives detailed descriptions of what the Beyond is like. Little by little, men come to realize the true nature of the world of the dead and death itself is accepted as a "rite of passage" to a spiritual mode of being. The ultimate fear of man—his fear of death—is greatly lessened because of shamanic reports of journeys to super-terrestrial realms.[1]

Shamanism in the Far East

Although most scholars have concentrated on shamanism among the tribes of northern Asia, the techniques and beliefs of the shaman can be found in China, Korea and Japan as well. In China shamanism has been closely associated with Taoism—not the Taoism of philosophers like Lao-tzu and Chuang-tzu but the folk Taoism of the holy man, fortune-teller and spiritual healer. During the imperial period, Chinese believed that serious sickness was caused by a flight of the soul from the body. Thus, in the event of grave illness the sorcerer was summoned to the patient's home so he could go into trance to pursue the fleeing soul, capture it and return it to its body. When someone died, a priest, friend or member of the family went up to the rooftop, displayed a fine new robe and pleaded for the soul to return home.[2]

Like the Taoist sorcerer, the shaman is one who can "fly up to heaven." Chinese said that "by means of feathers" shamans were able to leave the earth and ascend as Immortals. As a result, the Taoist holy man was appropriately designated as a "feather scholar" or a "feather guest."[3] Ecstatic dance was also involved in the

---

[1] Eliade, *Shamanism*. pp. 508-510. In this regard it is important to note that spiritualism and interest in psychic phenomena revived in the Western world about the middle of the 19th century when many felt overwhelmed by modern agnosticism, atheism and materialism. The Fox sisters' experience with mysterious table rappings in the 1840's aroused national attention and gave birth to spiritualist churches at the very time Marx was promoting dialectical materialism and Darwin was collecting evidence for his evolutionary hypothesis.

[2] Eliade, *Shamanism*, pp. 447-448.

[3] *Ibid*, p. 450.

shaman's ascent to heaven. Once a man or woman was caught up in the frenzy of the dance, he was open to possession by spirits. Then filled with the spirit, he could rise above the earth or descend beneath it.

To prepare for this experience of ecstasy, a Chinese sorceress would purify herself with perfumed water, dress in special ceremonial robes and dance until she was exhausted. At that moment—a time of physical weariness and spiritual receptivity—the *shen* entered. Henceforth, the body was that of the sorceress, but the spirit was supernatural. In the ecstatic experience the woman provided a body through which the *shen* could speak. Such mediums were called *wu* (female) or *hih* (male).[4] As intermediaries between the natural and supernatural realms, these Chinese shamans served as healers, fortune-tellers and mediums throughout most of the nation's history.

The shamanic dance in ancient China was also felt to be intimately related to the primitive innocence of animal life. Emperor Yü the Great, who ruled about 2208 B.C. according to traditional chronology, was one of the earliest models for the shamans and shamanesses of later Chinese history. By dressing up as a bear, he "became an incarnation" of the Bear Spirit.[5] As primitive people believed, by donning the skin of an animal, a man was transformed into that animal. By becoming the bear, Yü became greater and stronger than ordinary men: His fur robe enabled him to communicate with the deepest non-human levels of cosmic life, transcending the limitations and proprieties of humanity. By coming into sympathy with cosmic rhythms, he would achieve extra-human freedom and hence, bliss and immortality.[6]

Among the Japanese, shamanism has also been of primary importance. Even though the emperor was thought of as a divine descendent of the Sun Goddess, he was originally expected to obey

---

[4] Because women rather than men were most often gifted with shamanic powers, Chinese shamanism is often called *wu*-ism. In prehistoric times the bearskin-masked "dancing shaman" was a man, however.

[5] Eliade, *Ibid*, p. 458.

[6] *Ibid*, p. 460.

the commandments of the gods communicated to him through dreams and states of ecstasy. These trances—in which he was possessed by spirits—were produced by playing the *koto* and other musical instruments. As time passed, however, the emperor shared his priestly functions with designated religious dignitaries. Still, in theory the Japanese affirmed that the charisma of the emperor depended heavily on the ability of the shamanic diviner.[7] According to the ancient Shinto histories, the first emperor Jinmu (circa 660 B.C.) and the tenth emperor Sujin were both closely connected with shamans. Jinmu's mother may well have been a shamaness. As for Sujin, he was assisted by two shamans: his aunt and a diviner of humble birth. A later empress, Jingo, was praised for her ability to pacify troublesome spirits. Until the introduction of Buddhism and its adoption as the state faith, Shinto had neither a regular priesthood nor a fixed ecclesiastical organization. Some priestly functions were carried out by clan heads; others were performed by shamans who had special rapport with the spirits. After the government insisted that priests in both Buddhist and Shinto shrines become de facto public officials, the Japanese masses turned for personal religion to "unauthorized" holy men, healers and mediums. Often these wandering shamans called *ubasoku* were only nominal Buddhists. That is, they used Buddhist language and told Buddhist stories while continuing the shamanic practices of the older Shinto.[8] At this point we need merely note how deeply Shinto was rooted in shamanic soil and that this feature persisted behind the official cult of a later period. More detailed treatment of Shinto is reserved for another section.

Because Korean shamanism is not well known in the Western world yet exhibits all of the major characteristics of the faith, we shall use it as a case study. Except for minor variations, shamanism in Latin America, central Africa[9] or Polynesia resembles that to be found in Korea.

---

[7] Joseph M. Kitagawa, *Religion in Japanese History*, Columbia University Press, N.Y. 1966, p. 19.

[8] *Ibid*, pp. 19-45.

[9] For black versions of shamanism, see material on Haitian voodoo (i.e., Marcus Bach, *Strange Altars*, Bobbs-Merrill, Indianapolis, 1952) and the new independent Christian cults of Africa.

Korean Shamanism

Although shamans in Siberia can be classified into a few distinct types, the situation is quite different in Korea. For example, there are no definite classes of Black and White shamans, whereas in north Asia there is a recognized separation between those who invoke evil spirits and those who seek the aid of benevolent ones. In Korea shamanism is practiced by *Mudangs, Paksoos* and *Pansoos.* In addition there are experts in occult wisdom: the *Chikwan* (geomancers), *Ilkwan* (selectors of favorable days), and *Yubok* (blind female fortune tellers).

The *Mudangs* represent by far the greater number of shamans and are always women. A much smaller group, the *Paksoos*, are men. The *Pansoos*, who are not shamans in the strict sense, are blind experts in divination who because of their physical handicap are believed to possess an inner eye which enables them to foresee the future. Like their Siberian counterparts, the male Paksoo wears the outer dress of a woman while the female Mudang always wears the outer dress of a man. Possibly, as has been suggested, this curious use of ceremonial garments of the opposite sex may reflect a desire to appropriate the psychic energies of both the male and female. Or perhaps the robes of the shaman are intended to reflect the androgynous nature of the godhead. If the divine contains a polarity of yin and yang, it may be fitting for human instruments of sacral power to do likewise. Almost all scholars agree that the change from normal dress has some kind of mystic significance.

Mudangs wear on their ritual garb small round iron disks—flat, shield-shaped pieces, two to five inches in diameter. Whatever the original meaning of these decorations, they are now commonly said to possess unusual mantic power. When they shamanize, the Mudangs also wield crude iron swords or three-pronged forks which are supposed to generate supernatural power. In Siberia the male shaman's robe is decorated with iron breasts and he dresses his hair like a woman.

Like Siberian séances, those held in Korea are always conducted at night. Shamanic rites—called *Koots*—involve the beating of drums and ecstatic dancing. The Mudang accompanies her séance with blood sacrifices—often a chicken or pig. In the past, humans were also sacrificed, especially to the powerful and dangerous spirits of the sea. Pretty young girls were cast into the waves and drowned, presumably to satisfy the wild lusts of the ocean gods.[1] According to the Confucian historians who despised shamanism, this Korean practice was abruptly discontinued after a magistrate ordered that Mudangs be sacrificed instead of young girls.

In Korea shamanic incantations and techniques are not in any way standardized. Handed down from generation to generation by word of mouth, the methods for summoning and controlling spirits vary considerably from Mudang to Mudang. Although there are several books available—often imported originally from China—there are no sacred scriptures. Occasionally during a séance ancient Buddhist charm sentences will be recited from a book entitled the *Chunsoo Kyung*. Also held in high esteem is a brief booklet called the *Okchu Kyung* or "Nine Heaven Original Controlling, Thunder Shaking Chunchon Book."[2]

Women who become Mudangs are ordinarily extremely sensitive individuals. Unfriendly critics say they are usually neurotic,[3] a rather harsh and unfair judgment, it would appear. New Mudangs are sometimes recruited from among the children of practicing shamanesses or from nearby female relatives. In many cases there is no transmittal of psychic powers from mother to daughter. Koreans believe that when a Mudang dies, her spirit seizes control of another person. The spirits force the new person to serve them. Often a girl becomes a Mudang quite unexpectedly, occasionally against her conscious will. However, at least unconsciously the woman must have provided an opening for the spirits to enter her. In some instances, if the Mudang has no children of her own, she adopts an orphan or employs a young servant girl whom she

---

[1] Cf. the Mayan practice of drowning young girls in the sacred well of Chichen-itza who were said to become brides of the rain god Chac.

[2] Translated in full as an appendix to C.A. Clark, *Religions of Old Korea*, Christian Literature Society, Seoul, 1961, pp. 276-286.

[3] *Ibid*, p. 192.

gradually trains. If the child is of a properly nervous temperament, she may be able to receive visions after long years of apprenticeship. It would be fair to assume that such "trained" Mudangs are seldom the most reliable. For the true Mudang psychic sensitivity comes as an unexpected—or unwelcome—gift. Koreans are therefore traditionally fearful of "the falcon spirit," as it is termed, who swoops down on an unsuspecting woman much as a hawk suddenly seizes a baby chicken.

Shrines and Rites

Writing in 1900 for the magazine of the Royal Asiatic Society, a Christian missionary commented that behind the official state cult of Yi dynasty Confucianism—which was observed perfunctorily—the real, vital religion of Korea was shamanism. Twenty-five years later, another missionary correspondent for the same society noted that shamanism was still the strongest religious force in the country. In this connection it is important to recognize that shamanism retained its influence without government support, in spite of Confucian disdain and in the face of a well-financed, aggressive Christian missionary program. More significantly, shamanism did so without an organization, a trained clergy or impressive temples. Only during Queen Min's time was shamanism favored by the palace and this official patronage was of brief duration.[4] Although condemned publicly by Confucian literati, Protestant missionaries and Western-oriented reformers, Koreans of all classes openly or covertly turned to the Mudangs for guidance in periods of stress.

Nevertheless, shaman shrines, to be found everywhere, were always small and unpretentious. Even the National Spirit Shrine (Kooksa Dang), located on Seoul's South Mountain, was so tiny it could accommodate only fifty people. When hundreds of people gathered for shamanic worship to the *Sansin*, for example, services

---

[4] Queen Min (assassinated in 1895) was an ardent shamanist as well as a very remarkable woman. She elevated her favorite Mudang, Yi Chi Yong, to the rank of princess, encouraged the shamans to organize nationally so that they could be more powerful and forced the Confucian scholars to be respectful of the popular faith. This short-lived royal patronage came to a sudden halt when the queen was murdered.

were conducted on the mountain top in the open air. Mudangs hold no stated services comparable to the Sunday Bible classes or sermons of Christians. Nor are the shamanic shrines in any way visibly inspiring. Inside one may find a brightly colored red and yellow picture of the spirit, or a simple wooden tablet bearing his name, as well as wall charts inscribed with the names of spirits and deceased shamans. Ordinarily rites are held in private homes. The only impressive signs of shamanism in Korea are the great stone faces or heads called "Miryucks" (in honor of Maitreya, the Buddha-to-come) which were originally connected to Korea's pre-Buddhist faith.[5] But these no longer hold special meaning for the Mudangs.

More important than the shrine is the *Koot*, the Mudang's ecstatic dance and trance. Besides the special robes, iron trident and sword, the shamanic ritual involves the use of a special rattle (*Pangool*) and an hour-glass drum about three feet long. A small trumpet which makes a wailing, mournful sound is used by the Mudang's assistant.

The first step of the rite involves a chicken, pig or dog being sacrificed and a meal prepared. Once the food has been placed on a small table the Mudang begins her dance to the sound of the trumpet and drum. As she leaps about, whirling around like a Sufi dervish, she calls upon the spirits to join the revelry. Often the dancing goes on all night and sometimes has to be resumed for several evenings. Finally the spirit arrives and partakes of the sacrificial food. To dispel the spirit after it has eaten, the Mudang may show it a small horse made of straw. She begs the spirit to mount it. When he has done so, she seizes the horse, runs out the door and throws it into a stream or high up in a tree.[6]

---

[5] Some are carved in bas-relief on cliffs while others are statues. In the Diamond Mountains there is a carved face cut on a cliff sixty feet high. The statue of Eunjin near Kongju stands sixty-five feet high. Scores of smaller Miryucks can be seen in every part of Korea. Anthropologists often compare these to the stone heads on Easter Island in the South Pacific and rather different ones found in Mexico.

[6] This rite of exorcism to rid a sick person of the spirit which has "possessed" him has certain distinctive features which would vary from time to time. The key features are the use of the dance to induce ecstasy and the ability of the Mudang to summon the spirits, communicate with them and control them. In addition to serving as an exorcist, the shaman can hold a séance to speak with spirits, a service not necessarily connected to the performance of an ecstatic dance.

Worship of Spirits

Korean shamanism includes belief in numerous good and evil spirits: those of the earth and air, the waters and hills, rocks and trees, gods and goblins. Some are benevolent, some malicious and some just plain mischievous. Shamans therefore have traditionally provided a variety of articles (*Chiksung* or *Soosal Yungsan*) to ward off evil spirits. In olden days people used a screen with a picture of a tiger or dragon which they placed inside the gate of their house to frighten away demons. Similarly, at the road leading to a village they set a wooden goose on a pole to guard the area from demons. If an epidemic broke out, archways of bramble bushes were erected over the roads and the sacrificial blood of a bull or dog was poured on nearby stones, protecting the villagers from the disease-carrying spirits.

At the head of the Korean shamanic pantheon is the supreme God: *Hananim*. Worship of Hananim—Master of the sky—goes back to the earliest period when Tangun, the founder of Korea, worshipped Hananim on his high altar at Kangwha. This Supreme God is the creator of all; He sends the rain, is responsible for the harvest and gives us our life.[7]

Beneath Hananim are the divine Generals of the Five Points (*O Pang Chang Koon*), who rule the five separate regions of heaven: the Green General of the Eastern Sky, the Red General of the Southern Sky, the White General of the Western Sky, the Black General of the Northern Sky and the Yellow General of the Zenith. Hananim lets each of these rule supreme in his part of the sky and each has an army of spirits to carry out his bidding. When a shaman is called in to perform his rites, he first locates the offending demons in the proper ward of heaven and persuades the ruling *Chang Koon* to curb the offending spirit.

The *Chang Koons* are represented by carved posts set up at the village entrance. In autumn the villagers gather at these wooden pillars to offer sacrifices of rice bread and fruit. Each year a new post is erected but all of the older ones are left standing. Occasion-

---

[7] Korean Protestants use the word "Hananim" to denote the Biblical God YHWH, but Catholics prefer the Chinese term "Chunchu."

ally twin posts are set up, one for the General of the Upper Heavens and the other for Madame General of the Underworld.

The *Chang Koons* also have subordinates. These are called *Sinchangs* and there are said to be eighty thousand of them. A shaman seeks the good will and help of one or more *Sinchangs* because these spirit officers are in charge of great numbers of inferior spirits.

Shamans believe that special earth spirits protect and control the land. In pre-20th century Korea, every home had its *Tujoo* (site god) who controlled the ground upon which the house was built. *Tujoo*'s shrine was a small jar, perhaps containing a few coins, with a tent-shaped cover made of thatch. At least once or twice a year the family would offer the spirit a meal of cooked rice, rice bread or fruit, and pay their respects by bowing reverently.

Koreans worshipped mountain gods (*Sansin*) as well. Near the top of the mountains, they built small shrines to the Old Man Spirit which contained his picture, that of a venerable sage seated upon a tiger. He ruled everything on or within the mountain: its trees, minerals, birds and mammals. Consequently, hunters, miners and herb doctors who collected medicinal roots paid the mountain spirit special reverence. He also provided the water for the lowlands beneath the mountain; so in case of drought, the blood of sacrificial cows, pigs or dogs was poured on stones near his shrine. It was said that then the Old Man Spirit would have to send long-needed rains—to cleanse the blood-stained rocks which defiled his sanctuary.

In addition to mountain gods, there were believed to be mountain pass spirits (*Sunghwang Dang*). Wherever a road went through a pass, Koreans built a little roadside shrine, usually beside an old gnarled and twisted tree. Next to it they placed a pile of pebbles and one of the wooden pillars of the Five-Point Generals. Strips of colored cloth were attached to a straw rope in front of the shrine or hung from the branches of the sacred tree. Travellers left bits of their clothing as offerings to the mountain pass spirit. Some of the cloth, however, was a gift from brides who had to travel through the dangerous mountains on the way to the homes of their husbands. Fearing that angry spirits from her father's house might follow her, the girl spread a small feast at the shrine and left a bit of her clothing. By the time they had finished enjoying their meal, she would be out of reach and they would have to return home. Merchants paid respect to *Sunghwang Dang* by offering bits of silk. Farmers left rice to the spirit so that he would bless them with bountiful crops. Stable boys gave him tiny images of horses. Petitions for the spirit's aid were written on strips of paper and tied to branches of the tree.

Next to the shrine one found a curious pile of small rocks, the exact purpose of which is uncertain. Everyone passing by was expected to add a stone to the mound and spit upon it in disgust. While the stories told to explain this practice vary greatly, they all agree that the pile of rocks is a reminder of a faithless woman stoned to death as punishment for her adultery.[8]

Believed to preside over the plain and its farming villages are spirits called *Chunsin*. Connected with worship of these agricultural gods is an offering made to Ko Si. Before the farmer eats his mid-morning or noon lunch, he drops a spoonful of rice on the ground, crying, "Mrs. Ko, come and eat this!" Ko Si was the mother of the powerful Buddhist monk Tosun (10th century A.D.). After suffering from repeated crop failures, farmers in the two provinces south of Seoul requested help from Tosun. He rid the area of the evil spirits which had caused so much trouble, and since then the harvests have been bountiful. In gratitude the farmers pledged to offer perpetual sacrifices to Tosun's mother. For shamanists, reverence for spirits of the dead is as necessary as worship of the supernatural powers behind nature.

Water spirits too have an honored place in the Korean pantheon. Chief of these is the Dragon who rules rivers, lakes, wells, and the ocean. He resides in bottomless lakes and is worshipped by casting food upon the waters and saying prayers. While the Dragon is a benevolent spirit, quite the opposite are the spirits of any persons who have drowned. According to Korean folklore, those

---

[8] Cf. C.A. Clark, *Ibid*, p. 201 for three stories about the origin of the stone pile. Compare this with the rite of "stoning Satan" carried out by pilgrims to Mecca.

who drown are trapped in the water until they can pull in some unfortunate victim to take their place. Therefore, their spirits lurk around the water, forever trying to lure someone to his death. To appease and pacify these water ghosts, the Korean shamaness offered blood sacrifices at the water's edge. Furthermore, when Koreans in the past started off on a journey by boat, they first attracted all the nearby spirits by beating drums and gongs. Then they put food and incense on a straw raft and set fire to it. While the spirits were occupied with eating and enjoying the smell of incense, the boat sailed away out of their reach.

Koreans believed a special spirit (*Sungjoo*) dwelt in each home. When a new house was completed, the shamaness arrived to placate the spirit who would make it his dwelling place. She produced a paper envelope, filled it with rice and money, then soaked it in wine. After appropriate prayers, she pasted the envelope to the side of the ridgepole of the house. At harvest time and other important occasions, the house spirit was fed and prayers were recited to make it happy. If things went wrong in the household, this showed that the *Sungjoo* was angry or had deserted the place. In such cases, the shamaness had to be called back.

Among the other household spirits worshipped in Korea was the Hindu-Buddhist god Sakra. An earthenware jar full of dry rice was set up on a shelf and dedicated to him. This *Cheisuk Jar*, as it was called, was worshipped periodically. If the rice swelled and spilled out of the jar, it was a sign of good fortune to come; if it soured, the family could expect trouble. The *Samsin*, a trinity of spirits, were worshipped by women who longed for children. They also were believed to guard a child until he was ten years old. To provide a nest for these benevolent spirits, a shamaness hung a paper bag or gourd in the warmest and best part of the living room. Naturally, the *Samsin* were fed and worshipped regularly by the women of the family. Also venerated in most Korean households was the Taoist Kitchen God who nested in a bundle of cloths hung on the ridgepole. As a result of the introduction of the Confucian examination system to Korea, shamans encouraged the veneration of the Red Diploma Spirit (*Hongpi Kwisin*). Those who passed the

Confucian examinations for public officials were awarded sheepskin diplomas nearly three feet square and stained deep red. Since they were supposed to symbolize great power, the diplomas were often set up on the wall behind a curtain and worshipped. Of course, it was not the diploma itself but the spirit of it which was venerated.

The *Keullip* is the Korean god of wealth. He was believed to live in a great bunch of strings hung up against the wall of a house or the shop of a merchant. There are other good luck spirits who live in snakes and weasels. People were therefore pleased if these creatures made their home in the woodpile.

Tree worship was also a feature of Korean shamanism. However, unlike the Indians who worship the banyan, the Japanese who believed in the sacredness of the *sakaki* or the Germanic tribes who worshipped the oak, Koreans have not singled out any specific species of tree for worship. Any old, gnarled and twisted tree can become an object of veneration. Sometimes, a village would adopt a whole grove and assign each tree to a family. To show a tree is sacred, a rope of left-woven straw or a piece of thatch like a woman's apron was tied around it. Special tree worship took place on the fourteenth night of the first lunar month. After spreading red soil around the tree, the devout offered food and recited prayers to the tree spirit.

Finally, Korean shamanism affirmed the existence of numerous mischievous spirits. Goblins (*Tokeibis*) delight in inconveniencing people by misplacing articles which then have to be hunted for. *Namshakui* and *Duosuni* are the dangerous and vandal spirits of boys and young men who have died violent deaths. Even though they no longer have bodies, they have not been calmed down and made responsible or law-abiding. Among the dangerous demons none was more feared than the ghost of a young girl who died just prior to her marriage. Such frustrated souls would be particularly malicious. Consequently, their bodies were buried deep under much-travelled roads and roof tiles were attached to their heads to keep the spirits imprisoned in the grave. Members of the family would also put a basket of silk wedding clothes on a special shrine shelf in the home and carefully offer regular sacrifices to appease the troubled spirit. For Koreans, *Talki Kwisin* on the sixteenth night of the first lunar month is comparable to the western Halloween: all the evil spirits appear to show their power. Fortunately, if one hangs a sieve in the front doorway, the demons will become so preoccupied counting the holes in the sieve they will never get around to entering the house.

Messages from Spirit World

Shamanism testifies to the possibility of direct communication with spiritual entities—gods and goddesses, angels, demons or the souls of the departed. Whether practiced in Haiti or Hong Kong, the simple core of shamanism is unquestioning acceptance of the idea that even in ordinary, everyday life there exists two-way traffic between the supernatural and natural. For the worshipper, every human emotion has a matching and answering emotion in the realm of the divine. Implicit in the faith is a basic polarity between the visible and invisible worlds.

Although numerous examples of communication with the spirit world could be easily found, let us merely cite three dramatic illustrations from the Far East in our modern era. Each provides convincing evidence of the central affirmation of shamanism. Each gave birth to a religious movement of lasting value and perhaps most important, each has had an effect upon society at large.

The Taiping Movement (1837-1864)

At a time when the Manchu government of China was in a sad state of social, economic and political disintegration, a disappointed office-seeker named Hung Hsiu-ch'uan founded the God Worshippers Society. Their aim was no less than to remake the nation into the Heavenly Kingdom. In 1837 Hung went to Canton to try to pass the imperial examinations. Though he failed, while in the city he picked up a series of Christian tracts prepared by the London Missionary Society. He probably read them casually but they made no impression upon him at that time. When he went back to Canton the next year and again failed the tests, Hung became seriously ill and had to be carried to his village in a sedan chair. During this illness, he started having visions.

Hung feared he was dying and would be taken to Yen-lo, the Buddhist king of Hades. Instead, he was carried away by angels to a region of brilliant light. There he was washed at a river by an old woman. She cut out his vital organs and replaced them with new ones. Having been remade, he was brought to an elderly gentleman who complained that men were sinfully worshipping demons instead of himself. Then, Hung was given a sword and seal, tokens of his commission, and told to return to earth to destroy the demons.

As a result of this vision, Hung took on a marked change in personality. His depression was replaced by unusual self-confidence. Yet the following year Hung again could not pass the Confucian exams. But when he returned to his village, he started to read the Christian tracts he had bought years earlier. Entitled "Good Words to Admonish the Age," they gave Hung an explanation of his strange vision and new meaning to his life. On the basis of his scanty knowledge of Christian doctrine, he now believed that he had ascended to heaven, been baptized by the Heavenly Mother and commissioned by God the Father to wage war on the demons. Since Hung had also been introduced to a middle-aged man in heaven who treated him like a member of the family, he assumed that this must have been Jesus. Henceforth the Chinese seer thought of himself as the younger brother of Christ, called to establish God's kingdom on earth.

Hung's program promoted both individual and national regeneration. By worshipping only the one God and cultivating the heart, his followers would open up heavenly glories to man's view. On the basis of faith in the Fatherhood of God and belief that all men form a single clan, the God Worshippers Society would subjugate the demons and produce a new era of "great peace" (*Taiping*). Hung used the Ten Commandments as the code of behavior for his disciples. This meant forbidding opium smoking, concubinage, gambling, wine, fortune telling, banditry and prostitution. Since the Great God is the Father of all under heaven, Hung favored social equality, a new set of personal values and a new source of authority among brothers and sisters. All this to take place in a new religious commonwealth.

Though Hung combined Protestant teaching with the traditional Chinese emphasis on the family, his famous Taiping attack on idols gradually broadened into a revolution against the Confucian gentry and the whole status quo. The course of the Taiping revolt, its amazing successes and its ultimate suppression are not our concern. Suffice it to say that Hung's vision had enormous social, political, economic and religious consequences. Marx and Maoist writers have seen it as a valuable precursor to the Communist reconstruction of China. Nationalists have also paid glowing tribute to the Taiping movement. Sun Yat-sen was inspired by its ideals and felt he would carry to completion Hung's program.

Culturally, however, the crusade against idols led to the senseless destruction of innumerable art treasures, including the 260 foot Porcelain Pagoda of Nanking built in the 15th century. Though religiously the God Worshippers Society had created the only truly indigenous form of Christian faith China has ever had, they had, on the other hand, administered a nearly fatal wound to Buddhism in that nation. For good or ill, nevertheless, an essentially shamanic movement had made a profound effect in one very important period of China's modern history.[1]

Ch'ondogyo, the Heavenly Way

Ch'oe Che-u (1824-1864) was the founder of the religion called the Heavenly Way, which played a vital role in both the development of Korean nationalism and the struggle for independence. He began his work as a result of a vision in which he was

---

[1] Dr. Philip L. Wickeri has written about "Christianity and the Origins of the Taiping Movement," *Ching Feng* (Hong Kong), vol. XIX, no. 1, 1976, pp. 5-34. For sample anti-Taiping evaluations, see M.A. Nourse, *A Short History of the Chinese*, New Home Library, N.Y., 1942, pp. 214-227 and Daniele Varè, *The Last Empress*, Literary Guild, N.Y., 1936, pp. 105-118. A recent survey of the Taiping Rebellion as Chinese historians now interpret it can be found in Immanuel C.Y. Han, *The Rise of Modern China*, Oxford University Press, London, 1970. pp. 270-308.

commissioned by Heaven to create a new way of life based upon faith in God and man. Ch'oe was the son of a well-known Confucian scholar; but because his mother was a concubine, he was ineligible to become a civil or military official. Although his mother died when he was six years old and his father when he was sixteen, Ch'oe became well-educated in the Confucian classics, Buddhism, Taoism and the newly-introduced Roman Catholicism of the missionaries. It is important to note that he was physically frail as well as emotionally sensitive.

During the late spring of 1860 Ch'oe had a mystical experience in which he was given a twenty-one character "Sacred Formula":

> May the creative force of the universe be within me in abundant measure. May Heaven be with me and every creation will be done. Never forgetting this truth, everything will be known.[2]

From the Sacred Formula, Ch'oe derived his basic principle: man and God are one (*In nae ch'on*). When the individual exercises faith in the oneness of his own spirit and body in the universality of God, union between Heaven and man can be realized. One must harmonize all truth in a Tao based on this fundamental unity.

Ch'oe combined and reinterpreted certain principles of Buddhism, Confucianism and Taoism. From Buddhism he borrowed the ideal of a cleansed heart. From Confucianism he stressed the importance of the five relationships: father-son, ruler-subject, husband-wife, elder-younger and friend-friend. Taoism taught him the need for cleansing the body from physical and moral filth. When asked how his ideas differed from Roman Catholicism—then called "Western Learning" (*Sohak*)—he replied that his "Eastern Learning," *Tonghak,* is based on the incarnation of God in man, shows how to control one's temper and helps one to think

---

[2] *A Brief Guidance to Cheondogyo,* Cheondogyo Central Headquarters, Seoul, 1971, p. 1. See also C.A. Clark, *Religions of Old Korea,* pp. 144-172. For the Ch'ondogyo Bible translated in full, see Clark, *Ibid,* pp. 258-276.

clearly. By contrast Christians find the incarnation only in Jesus, do not really study to know God, have no spirit to inspire their physical development and lack the Sacred Formula.[3]

Ch'oe had a decidedly mystical bent—quite unlike the Chu Hsi Confucianism of his contemporaries. This can be explained in part by his admitted study of the *I Ching*. However, he also knew the Korean shamanist texts such as *Ch'amwisol*—the "Theory of Dream Interpretation." These writings encouraged spirit worship, stressed the value of sacred mantras and prophesied the fall of the decadent Yi dynasty. Nor should we forget that the establishment of Ch'ondogyo resulted from Ch'oe's direct communication with the spirit world.

Ch'ondogyo offered an idealistic and altruistic faith to Koreans in a period of social decay and turmoil. It gave comfort and hope to the masses who were oppressed politically, and in desperate straits economically. It combined deep mysticism with concern for social justice. It taught unselfish respect for one's fellow men: treat people as though they were God. As a leader, Ch'oe inspired intense personal devotion, so it was natural for his followers to call him "Great Divine Teacher" (*Taesinsa*). Within three years after his revelation, Ch'oe had attracted a large following of poor farmers, politically discredited members of the upper classes, social reformers, and some intellectuals. Like a messiah, Ch'oe proclaimed the possibility of heaven on earth (*chisang ch'on'guk*). As Yi Ton-hwa, a modern Ch'ondogyo theologian says, the oneness of God and man means that man has the ability to become divine and the present world the capability to become a paradise.[4]

Ch'oe's ministry lasted barely five years. Indignantly refusing to give a large sum of money to a corrupt official, he was imprisoned on charges of organizing a religion contrary to national principles. After months of abuse and torture in jail, Ch'oe was condemned for proclaiming the existence of a Lord of Heaven

---

[3] Benjamin B. Weems, *Reform, Rebellion, and The Heavenly Way*, University of Arizona Press, Tucson, 1964, pp. 7-8.

[4] *Ibid*, pp. 10-11. Quoted from *Essential of In Nae Ch'on*, Ch'ondogyo Central Headquarters, Seoul, 1925, pp. 199-201.

superior to the king. Equally disliked was his preaching of a religion resembling the hated Catholicism of the foreign missionaries. Found guilty of treason, he was finally hanged.

In 1871, seven years later, a *Tonghak* youth started an uprising in his home town, proclaimed himself a general and beheaded the local chief magistrate. He was caught and executed. In 1894 a far greater rebellion by the followers of the Heavenly Way took place. The frightened Yi monarch asked for Chinese troops to quell the insurgency. China promptly sent an army and Japan moved in to keep the Manchu empire from interfering with its own plans for subjugating Korea. The Yi dynasty had stopped the rebellion but paved the way for its own destruction, as Korea came under the subjugation of the foreign powers. *Tonghaks*, however, were outlawed and persecuted savagely, and their activities were restricted to purely religious matters. But Ch'ondogyo never abandoned its faith in a kingdom of God on earth. Their leaders were in the forefront of the 1919 independence movement and in our own time Ch'ondogyo has fought valiantly against communism.[5] Its social activism has always been a concrete application of its intense eschatological mysticism.[6]

Tenrikyo: Religion of Divine Wisdom

Scholars who study the many "New Religions" of Japan find that shamanistic practices play an important part in most of them.[7] For example, *Tenrikyo*—with several million adherents today—fits perfectly the pattern delineated by Eliade for archaic shamanism. The Religion of Divine Wisdom originated as a result of an experience of spirit-possession.[8] The founder of Tenrikyo,

---

[5] Ch'ondogyo leaders in Seoul plotted an uprising in North Korea in 1948 and again in 1950 (*A Brief Guidance to Cheon-do-gyo*, pp. 17-18).

[6] Cf. Key Ray Chong, "The Religious Meaning of Ch'oe Che-u's Tonghak Doctrine" in Robert J. Miller, ed., *Religious Ferment in Asia,* University of Kansas, Lawrence, 1974, pp. 64-79.

[7] Prof. Robert S. Ellwood, Jr. finds the same to be true of many of the new sects and cults which have become a major feature of post-World War II America. See his *Religious and Spiritual Groups in Modern America,* Prentice-Hall, Englewood Cliffs, N.J., 1973, pp. 28-31.

[8] Henry von Straelen, *The Religion of Divine Wisdom*, Veritas Shoin, Kyoto, 1957.

Nakayama Miki (1798-1887) was the wife of a big landowner and the mother of four children. From childhood she had been an unusually devout Pure Land Buddhist and at age nineteen had been initiated into one of the highest rites of the Jodo sect. When she was forty-one years old, she and her husband and son were suddenly subjected to great physical pains. As was the custom, a shaman was called in to cure them. Since the shaman's usual helper was not available, Miki agreed to serve as the medium in the rite of exorcism. During the ritual, Miki became possessed by a god and fell into a deep trance. Asked by the shaman to identify himself, the spirit replied: "I am the True and Original God. . . . I want to take Miki as the Shrine of God and mediatrix between God the Parent and man."

Everybody was awestruck by what had taken place. However, Miki's husband demanded that the god leave his wife's body because she was the mother of four children who needed all her attention. Speaking through the medium, the spirit thereupon threatened to destroy the whole family if his will was thwarted. A family council was convened and for three days Miki remained unconscious. When the husband concluded that nothing could be done but accept the god's wishes, Miki came out of her trance and the pains suffered by the husband and son completely disappeared.

According to Tenrikyo, the place where Miki became "possessed" was also the exact spot where the Divine Parent originally created the world and man. God's final revelation and first act of creation thus occurred at the same place. To commemorate these events and the unique holiness of this particular location, Tenrikyo worshippers erected an 8.2 foot wooden column (*kanrodai*) which has become the focal point of their devotions. Such a column bears a significant resemblance to the sacred pillar or tree of life which is so basic to archaic shamanism.

At present, the Patriarch of Tenrikyo—the great-grandson of the foundress—regularly leads a mystical dance around the holy column. He stands in the north position, his wife stands opposite him in the south, four men stand in the west and four women in the east. For ten minutes, the ten dancers perform a dance which is the most important rite of Tenrikyo. The Patriarch portrays the supreme male deity and his wife takes the role of the chief goddess. Each of the ten participants wears the mask of a traditional Shinto deity and their dance, conducted in secret, probably represents a mystical reenactment of creation. Another dance of three men and three women is publicly performed in front of the altar and lasts about an hour. This ceremony—the central act at all Tenrikyo temples in Japan—is accompanied by the beating of drums, creating a feeling of intense religious excitement.

On top of the sacred column sits a wooden cup which could hold over two gallons of liquid. Tenrikyo believes that sometime in the future the Heavenly Parent ("Tenri-O-no-Mikoto") will pour a special supernatural dew into this container. When the faithful drink the heavenly nectar, a messianic age will begin. Blessings will follow immediately. People will always be happy, be able to achieve perfect virtue and wisdom, and live to be 115 years old. Modern adherents of Tenrikyo still long for the consummation of this promise of ultimate bliss.

Miki claimed on the basis of revelation that God should be worshipped as "the Parent." According to her, He created the world and mankind in order that man should lead a cheerful life. To live joyfully, he should treat everything he has, even his body, as something loaned from God. To please the Heavenly Parent , we should be extremely careful in our care for our body because it does not belong to us; when we die we should return it to Him with much gratitude.

Tenrikyo affirms the essential and incorruptible goodness of creation. Evil is only dust covering man's true nature; God will therefore serve as the broom to clean the hearts of all the people in the world. Like Buddhists, Tenrikyo adherents believe in reincarnation. We return our body to the Creator at death but our immortal soul borrows a new one. To prepare for the age of perfect happiness to come, men should keep their minds free of the dust of sin and live now a joy-filled life.[9] Although many efforts have been made

---

[9] For a brief summary of Tenrikyo doctrine, see H. Thomsen, *The New Religions of Japan,* Tuttle, Tokyo, 1963, pp. 33-60. Also Takahito Iwai, *The Outline of Tenrikyo,* Tenrikyo Doyu-Sha, Nara, 1932, pp. 178-228.

to show how much Tenrikyo owes to Buddhism or Shinto, Miki and her followers affirm that the Religion of Heavenly Wisdom is the result of the Parent God's direct revelation—through the mouth of the prophetess in whose body He dwelt.

II. SHINTOISM
History of Shintoism

As THE indigenous faith of Japan, Shinto means the Tao of the Kami, the road to the gods. At first and for many subsequent centuries, it was an animistic and polytheistic faith which combined shamanistic practices with the rites of a primitive agricultural fertility cult. Reminders of this early religion can still be found in the Ise worship of the Sun Goddess, pilgrimages up the sacred Mt. Fuji, rice planting and harvesting ceremonies, veneration of holy trees, the doll festival on March 3 and boys' festival on May 5 every year. The chief characteristic of shrine Shinto is the *torii*, a gate made of two horizontal beams supported by two pillars, at the entrance to the palace of the Kami, as each place of worship is called.[1]

A new period opened with Buddhism's arrival. Beginning in the 6th century A.D. and lasting more than a millennium, Japan honored Mahayana Buddhism as the state faith. Buddhist priests took over Shinto shrines and reinterpreted Shinto beliefs in accordance with Buddhist metaphysics. However, because Buddhism is a tolerant faith, there were few changes in Shinto rites and careful preservation of Shinto shrines. Shintoists attempted to reconcile themselves to the new situation by claiming that Buddha taught the Way of the Kami and his fourfold truth came as a revelation from the Sun Goddess.

This Buddhist era ended when Japan opened her doors to the West and pure Shinto was revived as the basis for proud, self-assertive nationalism. Kamo Mabuchi (d. 1769), Motoori Norinaga (d. 1801) and Hirata Atsutane (d. 1843) promoted the recovery of Japan's heritage and a return to her original glory. Before, in their opinion, it had been "corrupted" by Chinese and Indian notions.[2] State Shinto henceforth became the ideological support for Japan's

---

[1] For details, see Hideo Kishimoto's revision of M. Anesaki, *Religious Life of the Japanese People,* Kokusai Bunka Shinkokai, Tokyo, 1961, pp. 12-29.

[2] Cf. J.A. Hardon, *Religions of the World,* Image Books, N.Y., vol. I, pp. 227-235. Also, Kitagawa, *Religion in Japanese History,* pp. 160-176.

"immanental theocracy," as it was called.[3]

Apologists for State Shinto were primarily interested in promulgating love for country, reverence for the emperor, filial piety and loyalty to the government to reinforce the concept of a strong centralized state. When they were criticized by Christians for denying men religious freedom, they replied that the compulsory rites of State Shinto were not anything more than patriotic exercises. By reducing Shinto in such a fashion, the way was opened for the birth of more enthusiastic Shinto sects which had no formal connection with the government but met popular need for a warm and vital religious life. Thirteen such sects sprang up and prospered under the guidance of charismatic founders, women as well as men.[4]

When Japan was defeated in World War II, the Allied occupation authorities abolished State Shinto and forced the emperor to renounce his claim to divinity. This left the ancient shrine Shinto and newer sectarian Shinto.[5] To these should be added several of the New Religions which grew out of Shinto. *Tenrikyo* is an example of sectarian Shinto and PL Kyodan (the Religion of Perfect Liberty) is an illustration of a new religion based on Shinto to some degree.[6]

Shinto Myths and Scriptures

In the opinion of Shinto priests and scholars, the pattern for man's daily life and worship can be found in the prehistorical Age of the Kami. *Kami*—loosely translated as "gods" or "spirits"—refers to the fundamental powers of creation: phenomena of nature

---

[3] Cf. D.C. Holtom, *The National Faith of Japan*, E.P. Dutton, N.Y., 1938 and *Modern Japan and Shinto*, University of Chicago Press, Chicago, 1947.

[4] For example, *Omoto-kyo* was founded on divine oracles received by a peasant shamaness Deguchi Nao (d. 1918) whose son-in-law Deguchi Onisaburo (d. 1948) was believed to be the messiah-Maitreya.

[5] In post-war Japan, Shinto found itself with a loss of government revenue, shortage of clergy and lack of a modern systematic theology. Worse, some said that the historic shrines were only cultural monuments which should be kept up by the government but they no longer had any religious meaning. Kitagawa, *Ibid*. pp. 284-289.

[6] Cf. H. Thomsen, *The New Religions of Japan:* Kurozumikyo, pp. 61-67, Konkokyo, pp. 69-78, Omoto and subsects, pp. 127-182.

like the sun, mountains, trees, wind, thunder and certain animals, as well as ancestral spirits, particularly those of the Japanese imperial family or outstanding national heroes. Anyone or anything with a "numinous" quality[7]—eliciting wonder, fascination or reverence—is divine, a dwelling place of the Kami.[8] Among the most important Kami are the Kami of the Center of Heaven (*Ame-no-minaka-nushi*), the two Kami of birth and growth (*Taka-mimusubi-no-mikoto* and *Kami-musubi-no-mikoto*), the heavenly Adam and Eve who gave birth to the islands of Japan (*Izangi-no-mikoto* and *Izanami-no-mikoto*), the Sun Goddess (*Ama-terasu*), the Earth Ruler (*Susa-no-o-no-mikoto*) and the Moon God who governs the realm of darkness (*Tsuki-yomi-no-mikoto*).

Shinto mythology reports that the Earth God behaved so badly toward his sister, the Sun Goddess, that she became angry and hid herself in a cave, causing the whole cosmos to be plunged into darkness. To persuade the goddess to come out a wild and merry dance was performed. When *Ame-no-Uzume* ("the Dread Female of Heaven") dressed up in strange clothes, kindled a fire and then danced on a tub, all the gods laughed. The Sun Goddess wondered how they could be so jolly while the world was wrapped in total darkness, so she peeped out of the cave. At once she was seized and prevented from hiding again. This folk tale obviously has several levels of meaning. It describes the natural rhythm from day to night and winter to spring. It shows the terrible effects of sin. Furthermore, it stresses the value of the shamanic dance as a means of banishing the realm of darkness and illuminating the soul of man.[9]

Shinto mythology also teaches that Japan is a "holy land" and her people are a "chosen people." The god *Izanagi* ("Male who

---

[7] Cf. Rudolph Otto, *The Idea of the Holy,* Oxford University Press, London, 1970. His definition of the Holy ("the numinous") as the *mysterium tremendum* is an apt description of the Shinto Kami-concept.

[8] Sokyo Ono, *Shinto: The Kami Way,* Bridgeway Press, Rutland, Vt., 1962, pp. 6-9.

[9] Masaharu Anesaki, "Japanese Mythology," J.A. MacCulloch, ed., *Mythology of All Races,* Cooper Square Publishers, N.Y., 1964, vol. VIII. Also, Jean Herbert, *Shinto,* Allen and Unwin, London, 1967, pp. 227-388.

invites") and the goddess *Izanami* ("Female who invites") marry and produce their special offspring: the islands, mountains, rivers, trees and grass of Japan. The Sun Goddess was also a product of their union. Some time later, she sent her grandson down to earth with three sacred treasures by which his descendents—the future emperors of Japan—could show that they ruled by divine right: a mirror, a sword and a jewelled necklace.[10] Her shrine—the imperial shrine of the Sun Goddess at Ise—is the main temple of Shinto.

There is no Shinto bible, mainly because the religion is shrine-centered and rite-centered rather than book-centered. However, records of ancient beliefs are found in *Kojiki* ("Record of Ancient Matters") and *Nihon Shoki* ("Chronicles of Japan"). Both date from the early years of the 8th century A.D. yet contain much older traditions.[11] Although the *Kojiki* and *Nihon Shoki* are of minor importance in shrine Shinto or the religious life of the masses, the stories in them were a standard part of primary school education from the Meiji period until the defeat of Japan in 1945.

Respect for the Dead

In Shinto there was originally no idea of a far-off heaven or a mysterious hell in the bowels of the earth. The departed spirits were thought of as constant presences, able to share the pleasures or pains of the living. Their real world was the place of burial. The spirits were believed to dwell in the tombs provided for them. They required food and drink and in return they would confer blessings on their benefactors. Although their bodies had disintegrated, their spirits linger on, living in a new plane of existence.[12]

The wicked man, however, becomes a spirit as surely as does the good man. All alike are *Kami*. In the afterlife, the wicked retain their evil inclinations. Hence, it is necessary to propitiate these wayward spirits with offerings of food, while playing the harp and

---

[10] These three sacred objects are believed to be connected with an early Japanese shamanic cult.

[11] Post Wheeler, *The Sacred Scriptures of the Japanese,* Schuman, N.Y., 1952.

[12] See "Spiritism" and "Ancestor Worship in Ancient Japan" in Genchi Kato, *A Study of Shinto,* Meiji Japan Society, Tokyo, 1926, pp. 32-47, 52-58.

the flute, singing and dancing or whatever else is likely to put them in good humor.

According to Shinto belief, to die is to enter into possession of superhuman power, i.e., to be capable of conferring benefits or inflicting misfortune by supernatural means. Even if while he was alive a man might be only a common laborer, once he died he inherited unusual spiritual powers. Consequently, his children pray to him for aid in their various undertakings. Yet, the dead are dependent on the living. According to Shinto belief, they need earthly nourishment and homage. Only through the devotion of their kindred—or other kindly people—can the discarnate souls find happiness and peace. Each spirit must have shelter—an appropriate tomb; and each requires suitable offerings. If he is respectably sheltered and adequately nourished, he will be happy and therefore bestow good fortune on his benefactors. However, deprived of a fitting sepulchre, proper funeral rites and regular offerings, the disembodied spirit will suffer from cold, hunger and thirst, feel miserable, resentful or angry, and therefore act malevolently toward those who have forgotten their duties.

Because of the decline of deep religious feelings in the modern world, it may be difficult for us to imagine how the happiness of the dead could depend upon material food. Among the ancestor worshippers of the Far East, the dead were believed to consume not the physical substance of the food but only to absorb and enjoy its invisible essence. However small the offerings of the living to the dead it was mandatory that they should be made regularly. The visible and invisible worlds are forever united and cannot be broken without dire consequences. Because the well-being of the dead and their surviving loved ones are bound together, neither can dispense with the help of the other.

Ancestor worship is founded upon five beliefs: 1) the dead remain in this world, haunt their tombs, frequent their former homes and enjoy the company of their living relatives; 2) all the dead become spiritual entities possessing supernatural powers, but retain the characteristics of their previous earthly existence; 3) as the happiness of the deceased depends upon respectful service from their descendents, so the happiness of the living is to some extent controlled by piety to the dead; 4) many natural events in the world are decisively affected by the influence of discarnate spirits; 5) all human actions, whether good or evil, are somewhat guided by the invisible workings of the spirits.[13]

Three Modern Japanese Thinkers
Ishida Baigan: Ethical Mysticism

Ishida (1685-1744) was an influential Japanese thinker of the shogun period whose movement called *Shingaku* attracted thousands of middle-class merchants and exerted enormous influence for more than a century. At twenty-three he decided to propagate Shinto, possibly as a result of a campaign by priests to encourage people to make a pilgrimage to the Ise shrine. While working as a clerk for a Kyoto merchant to earn a living, he devoted all his free time to study and lecturing. With the aid of a learned teacher who expounded Taoism, Buddhism and Confucianism, he achieved "enlightenment" at about age forty. As he put it, at last he felt like a cormorant plunging into the serenity of a great sea.[14] Within a few years he left his job to lecture. Living frugally and never marrying, Ishida concentrated upon learning the true nature of man and "knowing the heart." *Gakumon*, he taught, means behaving prudently, serving one's lord with righteousness, respecting parents, being faithful to friends, loving man at large and having pity on the poor. In his opinion, because men have been darkened by human desires, their original heart has been lost. By recovering his lost heart, one can become the heart of heaven and earth.[15] Recognizing the basic human predicament, Ishida compared people to sick men with paralyzed hands and feet. To recover man's true heart, he recommended meditation, an

---

[13] Cf. Lafcadio Hearn, *Japan's Religions,* University Books, New Hyde Park, N.Y., 1966. For a careful study of Chinese ancestor worship in modern times, see Francis L.K. Hsu, *Under the Ancestors' Shadow,* Routledge and Kegan Paul, London. 1949.

[14] The cormorant is a bird somewhat like a pelican trained to catch fish in Japan.

[15] Cf. Mencius whose thought was most important for Ishida.

austere life and devotion to one's social obligations. To be good is to unite with the heart of *Amaterasu*, the Sun Goddess, and act accordingly.

Shingaku espoused the importance of the work ethic. What one does—one's occupation—is what heaven has decreed, the basis for service to the nation and the foundation of the family. If one does not know his occupation, he is inferior to birds and beasts, declared Ishida. How can we neglect our job if we profess to be interested in righteousness? Because one's work is a holy calling, it is necessary to promote honesty, economy and only a just profit.

Ishida's theory made the merchant's life as noble as that of the samurai warrior. But he also underlined the duties of the money-maker. When a merchant was nearly wiped out because of a bad flood, he came to Ishida for advice. Ishida insisted that the merchant should sell everything he still possessed, even to selling his clothes, in order to repay his debts. In *Shingaku* thinking, if complete honesty be practiced, everybody within the realm of the four seas would become brothers. To the shrewd and enthusiastic Japanese bourgeois capitalists, Ishida argued that only the honest man has truly responded to the mirror-like mind of the Shinto gods. There is nothing shameful about selling; what is shameful is to practice dishonesty, live disjointed in heart and become a criminal in the eyes of the Shinto gods.

Ishida Baigan learned much from Taoism, Confucianism and Buddhism but he was essentially Shintoist. Because Japan is the special holy land and its emperor is the lineal descendent of the Sun Goddess, the Japanese should recover the lost heart and unite the way of Heaven with that of earth. Even if he uses Confucianist ideas, Ishida's initial interest was in Shinto, expressed in his veneration for the goddess of the Ise shrine and the belief that Japan is the Land of the Kami, superior to all other countries.[16]

---

[16] Robert N. Bellah, *Tokugawa Religion,* Free Press, Glencoe, Ill., 1957, pp. 133-177. Bellah somewhat differs from the above interpretation by insisting that Ishida was primarily Confucian rather than Shintoist.

Chikao Fujisawa: Concrete Catholicity

For Ishida Baigan, Shinto was interpreted as ethical mysticism; for Chikao Fujisawa, a 20th century Shinto apologist, it is a much-needed philosophy of "concrete universalism."[17] Shinto, in his opinion, brings man into existential communion with Nature and unites him to the material world. By combining spirituality and practical utility, it can overcome the dichotomy between transcendence and immanence. By reuniting scientific objectivity with religious subjectivity, Shinto bridges the chasm between the holy and the mundane. It asserts the vital connection of transcendental Heaven and immanent Earth.

A spiritual understanding of basic Shinto myths reveals the nature of concrete universalism. Shinto extols worship of the High Tree Deity (*Kukuno-Chi*) and the Sun Goddess—the former male, the latter female. The first represents the expansive male activity as the second symbolizes the contractive female principle. For Shintoists, every wedding is therefore a reminder of the cosmic union of the god Izanagi and the goddess Izanami which produced the islands of Japan.[18]

According to Fujisawa, Shinto myth furthermore shows how man has broken the unity between Heaven and Earth which the Kami designed for him. When the grandson of the Sun Goddess descended to earth to rule the world, the god of Mt. Fuji invited him to marry his two daughters, the divine princess of the cherry blossoms and the strong, but ugly Rock-Long-Princess. When the sun prince decided to wed only the lovely younger girl, the rejected sister became so ashamed and resentful that she cursed his marriage. Since he preferred delicate beauty, his children would be as short-lived as the cherry blossom. Also to show her anger, the Rock-Long-Princess caused a succession of explosive eruptions to devastate the area around Mt. Fuji. What this story means is that

---

[17] Chikao Fujisawa, *Concrete Universality of the Japanese Way of Thinking*, Hokuseido Press, Tokyo, 1958. This author, a professor of Nihon University, studied at the Universities of Berlin and Peiping and served at the Permanent Secretariat of the League of Nations in Geneva.

[18] Fujisawa, *Ibid*, p. 15.

man should love both aesthetic and utilitarian values.[19] Hence, when the Meiji leaders of the mid-19th century restored Shinto to its rightful place in Japanese life, they were justified in importing western technology to balance the traditional aestheticism of their culture. Shinto provides Japan with an all-inclusive faith in contrast to the otherworldliness of Buddhism and the mechanistic materialism of the Occident.[20]

Tokuchika Miki: Life as Art

Tokuchika Miki (b. 1900) founded one of Japan's new religions called *PL Kyodan* (Perfect Liberty Church) in 1946. His father had started a group—*Hito no Michi* (Religion of Man)—which attracted a million members in a single decade before its suppression by the government in 1937. Revived by the son when religious freedom was guaranteed by the American military authorities, the Religion of Man was then renamed the PL Religion.[21]

PL is clearly a Shinto faith brought up to date and purged of the nationalistic disadvantages of state Shinto, shrine Shinto and sect Shinto. The elder Miki based his Religion of Man on a revelation received after worshipping a sacred tree for five years. This tree had been planted in memory of his teacher: an itinerant priest, faith healer and spiritualist. The younger Miki adopted as the symbol of his PL faith the *Omitama*, a wheel-shaped gold emblem consisting of twenty-one rays emanating from a central hub signifying the sun. These two objects of veneration represent the most prominent Kami of ancient Shinto: the High Tree Deity and the Sun Goddess. For PL the shining sun symbolizes the noble and merciful God, who creates all things in accordance with a divine plan and endows every man with individuality and intelligence.[22] Following one of the twenty-one precepts of their faith,

---

[19] Fujisawa, *Ibid,* preface, pp. vi-ix.

[20] As Baigan used Confucian ethics to explain Shinto, Fujisawa finds support for his views in the 20th century Existentialist philosophies of Gabriel Marcel and Martin Heidegger.

[21] Cf. H. Thomsen, *New Religions of Japan,* pp. 183-198.

[22] From the prayer used at all PL services.

members "live radiantly as the sun."[23]

Everyone studying Japanese culture is impressed by its aesthetic emphasis—seen in scroll paintings, miniature gardens, flower arrangements, Noh plays and Kabuki dances. Since these grow out of the ancient Shinto love for the divine beauty of nature, Tokuchika Miki used this as the foundation for his religion of Perfect Liberty. "Life is Art," he said.

By contemplating Mt. Fuji or the delicate loveliness of cherry blossoms, one can see that God is the perfect artist. He provides the supreme example of creative talent by making everything distinctive. Whatever God does is an original creation. He gives to each thing He makes a certain unique individuality whether it be a person, a cloud, a flower or a rock. For millions of years God has been expressing His inner nature, always new and different in form, as if He simply had to make room for more examples of His inexhaustible creativity. Therefore, life is art.

If God is the supreme artist, we become truly human only to the degree that we make of our lives a painting, poem or piece of sculpture. What men possess—their land, money, position—are materials by which they are to display the artistry of their lives. Man's aesthetic intuitions are therefore signs of our kinship to the Kami. Because man possesses the essential qualities of God, he is God manifested in human form. He is an artist as his Creator is an artist. Hence, every man should regard his life as "a continuous succession of self-expressions." By using the things of nature as materials for self-realization, we become creative and learn the meaning of peace. Each individual exists for the ultimate joy and total satisfaction of an artistic life.[24]

Like ancient Shinto, PL is primarily interested in our every day, workaday world. It exhibits no concern for the sort of meditation which makes men hermits or monks. PL members seek to be consciously alive and alert, a hundred percent involved in daily tasks. For them, prayer simply means getting direction from God

---

[23] Listed in Thomsen, *Ibid,* pp. 188-189.

[24] Marcus Bach, *The Power of Perfect Liberty,* Prentice-Hall, Englewood Cliffs, N.J., 1971, p. 38.

so they can do well whatever they are called upon to do.[25] Prayer should be a method of finding guidance; hunches and intuitions are also ways God speaks to men.

Because man is God's noblest creation, he alone possesses the capabilities and artistic talent to create a better world. What makes humans distinctive is their conscious desire to surmount their natural limitations. God wants us to develop our unlimited potential. If one has a clear understanding of his relative position with his fellow men, society and the divine Universal Plan, he can overcome his limitations. Each individual—says Miki—should express his unique God-given personality but always in relationship to the divine Plan and always in reference to the ideal of the coming age of Great Peace.[26] By being aware of the unity of man and the cosmic power, by making work an act of God, PL reasserts the ancient Shinto principle that happiness for the individual and society results from working harmoniously with nature.[27] If we live artistic lives, Miki teaches, we can create a world of matchless beauty—a world mirroring God's creativity.

Thanks to sects such as Perfect Liberty, Shintoism, like its cousin Shamanism, is still a vital faith, subtly defying modern secular trends of thought and life in Japan. With Shamanism and Shinto, ancient traditions are being kept alive through the more modern, streamlined offshoots of the religion. In the Far East at least, new revelations of truth and new ways of looking at traditional messages continue to attract devotees and continue to point men towards Heaven.

---

[25] *Ibid*, p. 59.
[26] Bach, *Ibid*, p. 100.
[27] *Ibid*, p. 109.

BIBLIOGRAPHY FOR SHAMANISM & SHINTOISM

Masaharu Anesaki, *Religious Life of the Japanese People*, Kokusai Bunka Shinkokai, Tokyo, 1961.

"Japanese Mythology," J.A. MacCulloch, ed., *Mythology of All Races*, Cooper Square Publishers, N.Y., 1964, vol. viii.

Marcus Bach, *The Power of Perfect Liberty*, Prentice-Hall, Englewood Cliffs, N.J., 1971.

Strange Altars, Bobbs-Merrill, Indianapolis, 1952.

Robert N. Bellah, *Tokugawa Religion*, Free Press, Glencoe, Ill., 1957.

A Brief Guidance to Cheon-do-gyo, Cheondogyo Central Headquarters, Seoul, 1971.

Key Ray Chong, "The Religious Meaning of Ch'oe Che-u's Tonghak Doctrine" in Robert J. Miller, ed., *Religious Ferment in Asia*, University of Kansas, Lawrence, 1974.

Charles A. Clark, *Religions of Old Korea*, Christian Literature Society, Seoul, 1961.

Mircea Eliade, *Shamanism*, Princeton University Press, Princeton, N.J., 1964.

Robert S. Ellwood, Jr., *Religious and Spiritual Groups in Modern America*, Prentice-Hall, Englewood Cliffs, N.J., 1973.

Leonard Feinberg, "Fire Walking in Ceylon," N.E. Hoopes and R. Peck, ed., *Edge of Awareness*, Dell, N.Y., 1966.

Chikao Fujisawa, *Concrete Universality of the Japanese Way of Thinking*, Hokuseido Press, Tokyo, 1958.

Lafcadio Hearn, *Japan's Religions*, University Books, New Hyde Park, N.Y., 1966.

Jean Herbert, *Shinto*, Allen and Unwin, London, 1967.

D.C. Holtom, *The National Faith of Japan*, E.P. Dutton, N.Y., 1938.

Francis L.K. Hsu, *Under the Ancestors' Shadow*, Routledge and Kegan Paul, London, 1949.

Takahito Iwai, *The Outline of Tenrikyo*, Tenrikyo Doyu-sha, Nara, 1932.

Genchi Kato, *A Study of Shinto*, Meiji Japan Society, Tokyo, 1926.

Joseph M. Kitagawa, *Religion in Japanese History*, Columbia University Press, N.Y., 1966.

Sokyo Ono, *Shinto: The Kami Way*, Bridgeway Press, Rutland, Vt., 1962.

Henry van Straclen, *The Religion of Divine Wisdom*, Veritas Shoin, Kyoto, 1957.

Harry Thomsen, *The New Religions of Japan*, Tuttle, Tokyo, 1963.

Benjamin B. Weems, *Reform, Rebellion, and The Heavenly Way*, University of Arizona Press, Tucson, 1964.

Post Wheeler, *The Sacred Scriptures of the Japanese*, Schuman, N.Y., 1952.

POSTSCRIPT

HAVING EXAMINED a variety of living religions, one can better grasp the value of interfaith dialogue. On the basis of this introduction to the ways of thought and paths of life esteemed by millions of people in our contemporary "global village" it is my hope that every reader has broadened his knowledge and strengthened his own personal relationship with God. As we face the challenges and opportunities of His New Age, may we grow in respect for our fellow men and commitment to God's kingdom.

Over a decade ago, Dr. Stephen Neill, an official of the World Council of Churches, was invited to lecture on "The Christian Faith and Other Faiths" in the Anglican cathedral of Melbourne, Australia. As a former missionary and bishop in the Church of South India, Dr. Neill's devotion to the Christian cause had long been clear. Nevertheless, at the end of his first address he urged Christians to approach other faiths with the deepest humility. We must meet non-Christians at their best, exposing ourselves to everything that is most beautiful and convincing about their faiths. Rejoicing in all that they possess of high aspiration, we must be willing to go to school with them because they may have something we have not yet learned. If we really trust in Christ, we can open ourselves without fear to winds from any part of heaven, he said. Our commitment should become ever more intelligent and ever more complete, in order that in the last day nothing worthwhile will be lost when God's kingdom comes on earth.[1]

By knowing others we can better understand ourselves. By recognizing their idealism and spirituality, we can be inspired to deepen our own love for the God of heart. By working beside them and with them we can at long last realize the purpose of creation.

---

[1] S. Neill, *Christian Faith and Other Faiths*, Oxford University Press, London, 1961, pp. 18-19.

acknowledgements

Grateful acknowledgement is given to the following publishers whose works have been used:

Bantam Press, for excerpts from *The Humanist Way in Ancient China*, edited by Chai and Chai, copyright, 1965.

Beacon Press, for excerpts from *Taoism, The Parting of the Way*, by Holmes Welch, copyright, 1957.

Bobbs-Merrill, for excerpts from *The Way of Lao-Tze*, by Wing-tsit Chan, copyright, 1963.

Bookman Associates, for excerpts from *The Development of Neo-Confucian Thought*, by C. Chang, copyright, 1962.

E.J. Brill, for quotations from *The Buddhist Conquest of China*, by E. Zurcher, copyright, 1959.

The Buddhist Society of London, for excerpts from *The Jewel in The Lotus*, by John Blofeld, copyright, 1948.

Columbia University Press, for excerpts from *Sources of Chinese Tradition*, edited by W.J. de Bary, copyright, 1960; for excerpts from *Religion in Japanese History*, by J.M. Kitagawa, copyright, 1966.

Chondogyo Central Headquarters, in Iri City, Korea, for excerpts from *A Brief Guidance of Chondogyo*, copyright, 1971.

Doubleday and Company, for excerpts from *Buddhism or Communism*, by Ernst Benz, copyright, 1965; for material from *Three Ways of Thought in Ancient China*, by A. Waley, copyright, 1939.

Harper and Brothers, for excerpts from *Short History of the Chinese People*, by L. Carrington Goodrich, copyright, 1959.

Harper and Row, for excerpts from *The Wisdom of Buddhism*, by C. Humphreys, copyright, 1960.

Luzac and Company, for excerpts from Outlines of *Mahayana Buddhism*, by D.T. Suzuki, copyright, 1907.

McGraw Hill, for excerpts from *My Land and My People*, by the Dalai Lama, copyright, 1962.

David McKay Company, for excerpts from *The Living Thoughts of Confucius*, by A. Doeblin, copyright, 1960.

Mentor Books, for excerpts from *The Way of Life*, by R.B. Blakney, copyright, 1955.

Pelican Books, for excerpts from *Buddhism*, by C. Humphreys, copyright, 1969.

Penguin Books, for excerpts from *A Short History of Confucian Philosophy*, by Liu Wu-Chi, copyright, 1955.

Philosophical Library, for excerpts from *Religion in Chinese Garment*, by K. Reichelt, copyright, 1951.

Princeton University Press, for excerpts from *Buddhism in China*, by K. Ch'en, copyright, 1964; for excerpts from *History of Chinese Philosophy*, by Fung Yu-Lan, copyright, 1953; for excerpts from *Shamanism*, by M. Eliade, copyright, 1964.

Rainbow-Bridge Books Company, Taipei, for excerpts from *Liang Chi-chao and Intellectual Transition in China*, by Hao Chang, copyright, 1971.

Rider and Company, for excerpts from *The Zen Teachings of Hui Hai*, translated by J. Blofeld, copyright, 1962.

Stanford University, for excerpts from *Buddhism in Chinese History*, by A.F. Wright, copyright, 1959.

Charles E. Tuttle, Tokyo, for quotes from *The New Religions of Japan*, by H. Thomsen, copyright, 1963.

Yonsei University Press, Seoul, Korea, for excerpts from translation of *Samguk Yusa*, by Ilyon, copyright, 1972.

index

Ado, 51
Amida, 65, 66, 81
Amitabha Buddha, 4, 6, 18, 30, 31, 34, 50
Asvaghosha, 6
Avaloketsvara, 31

Bodhi, 3
Bodhicitta, 11
Bodhidharma, 32
Bodhisattva, 9-14, 18, 20, 32, 50
Bodhisattva Manjusri, 22
Boxer Rebellion, 37

Chai Jung, 15
Ch'an, 28, 31-34
Carsun Chang, 154-155
Chang Koon, 177-178
Chang T'ien-Jan, 118
Ch'en Tu-Hsiu 153-154
Ch'eng Hao, 144
Chiang Kai-shek, 37, 40, 42, 43, 45
Chiao Kioh, 11, 12
Chih-I, 28-30
Chikao Fujisawa, 198-199
Ching, 137
Chin Shan, 40
Chinhung, 53

Ch'oe Che-u 184-187
Chogyu Takayama, 77-78
Ch'ondogyo, 184-187
Chou Tun-Yi, 146
Chuang-Tzu, 97, 99-103, 109
Chu-Hsi, 144-148
Ch'un Ch'iu, 125
Chunsin, 179
Chun-tzu, 132-135
Chu Yang-Chang, 37

Daisaku-Ikeda, 74-75
Dalai Lama, 6-7, 47-49
Dharmakaya, 4-6
Dharmapala, 39
Dogen Zenshi, 63-69
Dosen, 38

Ech'adon, 52-53
Eisai Zenshi, 63-64
Emperor Ming, 15
Emperor Wen, 19
Emperor Wu, 17, 20, 36
Empress Tzu Hsi, 49

Fa-Tsang, 20
Feng-Fa Yao, 8
Feng, General, 42

Index

Five Elements School, 104-106
Fo-t'u-teng, 17
Fung Yu-Lan, 157-158

Genghis Khan, 22
Great Learning, 128-129
Han Fei-Tzu, 152
Han Shan-Tiung, 37
Honen Shonen, 63
Ho Yen, 113-114
Hsiao Ching, 130-132
Hsi Ch'ao, 8, 9
Hsuan, 141
Hsün Tzu, 107, 108, 140, 142, 144
Huai-nan Tzu, 107
Hui Hai, 33
Hui-Yuan, 16, 17
Hung Hsiu-Ch'uan, 182-184
Hwarjiang, 57
Hwarang Do, 53-55
Hygiene School, 104

I Ching, 126, 146
I-Kuan Tao, 118
Ishida Baigan, 196-197

Jen, 133-134, 141, 149, 156
Jinmu, 172
Jizo, 65
Josei Toda, 74

Kami, 192-194
K'ang Yu-Wei, 125, 151
Kobo Daishi, 63
Koot, 173, 176
Koguryo Buddhism, 51
Koryo Buddhism, 58-60
Kotami Kimi, 71
Kuo Hsiang, 114
Kuan-yin, 14, 31, 116
Kublai Khan, 22
Kubo Kakutaro, 71
Kuei-I-Tao, 117
Kyo Buddhism, 51

Li, 137-138, 143, 145-146, 148
Liang Ch'i-ch'ao, 49-51

Liang-Chih, 149
Li Chi, 125, 137
Lieh Tzu, 110-112
Li T'ing'yu, 117
Lotus Sutra, 28, 29, 62, 65, 67, 71

Maitreya, 34-36, 37, 38
Makiguchi, 76-77
Malalasekera, 40
Mao Tse-tung, 37, 43-49, 152-153
Mencius, 89, 107, 108, 112, 139-142
Miao-suan, 14
Milo Fo, 34-36, 37, 38
Marquis of Lu, 100
Mudang, 173-176

Nagarjuna, 3
Naganuma Myoko, 72
Nakayama Miki, 188-190
Nichiren, 66-67, 70, 74
Nichiren Buddhism, 70-78
Nikko, 71, 74
Nirmanakaya, 5
Niwano Nikkyo, 72

Omitama, 199

Paekche, 62
Paksoos, 173
Pang Hu, 37
Paksoos, 173
Peng-Tzu, 111
Perfect Liberty (PL), 199-201
Pophung, 52
P'u, 95
Pure Land School, 28, 30-31, 50
Pure Land Sutra, 30

Reiyukai, 71-72
Rinzai Zen, 67
Rissho Kosei Kai, 72-73

Sambhogakaya, 5, 6
Samyungdang, 60
Sansin, 175
Shao Yung, 146-147
Shen, 171

Index

Shen-Hsiu, 8
Shih Ching, 125
Shi-Huang Ti, 153
Shih King, 137
Shingaku, 196-197
Shinran, 66
Shotoku, 62, 64
Shu Ching, 125
Sinchangs, 178
Siva, 10
Soka Gakkai, 73-77
Sosan Daesa, 60, 61
Sosoorim, 51
Soto Zen, 67
"Suchness", 3-4
Sun (Ch'an) School, 51
Sunghwang Dang, 178
Sun Yat-sen, 37, 39, 41
Sutra in Forty-Two Sections, 15
Suzuki, D.T., 5-6

T'ai-Chi, 146
T'ai-hsu, 39-40
Taiping Movement, 182-184
T'an Ssu-T'ung, 41
Tao, 89-91, 93, 99, 101
Tao-an, 34
Tao-Te-Ching, 89-99, 104, 105
Te, 92
Tenrikyo, 187-190, 192
T'ien-t'ai, 28-31
Ti'-tsang, 11-12
Tokuchika Miki, 199-201
Tongbulgyo, 55, 57
Torii, 191
Tripitaka, 22
"True Man," 102, 103

True Pure Land Sect, 66, 68
Tsai-li Society, 116
Tseng Kuo-Fan, 149-150
Tujoo, 178
Tsung-Yang, 41
Tzu-Ssu, 127

Ubasoku, 64, 172
Uichum, 59, 61

Vishnu, 10

Wang Ch'ung, 109-110
Wang Pi, 113
Wang Tse, 36
Wang Yang-Ming, 148-149
Weber, Max, 95
White Lotus Society, 36-37, 117
Wonhyo, 55-58
World Tree, 165
Wu Chih-hui, 153
Wu-wei, 92-94, 96, 97

Yakut, 163
Yang Chien, 19
Yang Chu, 111-112
Yang Hsiung, 107-109
Yang T'sun-jen, 116
Yang Wen Hui, 38-39
Yellow Turban Taoists, 16
Yi, 140
Yin-Yang Philosophy, 104-106
Yin Yeng-sheng, 116
Yuan-Hsien, 23

Zen, 31-34